Ontologies in Urban Development Projects

Advanced Information and Knowledge Processing

Series Editors
Professor Lakhmi Jain
lakhmi.jain@unisa.edu.au

Professor Xindong Wu
xwu@cems.uvm.edu

For further volumes:
http://www.springer.com/series/4738

Gilles Falquet • Claudine Métral
Jacques Teller • Christopher Tweed

Ontologies in Urban Development Projects

 Springer

Dr. Gilles Falquet
Centre universitaire d'informatique
University of Geneva
Carouge
Switzerland
gilles.falquet@unige.ch

Dr. Claudine Métral
Centre universitaire d'informatique
University of Geneva
Carouge
Switzerland
claudine.metral@unige.ch

Dr. Jacques Teller
LEMA Université de Liège
Liège
Belgium
jacques.teller@ulg.ac.be

Dr. Christopher Tweed
Welsh School of Architecture
Cardiff University
Wales, United Kingdom
tweedAC@cardiff.ac.uk

ISSN 1610-3947
ISBN 978-1-4471-2697-3   ISBN 978-0-85729-724-2 (eBook)
DOI 10.1007/978-0-85729-724-2
Springer London Dordrecht Heidelberg New York

British Library Cataloguing in Publication Data
A catalogue record for this book is available from the British Library

Printed on acid-free paper

Springer is part of Springer Science+Business Media (www.springer.com)

Contents

Contributors

Chantal Berdier Institut National des Sciences Appliquees (INSA) de Lyon, France, chantal.berdier@insa-lyon.fr

Roland Billen Geomatics Unit, University of Liege, Belgium, rbillen@ulg.ac.be

Sylvie Calabretto Institut National des Sciences Appliquées de Lyon (INSA-Lyon), France, sylvie.calabretto@insa-lyon.fr

Eduardo Camacho-Hübner Région de Genève, Suisse, eduardo.camacho-huebner@transitec.net

Oscar Corcho Departamento de Inteligencia Artificial, Facultad de Informática, Universidad Politécnica de Madrid (UPM), Spain, ocorcho@fi.upm.es

Anne-Françoise Cutting-Decelle CODATA France and Ecole Centrale Paris/ LGI, Grande Voie des Vignes, F-92295 Châtenay-Malabry, France, afcd@skynet.be

Gilles Falquet Centre universitaire d'informatique, Universiy of Geneva, Switzerland, Gilles.Falquet@cui.unige.ch

Jacques Guyot Centre universitaire d'informatique, Université de Genève, Switzerland, guyot@cui.unige.ch

Anssi Joutsiniemi Institute of Urban Planning and Design, School of Architecture, Faculty of Built Environment, Tampere University of Technology, Finland, anssi.joutsiniemi@tut.fi

Myoung Ah Kang Laboratory of Computer Science, Modelling and System Optimization, Blaise Pascal University, Clermont Ferrand, France

Javier Lacasta Computer Science and Systems Engineering Department, University of Zaragoza, Spain, jlacasta@unizar.es

Jarmo Laitinen ICT in Construction, Department of Civil Engineering, Faculty of Built Environment, Tampere University of Technology, Finland, jarmo.laitinen@tut.fi

John Lee Graduate School of Arts, Culture and Environment, University of Edinburgh, Alison House,12 Nicolson Square, Edinburgh EH8 9DF, Scotland, UK, J.Lee@ed.ac.uk

School of informatics, University of Edinburgh, Alison House,10 Crichton Street, Edinburgh EH8 9AB, Scotland, UK

F. Javier López-Pellicer Computer Science and Systems Engineering Department, University of Zaragoza, Spain, fjlopez@unizar.es

Juho Malmi Virtual Building Laboratory, Department of Civil Engineering, Faculty of Built Environment, Tampere University of Technology, Finland, juho.malmi@tut.fi

Claudine Métral Centre universitaire d'informatique, Universiy of Geneva, Switzerland, Claudine.Metral@unige.ch

Javier Nogueras-Iso Computer Science and Systems Engineering Department, University of Zaragoza, Spain, jnog@unizar.es

Francois Pinet French Institute for Agricultural and Environmental Engineering, Clermont Ferrand, France, Francois.Pinet@cemagref.fr

Francesco Rotondo Dipartimento di Architettura e Urbanistica, University of Basilicata, Bari, Italy, f.rotondo@poliba.it

Catherine Roussey LIRIS, Université de Lyon, France, catherine.Roussey@cemagref.fr

Jacques Teller LEMA Université de Liège, Belgium, Jacques.Teller@ulg.ac.be

Stefan Trausan-Matu Computer Science Department of the Politehnica University of Bucharest, Romania, trausan@gmail.com

Christopher Tweed BRE Centre for Sustainable Design of the Built Environment, Welsh School of Architecture, Cardiff University, UK, TweedAC@cardiff.ac.uk

Jussi Vakkilainen Virtual Building Laboratory, Department of Civil Engineering, Faculty of Built Environment, Tampere University of Technology, Finland, jussi.vakkilainen@tut.fi

Luis M. Vilches-Blázquez Ontology Engineering Group, Universidad Politécnica de Madrid, Spain, lmvilches@fi.upm.es

Part I
Ontology Fundamentals

Chapter 1
Introduction

Gilles Falquet, Claudine Métral, Jacques Teller, and Christopher Tweed

Ontologies are increasingly recognized as essential components in many fields of information science. Ontologies were first employed in artificial intelligence, as a means to conceptualize some part of the real world. The first aim was to enable software system to reason about real-world entities. The CyC ontology (Lenat 1995) is typical of this perspective, it is comprised of several thousand concepts and tens of thousand facts, expressed as logical formulae. A second aim of ontologies was to provide a common conceptualization of a domain on which different agents agree. It is certainly this aspect of ontologies that triggered widespread interest in this knowledge engineering artifact in fields such as information system design, system integration and interoperation, natural language processing, or information retrieval. For instance, the Gene ontology (The Gene Ontology Consortium 2001) provides a common vocabulary to standardize the representation of gene and gene products.

Although the concept of ontology is now well understood and equipped with an array of theoretical and practical tools (there are currently several dozens of books on ontology engineering), the practical implementation of ontologies in a specific applicative context remains a challenging task. Moreover, the effectiveness

G. Falquet (✉) • C. Métral
Centre universitaire d'informatique, University of Geneva, Switzerland
e-mail: Gilles.Falquet@cui.unige.ch; Claudine.Metral@unige.ch

J. Teller
LEMA Université de Liège, Belgium
e-mail: Jacques.Teller@ulg.ac.be

C. Tweed
Welsh School of Architecture, Cardiff University, UK
e-mail: TweedAC@cardiff.ac.uk

G. Falquet et al., *Ontologies in Urban Development Projects*, Advanced Information and Knowledge Processing 1, DOI 10.1007/978-0-85729-724-2_1,
© Springer-Verlag London Limited 2011

or cost-benefit evaluation of ontology-based approaches still requires more research. One of the purposes of this book is to explore these questions in the urban domain.

1.1 Ontologies in Information Science

1.1.1 Defining Ontologies

Over the last two decades, several definitions of the term ontology have been proposed (Gruber 1993; Guarino and Giaretta 1995). From a very general perspective, an ontology is a specification of some conceptualization of a domain. A conceptualization is an abstract model that represents the entities of a domain in terms of concepts, relations, and other modelling primitives. In principle, the specification of this conceptualization could take any form. However, the most commonly used ontological languages specify the meaning of concepts with some form of explicit definition. Thus an ontology is comprised of

- a representational vocabulary with different types of symbols (class names, relation names, etc.)
- a set of definitions that specify the meaning of the vocabulary

Each ontological language has its own types of symbols and definition expression language. For instance, in description logics the representational vocabulary consists of concepts, properties, and individuals; definitions are expressed as logical axioms that state, among others, equivalences, inclusions or exclusions between concepts as well as constraints on properties. The vocabulary of an ontology defined by UML class diagrams is made of classes, attributes, associations, etc. Definitions are graphically expressed by diagrams that can represent generalization/specialization or part/whole constraints between classes, as well as constraints on the associations between classes.

In this book, we take a rather broad view of ontologies. We admit that definitions can be expressed in a language that has no formal interpretation, in particular in natural language. Nevertheless, the expression must be sufficiently precise to enable the intended users (human or software agents) to *commit* to the ontology. By committing to an ontology an agent agrees to use the vocabulary in a way that is consistent with the definitions given in the ontology. It is clear that a software agent can only commit to an ontology expressed in a formal language, while a human being can commit to definitions expressed in natural language.

Following this view, it appears that some knowledge resources cannot be considered as ontologies. For instance, a thesaurus whose main purpose is to define an indexing vocabulary for a document corpus does not precisely define the meaning of each term. Hence, an agent cannot commit to meanings defined in this thesaurus. Conversely, other thesauri (such as the English Heritage Thesaurus) provide a much more precise definition (in English) for each term and organize them in a consistent generic-specific hierarchy. In this case a human agent can commit to these definitions and consider these thesauri as ontologies.

1.1.2   Current State of Ontologies and Ontology Engineering

Recent years have witnessed a rapid increase in the number of publicly available ontologies.[1] These ontologies are not all of high quality and some are very restricted in scope. However, this shows that the development of ontologies is no more the preserve of large projects with significant funding. This is probably due to several factors, including:

- the availability of numerous books, tutorials, and courses on ontologies and ontology engineering;
- the semantic web initiative that stressed the importance of ontologies and lead to the development of the RDF/S and OWL web ontology languages. These languages have been widely accepted for the expression and interchange of re-usable ontologies;
- publicly available ontologies certainly create a kind of network effect, helping others to develop and share new ontologies;
- theoretical developments in description logics that lead to a much better understanding of theses logics. We know more precisely which logics have decision procedures for reasoning tasks, and what is the computational complexity of these procedures;
- work on reasoning algorithms resulted in practical reasoners that are highly optimized and applicable on large ontologies; and
- the availability of ontology engineering methodologies and associated tools such as editors, viewers, refactoring tools, etc. have popularized the ontology development process.[2]

Despite all these advances, ontology engineering is not yet an integral component of practical methods and tools in information engineering. For instance, the link between databases and ontologies still requires research and development work, as well as the integration of ontology-based reasoning in business processes.

1.2   Ontologies in the Urban Domain

Arguably, interest in ontologies for use in the urban domain was initially triggered by technological challenges related to interoperability of urban and territorial databases.

---

[1]For instance the Swoogle ontology search engine (http://swoogle.umbc.edu/) announces more than 10,000 indexed ontologies.

[2]The Protégé ontology editor has more than 100,000 registered users.

As information about urban areas and urban developments became more and more easily available and abundant, the need to interconnect different databases in order to perform complex tasks (traffic modeling, environmental management, urban forecasting etc.) appeared more urgent than ever. Since these databases are usually characterized by different purposes, spatial resolutions and quality of information, their interoperability obviously raised new demands in terms of ontology design and mapping. Difficulties in connecting different urban databases not only appeared in such complex modeling tasks, but also in apparently simple or routine tasks like the interconnection of spatial databases indexed by street names.

Reengineering of existing urban databases constituted another technological challenge that urgently called for urban ontologies. Actually, many of urban databases had been characterized by an incremental development since the diffusion of Geographical Information Systems amongst urban experts. Hence, it appeared that the conceptual schema of some of these databases were no longer consistent, given their progressive and unplanned evolution. A further upgrading of these databases to make them more easily available and to connect them with other data sources hence appeared impossible without a deep restructuring of their content. Given the magnitude and complexity of the task, ontology engineering was seen as a necessary step to manage both conceptual soundness and continuity with previous versions of the database.

European integration of databases constituted a third technological motivation for developing urban and territorial ontologies. It was mainly driven by growing demands related to cross-boundary integration of territorial databases, and the transposition of the INSPIRE European directive in all Member States. Such an exercise rapidly appeared far from trivial given existing discrepancies between national and regional databases. It especially revealed that some of these discrepancies, and especially terminological differences, often concealed serious ontology divergences.

Though, besides such real technological concerns, ontologies were rapidly considered as a conceptual challenge *per se* in the urban domain. Urban sciences have long been characterized by their hybrid nature, in that they usually convey different disciplinary backgrounds: architecture, law making, social sciences, construction, geography etc. Adopting a global conceptual framework, shared by all those disciplines involved in the urban environment, once appeared as neither realistic nor desirable. Though the lack of common grounds to exchange between these different world views should be considered as a major drawback in the circulation of knowledge between these disciplines as well as, and probably more importantly, between scientists, experts and daily urban practitioners.

Furthermore, urban sciences are characterized by the emergence and rapid diffusion of fuzzy concepts, like sprawl or urban sustainability, which by nature resist precise and generalized definitions. Such a profusion of neologisms should always be regarded with skepticism as they often hide a lack of conceptualization and scientific consensus. Still, it should also be acknowledged that they are also nurtured by new ways to frame urban issues, as in the case of urban sustainability, as well as rapid changes in the human-made environment, as in the case of sprawl. Such changes are usually driven by background forces, common to all cities, usually altered by local characters. To keep on the same examples, urban sustainability and sprawl are in some sense both universal and place-driven, which largely explains the difficulty to reach a consensus about related concepts in the urban domain.

Finally, if a number of models have been proposed to characterize urban structures since the early 1960ies and the seminal works of Forrester (1969), it should be acknowledged that the way cities are actually designed and produced by its actors, has hardly been formalized in the past. Here again, this may be related to place-based specificities of urban decision-making. Some authors further relate such a lack of conceptualization to the complex and unpredictable nature of communications in urban development project, while others would rightly raise concerns about the prescriptive nature of any conceptualization model in this domain. Still, the reluctance to propose tentative models to formalize communication flows between actors of urban development is certainly a serious impediment for the transformation and enhancement of existing decision systems. Here again designing urban ontologies has been viewed as a stimulating conceptual challenge in that it would force a clarification of communication means and purpose between the different actors involved in urban development: engineers, urban planners, constructors, architects, citizens, etc. As such, it appears as a way to engage a reflective exercise about the nature and conditions of urban development.

The need for comprehensive models of urban systems as an aid to future urban development has never been more urgent. The challenges policy makers and practitioners face in this turbulent period of human history demand new understandings and new approaches. The emerging "low carbon" agenda, together with the requirements of social and economic sustainability, all suggest systemic approaches, in which we can expect the explicit development of ontologies to play a major role.

Interestingly these two ways to frame the issue, as both a technical and a conceptual challenge, once met in the COST Action C21, which specifically aimed at prospecting the potential of ontologies as a way to enhance communications in urban development projects.

1.3 Structure of the Book

The first part of the book is a presentation of the fundamental concepts and issues of ontology engineering. An introduction to ontologies and ontology engineering provides a detailed view of the different types of ontologies, according to their level of formalization and their purpose. This introduction also presents a typology of the ontology design approaches. The subsequent chapters address issues in ontology engineering that are particularly relevant in the urban domain: using ontologies to ensure interoperability; dealing with heterogeneity and differences in viewpoints; and dealing with multilingualism in ontologies.

The second part focuses on methods and tools to apply ontology engineering in the urban domain. It covers the geographical aspect of urban ontologies; the interconnection of urban models through ontologies; the interconnection through different representation scales; the development of urban knowledge based systems; and the creation of ontologies from existing urban knowledge resources.

The third part is a collection of case studies in the construction and use of urban ontologies. Each case study is described using a common template to facilitate comparison and to ensure a suitable coverage of each case. The cases are drawn from a wide variety of domains loosely related to urban development. Their diversity—ranging from building information models to urban scale public participation—underlines the potential for widespread application of ontology engineering. This part concludes with an overall analysis that highlights lessons learned and questions to solve.

References

Forrester, J.W.: Urban Dynamics. MIT Press, Cambridge/London (1969)

Gruber, T.R.: A translation approach to portable ontology specifications. Knowl. Acquis. **5**(2), 199–220 (1993)

Guarino, N., Giaretta, P.: Ontologies and knowledge bases: Towards a terminological clarification. In: Mars, N. (ed.) Towards Very Large Knowledge Bases: Knowledge Building and Knowledge Sharing, pp. 25–32. IOS Press, Amsterdam (1995)

Lenat, D.B.: Cyc: a large-scale investment in knowledge infrastructure. Commun. ACM **38**(11), 33–38 (1995)

The Gene Ontology Consortium: Creating the gene ontology resource: design and implementation. Genome Res. **11**, 1425–1433 (2001). doi:10.1101/gr.180801

Chapter 2
An Introduction to Ontologies and Ontology Engineering

Catherine Roussey, Francois Pinet, Myoung Ah Kang, and Oscar Corcho

2.1 Introduction

In the last decades, the use of ontologies in information systems has become more and more popular in various fields, such as web technologies, database integration, multi agent systems, natural language processing, etc. Artificial intelligent researchers have initially borrowed the word "ontology" from Philosophy, then the word spread in many scientific domain and ontologies are now used in several developments. The main goal of this chapter is to answer generic questions about ontologies, such as: Which are the different kinds of ontologies? What is the purpose of the use of ontologies in an application? Which methods can I use to build an ontology?

There are several types of ontologies. The word "ontology" can designate different computer science objects depending on the context. For example, an ontology can be:

- a thesaurus in the field of information retrieval or
- a model represented in OWL in the field of linked-data or
- a XML schema in the context of databases
- etc.

C. Roussey (✉)
LIRIS, Université de Lyon, France
e-mail: Catherine.Roussey@cemagref.fr

F. Pinet
French Institute for Agricultural and Environmental Engineering, Clermont Ferrand, France
e-mail: Francois.Pinet@cemagref.fr

M.A. Kang
Laboratory of Computer Science, Modelling and System Optimization, Blaise Pascal University, Clermont Ferrand, France

O. Corcho
Departamento de Inteligencia Artificial, Facultad de Informática, Universidad Politécnica de Madrid (UPM), Spain
e-mail: ocorcho@fi.upm.es

G. Falquet et al., *Ontologies in Urban Development Projects*, Advanced Information and Knowledge Processing 1, DOI 10.1007/978-0-85729-724-2_2,
© Springer-Verlag London Limited 2011

It is important to distinguish these different forms of ontologies to clarify their content, their use and their goal. It is also needed to define precisely the vocabulary derived from the word ontology. For example what is the difference between a core ontology and a domain ontology? First, we introduce and define the different types of ontologies. Second, we present some methodologies to build ontologies. Some of the illustrative examples will be taken from project presentations made in the context of the COST UCE Action C21 (Urban Ontologies for an improved communication in UCE projects TOWNTOLOGY) or, in general, in the area of Geographic Information Systems (GIS).

2.2 Ontology Classifications

Several classifications of ontologies have been presented in the literature (Lassila and McGuinness 2001; Gomez-Perez et al. 2004; Borgo 2007, etc). Each of them focused on different dimensions in which ontologies can be classified. This section focuses on two of these classifications: the first one classifies ontologies according to the expressivity and formality of the languages used: natural language, formal language, etc.; the second one is based on the scope of the objects described by the ontology.

2.2.1 Classification Based on Language Expressivity and Formality

Depending on the expressivity of an ontology (or, in general, of a knowledge representation language), different kinds of ontology components can be defined (concepts, properties, instances, axioms, etc.). Figure 2.1 presents the set of components that we will use to provide our classification based on language expressivity. For example, if we focus on concepts, which are one of the main components of ontologies, the UML class diagram of Fig. 2.1 shows as that they can be defined in different (and complementary) ways:

- By their textual definitions: For example the concept "*person*" is defined by the sentence "*an individual human being*",
- By a set of properties: for example the concept "*person*" has the property "*name*", "*birth date*" and "*address*"; note that a property can be reused for several concepts.
- By a logical definition composed of several formulae: for example the concept "*person*" is defined by the formula "*LivingEntity ∩ MovingEntity*".

A concept can also be defined by the set of instances that belong to it. For example, "*Martin Luther King*" is an instance of the concept "*person*". This last definition is called the extensional definition of a concept and the three former definitions are called intensional definitions of a concept.

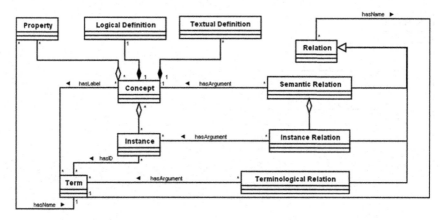

Legend:

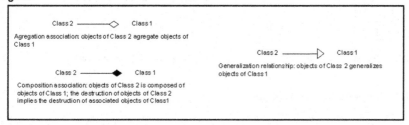

Fig. 2.1 UML class diagram representing ontology components and their relationships

Concepts, instances and properties are referenced by one or more symbols. Symbols are terms that humans can rapidly understand roughly by reading them. And finally all these ontology components are connected through relations. Semantic relations link only concepts together: for example the location relationship indicates that city concept is localized in a country concept. Instance relations connect only instances and instance relations are often instances of semantic relations, although it is not always the case. Some relations between instances can be contextual and cannot be generalized to all instances of their concept. An example of instance relation is that the city instance named Paris is localized in the country instance named France. All cities are localized in a country. A contextual instance relation can be that the person instance named "John Travolta" is localized in the city instance named "Paris" at the point in time 31 January 2010. The terminological relations express the relationships that terms can have: for example the term *"person"* is synonym to the term *"human being"*

According to the usage of these components, in the following sections we present four kinds of ontologies. In each section we explain which type of language is normally used to define the ontology and we provide some examples for illustration purposes. The classification starts using the less formal languages to the more formal one.

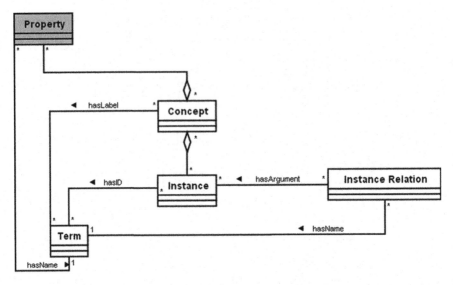

Fig. 2.2 UML schema of information ontology component and their relationships

2.2.1.1 Information Ontologies

Information ontologies are composed of diagrams and sketches used to clarify and organize the ideas of collaborators in the development of a project. These ontologies are only used by humans. The characteristics of information ontologies are:

- Easily modifiable and scalable
- Synthetic and schematic
- They are normally used during a design process of a project: for example, information ontology can be used during the conception phase of information system development project or during the design of floor plan in architectural construction project.

As shown in Fig. 2.2, information ontologies focus on concepts, instances and their relationships. Their goal is to propose an overview of a current project in order to express the state of this project. The grey color of the property elements means that properties are not always well defined by information ontologies.

Information ontologies are normally described by means of visual languages, so that they can be easily understood by humans. A Mind Map is a good example of this type of visual language. For example the OnToKnowledge project about methodology for ontology design propose to add a Mind Map plug-in called Mind2Onto in their ontology editor called OntoEdit (Sure and Studer 1999). They notice that Brain Storming is a good method to quickly and intuitively start a project. Their Mind Map plug-in is a support for discussion about ontology structure. Mind Map descriptions will be followed by three examples of information ontologies: one example will be taken from urban planning project, another one come from architectural design and the latter is used in a construction project.

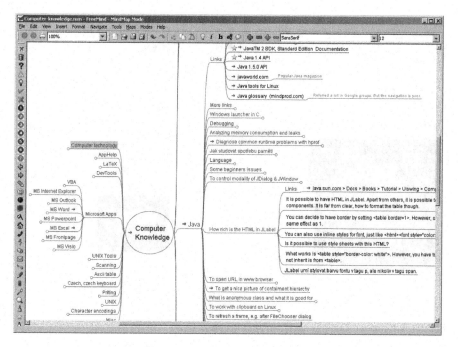

Fig. 2.3 Screenshot of a free mind mapping software called FreeMind (http://freemind.sourceforge.net/wiki/index.php/Main_Page)

Language: Mind Map

Mind Map were originally developed to support more efficient learning and evolved to a management technique used by numerous companies (Buzan 1974). Mind Map provides information about a topic that is structured in a tree (see Fig. 2.3 for example). Mind maps are used to generate, visualize, structure, and classify ideas, and as an aid in study, organization, problem solving, decision making, and writing.

Example: Information Ontology of Architectural Design

Bouattour et al. (2005) propose also a new set of concepts for information ontologies adapted to architectural design. These concepts could be seen as an upper layer of IFC classes (see section "Example: Industry Foundation Classes" (Ferreira da Silva and Cutting-Decelle 2005, p. 9)). Their information ontology is composed of actors, objects, activities and documents. All these components are in relation during the cooperative process of design building. Thus it is preferable to follow the decisions taken by each actor to understand the project development, to save time and to avoid errors. Their information ontology presents the state of architectural design components by following the decision process of each actor about this component.

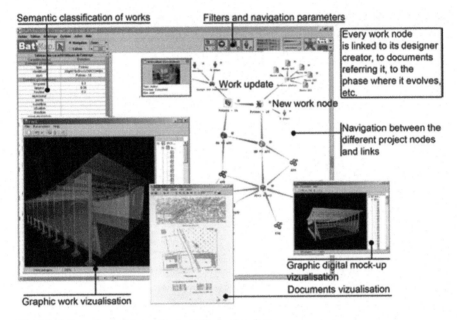

Fig. 2.4 Information ontology about architectural project

The information ontology representing the current state of an architectural project is composed of instantiation of their concepts. These ontologies are implemented in information system in order to compute some 3D representations of the building called mock up. These mock-ups synthesize the evolution of the project. This work is still in development, Bouattour et al. (2007) presents an on-going research aimed at computer-aided cooperative design for architectural project (Fig. 2.4).

Example: Information Ontology of Urban Planning

Kaza and Hopkins (2007) presents a set of concepts to formalize information ontologies used during urban planning process. Their information ontologies show the different alternatives of a decision in a plan. Plans could present effective decisions, alternative decisions and realizations in order to facilitate the communication between several actors. Moreover this type of plans can help stakeholders during their decision process in order to have a general overview of the city evolution. All these concepts (decisions, alternative, actors, etc.) and their instances compose an information ontology of urban planning (Fig. 2.5).

In this example the information ontology does not look like a Mind Map but it still uses a visual language similar to that used in a plan. This type of information ontology focuses on the location of the concept instance not on their internal structure description.

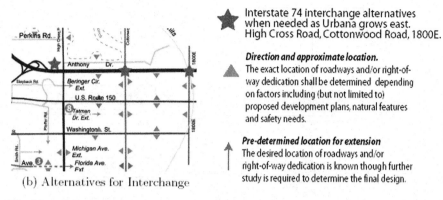

(b) Alternatives for Interchange

Fig. 2.5 Information ontology about urban planning process

Example: Information Ontology of Construction Project

Lee and McMeel (2007) propose to build an information ontology in order to ease the communication between the different actor groups involved in a construction project. These information ontologies represent some general patterns that have to be modified in order to resolve the specific problem of the construction project. The first stage of problem solving is to understand the language convention of each actor group based on the ontology element. Then negotiation and collaborative works can begin to find the appropriate solution of the construction problem. This type of ontology has to be heavy adaptable and modifiable.

2.2.1.2   Linguistic/Terminological Ontologies

Linguistic ontologies can be glossaries, dictionaries, controlled vocabularies, taxonomies, folksonomies, thesaurii, or lexical databases. As shown in Fig. 2.6 this type of ontology mainly focuses on terms and their relationships.

Unfortunately, terms are ambiguous. A concept can be referenced by several terms (for example: "computer science", "computing", "information technology" are synonyms) and a term can reference several concepts (for example the term "bank" can be used to reference a "river bank" or a "commercial bank"). The roles of linguistic ontologies are twofold: The first one is to present and define the vocabulary used. This is achieved by a dictionary for example which list all the terms actually used in language. Secondly, linguistic ontology is the result of a terminology agreement between a users' community. This agreement defines which term is used to represent a concept in order to avoid ambiguity. This process is called vocabulary normalization. When a concept could be described by two synonym terms, the normalization process selects one of those to be the preferred label of the concept. It means that in Fig. 2.6 the cardinality of the hasLabel and hasID relationship is changed

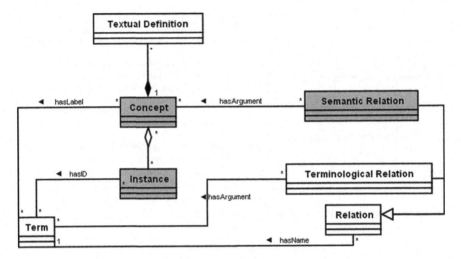

Fig. 2.6 UML schema of linguistic ontology components and their relationships

from * to 1 compared to Fig. 2.1. Taxonomy and thesaurus organized their normalized vocabulary so that the a priori relationships between concepts are made explicit. That is the reasons why in Fig. 2.6 concept and semantic relation are in grey to express that some linguistic ontologies try to explicit these components. Unfortunately the distinction between concepts and their instances are not taken in account: Instances are considered like concepts. A thesaurus has three basic relationships among terms: equivalence, hierarchical and associative. Let us point out that the last two relations hide several semantic relations. Associative relation between two terms means that there exists a semantic link between concepts labeled by these terms but no information is given on this semantic link. Hierarchical relation between two terms can hide an "instance of" relation between a concept and one of its instances (in grey in Fig. 2.6), a "specialization" relation between two concepts, a "part of" relation between concepts and so on. More information on thesaurus development are available in (ISO 2788 and ISO 5964).

Now we describe two languages that can be used to describe this type of ontologies: SKOS is used to define thesaurii and RDF is used the defined web metadata. Next we present four different thesaurii belonging to different domains: urban planning, environmental domain and cultural heritage; followed by a taxonomy used in architectural design.

Language: Simple Knowledge Organization System (SKOS)

Simple Knowledge Organization System (SKOS) is a semantic web activity proposed by the W3C. They are developing specifications and standards based on XML to support the use of knowledge organization systems such as thesauri, classification schemes, subject heading systems and taxonomies within the framework of the Semantic Web [see http://www.w3.org/2004/02/skos/intro for more details].

Language: Resource Description Framework (RDF)

The Resource Description Framework (RDF) is a general-purpose language for representing information in the Web. RDF is a recommendation from the W3C for creating meta-data structures that define data on the Web. RDF is used to improve searching and navigation for Semantic Web search engine (Web 3.0 applications).

RDF is implemented in XML. RDF is composed of Triples: (1) the subject (the web page), (2) a property or predicate (an attribute name) and (3) an object (the actual value of the attribute for the web page).

1. The subject is a resource. Resource is anything that can have a Unique Resource Identifier (URI); this includes all the world's web pages, as well as individual elements of an XML document.
2. The property is a resource that has a name. For example the Dublin Core Metadata Initiative propose to use the name "dc:creator" to represent the author property. Property can be associated to a property type defined in an RDF Schema (RDFS). RDFS defined a RDF vocabulary composed of property type and resource type.
3. The object can be a URI, a literal (a string of character representing a number, a date, a noun etc.) or a blank node.

For example, the triple (1) http://www.textuality.com/RDF/Why.html (2) dc:creator (3) "Tim Bray" means "The Author of http://www.textuality.com/RDF/Why.html is Tim Bray" [see http://www.w3.org/RDF/ for more details].

Example: URBAMET Thesaurus. Urban Planning, Housing and Construction News and Records

URBAMET is the French library databank on urban development, town planning, housing and accommodation, architecture, public facilities, transport, local authorities etc. Since the creation of the data bank in 1986, the hierarchical organization of all these topics gave place to the construction of thesaurus URBAMET. The thesaurus is accessible in French, Spanish and English. A study of this thesaurus is presented in Chap. 10.

Example: GEMET Thesaurus

GEMET, the General Multilingual Environmental Thesaurus is the reference vocabulary of the European Environment Agency (EEA) and its Network (Eionet). It has been developed as an indexing, retrieval and control tool for the EEA.

GEMET was conceived as a "general" thesaurus, aimed to define a common general language, a core of general terminology for the environment. The language used in GEMET are: Basque, Bulgarian, Czech, Dutch, Danish, English, Estonian Finnish, French, German, Greek, Hungarian, Italian, Norwegian, Polish, Portuguese, Russian, Slovenian, Slovak, Spanish, Swedish etc. [see http://www.eionet.europa.eu/gemet for more detail] (Fig. 2.7).

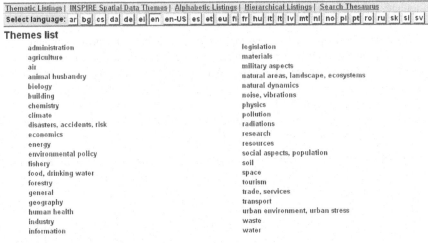

Fig. 2.7 The theme list of the GEMET thesaurus

Example: Agrovoc Thesaurus

In environmental domain, the well-known AGROVOC thesaurus is used to develop the Agricultural Ontology Service (AOS) project (AGROVOC). AGROVOC is a multilingual thesaurus designed to cover the terminology of all subject fields in agriculture, forestry, fisheries, food and several other environmental domains (environmental quality, pollution, etc.). As presented in (AGROVOC), "it consists of words or expressions (terms), in different languages and organized in relationships (e.g. 'broader', 'narrower', and 'related'), used to identify or search resources". AGROVOC was developed by the FAO and the Commission of the European Communities, in the early 1980s. It is an excellent example of linguistic ontology resulting of a terminology agreement between a community. The terms of AGROVOC can be used to reference document contents (Wildemann et al. 2004) or to find the similarity degree between several words corresponding to the same idea. AGROVOC is available in the following languages: English, French, Spanish, Arabic, Chinese, Portuguese, Czech, Thai, Japanese, Lao Hungarian, Slovak, German, Italian, Polish, Farsi (Persian), Hindi, Telegu, Moldavian [see http://www.fao.org/aims/tools_thes.jsp for more detail].

Example: HEREIN Thesaurus

The European Heritage Network is an information system gathering governmental services in charge of heritage protection within the Council of Europe. The HEREIN project focuses is on cultural heritage, particularly on architectural and on archaeological heritage. The multilingual thesaurus attached to the HEREIN project intends to offer a terminological standard for national policies dealing with architectural

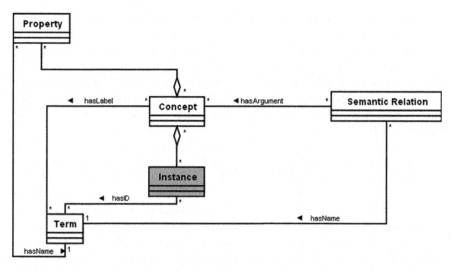

Fig. 2.8 UML schema of software ontology components and their relationships

and archaeological heritage [see http://www.european-heritage.net/sdx/herein/index.xsp for more detail]. This thesaurus is described in Chap. 15.

Example: DesignScape Project

The research developed in the project DesignScape focuses on the modeling of the different steps of the architectural design (Kim and Kim 2007). The works formalize the typical building design process by a linguistic ontology. More precisely, the ontology is a taxonomy describing the relationships between different activities related to architectural design. The main basis activities modeled are: pre-design, site analysis, schematic design, space zoning, site zoning, objectives definition, analysis, synthesis, evaluation. Numerous concepts around the architectural design activity are represented in the considered ontology.

2.2.1.3   Software Ontologies

Software ontologies (or software implementation driven ontologies) provide conceptual schemata whose main focus is normally on data storage and data manipulation, and are used for software development activities, with the goal of guaranteeing data consistency. As shown in Fig. 2.8, a concept is composed of a set of properties; all concepts are also defined thanks to each other's by the relations they have. These relations are also associated to constraints. At execution time, data are stored in the properties of object, that is to say an instance of a concept. Thus, data could be processed in various treatments (called methods). Nevertheless, software ontologies goal is not to describe particular instances during execution time; that is the reason why instance is colored in grey in Fig. 2.8.

Software ontologies are normally defined with conceptual modeling languages used in software and database engineering. These languages are used during software design procedure: for example Entity-Relationship Model language or Object Model Language. The next section presents the most well known one called UML. UML presentation will be followed by one example of software ontology[1] used in building construction.

Language: Unified Modeling Language (UML)

The Unified Modeling Language (UML) is a standard used mainly for modeling software and information systems. UML is a graphical language for visualizing, specifying and constructing any parts of software components. UML is a semi-formal formalism, because the official document defining the semantics of UML is mainly composed of informal descriptions in English (OMG 2003). Thus, UML is not sufficient to represent all the details required by complex reasoning processes (Cranefield 2001) like: deducing new knowledge, compute the logical correctness of a formal ontology, etc. UML propose several diagrams, the ones used to specify software ontology are UML class diagram and UML object diagram. Figures 2.1, 2.2, 2.6, 2.8, 2.9 are examples of UML class diagram.

Example: Industry Foundation Classes

The Industry Foundation Classes (IFC) has been progressively developed by the International Alliance for Interoperability (IAI) since 1995. There have been several releases of the model that have been implemented. The IFC is a response to interoperability requirements within building construction by a significantly large group of industry practitioners including government and other statutory bodies, clients, consultants and contractors together with a substantial number of software vendors. The primary target of the IFC Model is the interoperability among software applications within the building and construction market sector (Ferreira da Silva and Cutting-Decelle 2005). IFC classes are therefore defined according to the scope and the abstraction level of software systems dealing with building and construction specific content. Such a model has been primarily developed to enable the exchange and sharing of Building Information Models (BIM) to increase the productiveness of design, construction, and maintenance operations within the life cycle of buildings. The IFC model therefore describes an object model with concepts (classes), relations (as direct associations or objectified relationships), and properties (or attributes).

---

[1]Software ontology can be also name semi formal ontology in the literature because UML is a semi-formal formalism.

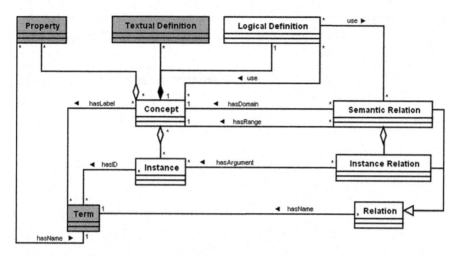

Fig. 2.9 UML schema of formal ontology components and their relationships

IFC classes are first built in the express language, and now an XML version is available. They are now widely accepted by industry and major Computer Aided Design software systems support IFC classes for file based exchanges with planning tools and cost evaluation applications. The IFC standard is studied in several chapters of this book, especially in Chap. 8.

2.2.1.4 Formal Ontologies

Formal ontologies require a clear semantics for the language used to define the concept, clear motivations for the adopted distinctions between concepts as well as strict rules about how to define concepts and relationships. This is obtained by using formal logic (usually first order logic or Description Logic) where the meaning of the concept is guaranteed by formal semantics (Borgo 2004). As you can see in Fig. 2.9, this ontology type is the only one that contains logical definition.

For example, Knowledge Bases (KB) are formal systems that capture the meaning of the adopted vocabulary via logical definitions. The logical definition of a concept is composed of one or more logical formulae. A logical formula (or axiom) is a combination of concepts and semantic relations. A KB contains more expressive components than a conceptual schema (Notice in Fig. 2.9 that formal ontology has all the components of software one). The purpose is not simply retrieval and storage of data but reasoning. Compared to software ontology, data are not associated to method in order to make some calculation; data are stored in property only to be retrieved (That is the reason why property is in grey in Fig. 2.9). For example, Fig. 2.10 presents an ontology about urban development and civil engineering, which defined knowledge related to getting urbanism authorizations for new buildings.

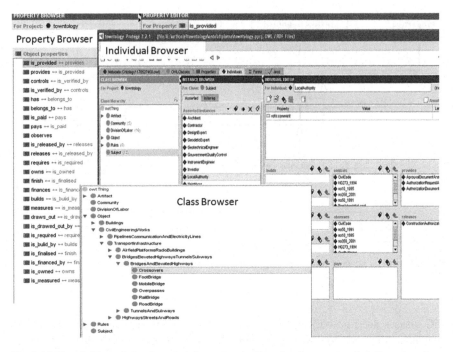

Fig. 2.10 **Protégé knowledge base ontology about urban development and civil engineering ontology**

This Knowledge Base is defined with the Protégé system (Protégé 2005). Thanks to these formal definitions and rules, the inference engine can enters into a dialog with a user (see Chap. 9). Formal ontology does not focus on term and textual definition even if they could be defined in the ontology. Terms are only used as symbol in order to help user during the manipulation of logical formula.

There exist different formal languages used to describe formal ontology like Description Logics (DL), Conceptual Graphs (CG), First Order Logic (FOL), etc. We chose to present OWL, the standard recommended by W3C. OWL presentation is followed by three examples of formal ontologies belonging to urban planning field, architecture domain and pervasive environment.

Language: Web Ontology Language (OWL)

The OWL Web Ontology Language is a standard recommended by the W3C. It is designed for use by applications that need to process the content of information instead of just presenting information to humans. OWL facilitates greater machine interpretability of Web content than that supported by XML, RDF, and RDF Schema (RDF-S) by providing additional vocabulary along with a formal semantics. The OWL is intended to provide a language that can be used to describe concepts and relations between them that are inherent in Web documents and applications. OWL language is used for:

1. formalize a domain by defining concepts called classes and properties of those classes,
2. define instances called individuals and assert properties about them,
3. reason about these classes and individuals to the degree permitted by the formal semantics of the OWL language.

The OWL language provides three increasingly expressive sublanguages designed for use by specific communities of implementers and users.

- OWL Lite supports those users primarily needing a classification hierarchy and simple constraint features. For example, while OWL Lite supports cardinality constraints, it only permits cardinality values of 0 or 1. It should be simpler to provide tool support for OWL Lite than its more expressive relatives, and provide a quick migration path for thesauri and other taxonomies.
- OWL DL supports those users who want the maximum expressiveness without losing computational completeness (all entailments are guaranteed to be computed) and decidability (all computations will finish in finite time) of reasoning systems. OWL DL includes all OWL language constructs with restrictions such as type separation (a class can not also be an individual or a property, a property can not also be an individual or class). OWL DL is so named due to its correspondence with Description Logics, a field of research that has studied a particular decidable fragment of first order logic. OWL DL was designed to support the existing Description Logic business segment and has desirable computational properties for reasoning systems.
- OWL Full is meant for users who want maximum expressiveness and the syntactic freedom of RDF with no computational guarantees. For example, in OWL Full a class can be treated simultaneously as a collection of individuals and as an individual in its own right. Another significant difference from OWL DL is that a owl:DatatypeProperty can be marked as an owl:InverseFunctionalProperty. OWL Full allows an ontology to augment the meaning of the pre-defined (RDF or OWL) vocabulary. It is unlikely that any reasoning software will be able to support every feature of OWL Full.

Each of these sublanguages is an extension of its simpler predecessor, both in what can be legally expressed and in what can be validly concluded. The following set of relations hold. Their inverses do not [see http://www.w3.org/TR/owl-features/ for more details].

Example: Formal Ontology About Urban Development and Civil Engineering

Chapter 9 of this book contains a description of an expert system able to dialog with a user in order to inform him about which document is necessary to have the authorization to construct a new building. The goal is not only to give a list of documents but to explain where and how to find this document and where to send this document... Moreover the process could be an incremental process to ask for this document you will need this one and so on... This expert system consists of a formal ontology about urban development and civil engineering and an the rule-based inference engine Jess.[2]

This ontology contains concepts called classes, instances called individuals and relations called properties. For example, the "Subject" class has 12 instances (see Fig. 2.10). One of these, the "LocalAuthority" instance has several relations ("provides", "releases", "controls", etc.) with other individuals.

Example: Formal Ontology for the Korean Architectural Domain

A research project has been initiated in South Korea to model an ontology for the Korean architectural domain (Kim 2005). The author has built the formal description of the ontology in using OWL and Protégé. A prototype based on this ontology has been developed to help learn the History of the main Korean historical buildings.

The goal is to precisely and formally model information related to monuments (temples, towers, famous places, etc.) and their history. The main classes of the ontology are:

- Buildings,
- Architectural Styles,
- Artifacts e.g. important monuments associated to buildings; artifacts are linked to buildings by the relationship "belong to"
- History; this class has three subclasses (1) Event, (2) Fact, (3) Story i.e. legend and non-verified information,
- People,
- Media (image, sound, text, etc.).

For instance, the ontology can be used to model that two towers Dabo-Pagoda and Seokga-Pagoda (i.e. two instances of Artifacts) belong to the Temple Bulgulsa (i.e. an instance of Building). In this example, historical Events associated to the temple can be "thievery" or "fire". An example of Facts is "KimDaesung has constructed the temple". In the ontology, the person KimDaesung is an instance of People. All the media providing significant information are instances of the class Media.

Example: CoBra Ontology

In another context, the CoBra ontology has been defined in order to facilitate the pervasive computing environment (Chen et al. 2003). The ontology has been modeled in OWL to enable reasoning about knowledge.

---

[2]http://www.jessrules.com/

In a pervasive environment, different intelligent agents have specific tasks and they can communicate each other thanks to a common network. Agents must exchange their knowledge and cooperate together to understand a local context and reach their goals. This requires to reason with contexts and to help agents maintaining consistent contextual knowledge and cooperating. The authors implemented an intelligent meeting room system on the campus of an university. The ontology (consisted of 17 classes and 32 properties definitions) defines some of the common relationships and attributes that are associated with people, places and activities in an intelligent space. When a person enters into a conference room, the system detects his presence and acquires situational information from heterogeneous sources such as the Web, corporate databases, etc. The situational information may concern data about the person, schedule, time, technical characteristics of the devices installed in the room, etc. Then, the system deduces the role and the intention of the person by reasoning with the context and by interpreting situational information (e.g. he is expected to present something in this room at that time). The system informs other agents in order to help this person e.g. the projector agent can obtain automatically the presentation from system and run the slideshow.

This use of formal ontologies could have several direct applications in the management of urban areas. Different agents could be implemented in the infrastructure of the city (public transport, automatic distributor teller, etc.). Each agent will deduce what people need thanks to contextual information and a formal ontology.

2.2.2 Classification Based on the Scope of the Ontology, or on the Domain Granularity

Figure 2.11 presents the second classification based on the scope of the objects described by the ontology. For instance, the scope of a local ontology is narrower than the scope of a domain ontology; domain ontologies have more specific concepts than core reference ontologies, which contains the fundamental concept of a domain. Foundational ontologies can be viewed as meta ontologies that describe the top level concepts or primitives used to define others ontologies. Finally, general ontologies are not dedicated to a specific domain thus its concepts can be as general as those of core reference ontologies.

2.2.2.1 Local Ontologies/Application Ontologies

Local or application ontologies are specializations of domain ontologies where there could be no consensus or knowledge sharing. This type of ontology represents the particular model of a domain according to a single viewpoint of a user or a developer.

Fonseca et al. (2000) present this kind of ontology as a combination of domain ontology and task ontology in order to fulfill the specific purpose of an application.

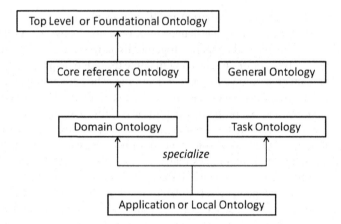

Fig. 2.11 Ontology classification based on domain scope

The task ontology contains knowledge to achieve a task, on the other hand the domain ontology describes the knowledge where the task is applied.

2.2.2.2 Domain Ontologies

Domain ontology is only applicable to a domain with a specific view point. That is to say that this viewpoint defines how a group of users conceptualize and visualize some specific phenomenon. This domain ontology could be linked to a specific application: electric network management system for example.

Example: Urban Sprawl Ontology

Cagiloni and Rabino (2007) use the Lowry Model of the city in order to have a simplified view of the urban sprawl phenomenon. The Lowry Model is a simplified model of the city that modelized the relation between transportation and land use. This model has a mathematical formulation taking as input values the employment, the population, the residential sector, the travel cost etc..This ontology is a domain ontology, it is applicable only on urban morphological evolution.

2.2.2.3 Core Reference Ontologies

Core reference ontology is a standard used by different group of users. This type of ontology is linked to a domain but it integrates different viewpoints related to specific group of users. This type of ontology is the result of the integration of several domain ontologies. A core reference ontology is often built to catch the central concepts and relations of the domain.

Example: Hydrontology

Vilches Blazquez et al. (2007) present the development of a core reference ontology untitled hydrontology describing hydrographic features. They gather different sources of information. These sources are chosen based on their reliability that is to say they come from well-known institution. Their goal is to harmonize all the different representations of hydrographic phenomenon in order to propose a standard. Hydrontology is presented in the Chap. 6.

Example: CityGML

CityGML is an OpenGIS® Encoding Standard for the representation, storage and exchange of virtual 3D city and landscape models. CityGML is implemented as an application schema of the Geography Markup Language version 3.1.1 (GML3).

CityGML models both complex and georeferenced 3D vector data along with the semantics associated with the data. Indeed, CityGML defines the classes and relations for representing the most relevant topographic objects in cities and regional models with respect to their geometrical, topological, semantical, and appearance properties. Thus CityGML can be seen as a core reference ontology dealing with 3D City Model. Nevertheless, CityGML is only appropriate for visualization purpose and it is not sufficient for touristic or environmental application. For these specific domain areas, CityGML also provides an extension mechanism to enrich the data with identifiable features. Thus, to our point of view, CityCML is a core reference ontology based on the GML foundational ontology and it can be derived to build domain ontology [see http://www.citygml.org/ for more details]. CityGML is also discussed in Chap. 7.

2.2.2.4 General Ontologies

General ontologies are not dedicated to a specific domain or fields. They contain general knowledge of a huge area.

Example: OpenCyc Ontology

Cyc technology is a general knowledge base and commonsense reasoning engine. The entire Cyc ontology containing hundreds of thousands of terms, along with millions of assertions relating the terms to each other, forming an general formal

ontology whose domain is all of human consensus reality. The OpenCyc ontology
is available in OWL format [see http://www.opencyc.org/ for more detail].

2.2.2.5 Foundational Ontologies/Top Level Ontologies/Upper Level Ontologies

Foundational or top level ontologies are generic ontologies applicable to various
domains. They define basic notions like objects, relations, events, processes and so on.
All consistent ontology has a foundational ontology. Foundational ontology can be
compared to the meta model of a conceptual schema (Fonseca et al. 2003). The most
well known foundational ontology are the Descriptive Ontology for Linguistic and
Cognitive Engineering (DOLCE)[3] and the Basic Formal Ontology[4] (BFO). These two
ontologies are formal and propose a different logical theory for representation of
world assumption. Thus, domain or core reference ontologies based on the same foundational ontology can be more easily integrated. For example, Fonseca et al. (2006)
describes a top level ontology of geographic objects and a similarity measure to evaluate
the interoperability of domain ontologies based on this top level ontology.

Example: Descriptive Ontology for Linguistic and Cognitive
Engineering (DOLCE)

Descriptive Ontology for Linguistic and Cognitive Engineering (DOLCE) contains
abstract concepts aimed at generalizing the set of concepts that we may encounter
in different domains (Masolo et al. 2003).

DOLCE is a formal ontology of particulars, in the sense that its domain of
discourse is restricted to them. The fundamental ontological distinction between
universals and particulars can be informally understood by taking the relation of
instantiation as a primitive: Particulars are entities which have no instance; universals are entities that can have instances. Properties and relations are usually considered as universals.

DOLCE describes particulars that can be physical object (endurant), events
(perdurant), quality (quality) and quale (quality value).

- Endurants are entities enduring in time. Within endurants, physical objects are
distinguished from non-physical objects, since only the former possess direct
spatial qualities. The domain of non-physical objects covers social entities and
cognitive entities.
- Perdurants are entities that happen in time and in which endurants participe.
Among perdurants, one defines actions that are intentionally accomplished,
i.e. controlled by an agent.

---

[3] See http://www.loa-cnr.it/DOLCE.html for more details.
[4] See http://www.ifomis.org/bfo for more details.

- Endurants and perdurants have inherent properties (qualities) that we perceive and/or measure.
- These qualities take a value (quale) within regions of values which are abstract.

In this context spatiality is expressed by a spatial quality which quale belongs to a spatial region at a point in time (Bateman and Farrar 2004).

For example, to express the fact that this paper (paper#1) is a Physical Endurant which has a Physical Quality (spatialQuality#1), we can say that there exists a relation QT between these two elements. This is formally expressed by the formula:

PhysicalEndurant(paper#1) $\wedge$ PhysicalQuality(spatialQuality#1) $\wedge$ QT(paper#1, spatialQuality#1).

To define the value of this spatial quality we need a Physical Region (location#1) which can be a point. This Physical Region is part of a space region (space region) and they are linked at a point in time t by a quale relationship QL.

This is expressed by the formula:

PhysicalRegion(location#1) $\wedge$ PartOf(location#1, space region) $\wedge$QL(location#1, spatialQuality#1, t).

Example: Socio Cultural Ontology

Trausan-Matu (2007) presents the top level concept of a socio cultural ontology. These top level concepts come from the Activity theory of Engestrom. Yrjö Engeström's (1987) theory emphasizes categories (subjects, objects, and communities) and mediators (general artifacts, social rules and division of labor). Thus we could say that these six general concepts composed the foundational ontology of socio cultural ontology.

Example: Geography Markup Language GML

The Geography Markup Language (GML) is an OpenGIS® Encoding Standard for the representation, storage and exchange of geographical features. GML serves as a modeling language for geographic systems as well as an open interchange format for geographic transactions on the Internet. The concept of feature in GML is a very general one and includes not only conventional "vector" or discrete objects, but also coverage and sensor data.

To a technical point of view, GML is an XML grammar proposed by the Open Geospatial Consortium (OGC) to describe generic geographic data sets that contain points, lines and polygons. Thus GML contains a foundational ontology of geographic features. Moreover, GML can be extended to define core reference ontology called community-specific application schemas like CityGML.[5] Using application schemas, users can refer to roads, highways, and bridges instead of points, lines and polygons.

---

[5] see http://www.opengeospatial.org/standards/gml and http://en.wikipedia.org/wiki/Geography_Markup_Language for more details.

2.3   Different Ontology Design Approaches

Several methodologies for ontology engineering are proposed to design ontologies. The most complete ones are Methontology (Gomez-Perez et al. 2004) and On-to-knowledge (Sure et al. 2003). Nevertheless, this research area is still in development; see for example the NeON project [http://www.neon-project.org/web-content/]. All these methodologies are composed of several activities. The development process is not a linear process but a refinement one where each activity can be repeated several times. Among all the activities the most important are:

- Ontology specification
- Knowledge acquisition
- Conceptualization
- Formalization
- Implementation
- Evaluation
- Maintenance
- Documentation

2.3.1   Classification Based on Taxonomy Construction Direction

The conceptualization activity is composed of several tasks. One of them is the construction of the concept taxonomy.

To build the taxonomy of concepts, several approaches have been opposed in literature (Gandon 2002):

- *Bottom-Up approach.*
- *Top-Down approach.*
- *Middle-Out approach*

2.3.1.1   Bottom Up Approaches

Bottom-Up approaches start from the most specific concepts and build a structure by generalization; the ontology is built by determining first the low taxonomic level concepts and by generalizing them. This approach is prone to provide tailored and specific ontologies with fine detail grain concepts (Gandon 2002).

Example: Spatial Database Ontology

Chaidron et al. (2007) investigate a bottom up approach of local ontology construction. Their goal is to define a local ontology describing objects stored in a spatial database.

Thus, this local ontology is used as a DB documentation. Moreover, it facilitates the database reengineering by differentiating the attended use and the effective use of object type. This work is presented in Chap. 6.

Example: Urban Network Ontology

Nogueras-Iso et al. (2007) propose an automatic bottom up method of ontology construction based on Formal Concept Analysis approach. Their goal is to analyze several databases of street type and personal or land addresses in order to build a core reference ontology of street types. Thus this ontology is the result of merging different street categorizations. Each database has its own street categorization. This core reference ontology could be used afterward to query all these databases together in a general system (see chapter object interoperability).

Example: The Phenomen Ontology

Gomez-Perez et al. (2008) propose to study a cartographic database of the National Geographic Institute of Spain to build automatically a first draft of a domain ontology about geographic feature types. They used a combination of criteria to build taxonomy of concepts. First of all, the code of each feature instance stores a three level classification. Secondly, they notice that the several features names can begin with a common lexical part (for example: "highway", "divided highway", "toll highway"). The common part "highway" is the super class of the others feature types.

2.3.1.2   Top Down Approaches

Top-Down approaches start from the most generic concept and build a structure by specialization; the ontology is built by determining first the top concepts and by specializing them. The top concepts can be chose in a foundational ontology These approaches are prone to the reuse of ontologies and inclusion of high level philosophical considerations which can be very interesting for coherence maintenance (Gandon 2002).

Example: Socio Cultural Ontology

Human activity creates some geographical object like state, city, administrative border. These types of geographical objects are opposed to physical object like mountains, rivers. Trausan-Matu (2007) describe urban development as the consequence of human activity. He uses a top down approach to develop its socio cultural ontology. This ontology explains the human interaction inherent in urban development. He adapts the John Sowa's methodology of classification (Sowa 1999) to the activity theory of Engestrom. This ontology is presented in the Chap. 9.

Example: Urban Morphological Process Ontology

Camacho-Hubner and Golay (2007) propose to use John Sowa's methodology to develop an ontology of urban morphological change. Their goal is to explain the change of urban morphology by studying 3 aspects: time, historical context and morphological process.

2.3.1.3 Middle Out Approaches

Middle-Out approaches identify central concepts in each area/domain identified; core concepts are identified and then generalized and specialized to complete the ontology. This approach is prone to encourage emergence of thematic fields and to enhance modularity and stability of the result (Gandon 2002).

Example: Hydrotonlogy

Vilches Blazquez et al. (2007) presents an experiment in building a core reference ontology of hydrographic features. They use the Methondology ontology development method based on middle out approach. First they build a dictionary of most important terms. These terms enable to start the development of the concept hierarchy using four taxonomic relations: subclass of, disjoint-decomposition, exhaustive decomposition and partition. A dictionary was drawn up and used to validate the correctness of the taxonomy. The ontology was enriched by adding ad-hoc relationship between ontology concepts. The last step was the attribute specification for every concept. For more detail see Chap. 6.

2.3.2   Classification Based on the Type of Sources

As shown previously ontology design contains the activity of knowledge acquisition. This activity is based on elicitation techniques. The task of knowledge elicitation from resources gave rise a new research field called ontology learning. The second ontology design classification is made according to the type of information sources used to extract knowledge. You will find a more precise description on all the possible techniques to build an ontology from different resources in Chap. 10.

2.3.2.1 Based on Text

Texts contain unstructured data not meaningful for a computer system. Nevertheless textual corpus is a huge source of information. Texts can be used to extract terms thanks to Natural Language Processing technique (lots of parser are available like tree tagger).

Then statistical techniques like co-occurence evaluation can be applied in order to extract the most important terms appearing in the corpus or the most important couple of terms in order to detect relation between terms. Linguistic pattern can also be extracted thanks to statistical technique. Those patterns identify specific semantic relations thanks to verb extraction.

For example, Aussenac Gilles et al. (2000) presents an experiment of corpus analysis in order to help the knowledge engineer during the design of domain ontology. The design process is still manual but corpus analysis tools minimize time and efforts spent in knowledge extraction.

Buitelaar et al. (2005) present an overview of different techniques applied on text in order to extract knowledge. Knowledge can be: terms, synonyms and multilingual variants, concepts (concept can be identified as a set of instances or a cluster of terms or a textual definition), concept hierarchies, non-hierarchical relations and rules. These elicitation techniques come from Information Retrieval methods, Natural Language Processing tool, text mining methods or statistics.

Mounce et al. (2009) presents an example of semi automatic creation of ontology in the water field. They use the ontology learning tool Text2Onto applied on corpora of documentation about water management.

2.3.2.2 Based on Thesaurus

Thesaurii are linguistic ontologies that can be used to extract a first draft of software or formal ontology.

For example Lacasta et al. (2007) presents an experiment in using several multilingual thesaurus (AGROVOC, EUROVOC, GEMET, UNESCO, URBISOC thesaurus) in order to build a first draft of a domain ontology in urbanism. Their goal is to extract concepts and semantic relations from terms and linguistic relations. Notice that this work is detailed in the Chap. 10. The process is composed of several steps:

- Thesaurii are transformed in the same format.
- Terms of different thesaurus are gathered when they share at least a common synonym. Thanks to these clustering techniques a concept is considered as a cluster of terms.
- The probability of concept is proportional to the number of synonyms shared by different thesaurii.
- Semantic relations are extracted from linguistic relations between concepts contained in different thesaurii.
- Semantic relation probability is proportional to the number of linguistic relations between terms contained in different thesaurii.

2.3.2.3 Based on Relational Database

Relational databases are valuable resources for software or formal ontology learning. Due to the structural nature of database, a better accuracy of ontology design process can be expected than from textual corpora. In relational database two aspects can be explored to design ontology: the structure of the database and the data stored in the database. The structure can be used to extract concepts, semantic relations and properties. Li et al. (2005) and Astrova and Kalja (2008) works are based on rules to transform a well-formed relational database into an object oriented conceptual schema. Nevertheless the resulting ontology has a flat concept taxonomy. We need to extract more hierarchical relation from data. For example Nogueras-Iso et al. (2007) use the Formal Concept Analysis techniques applied on the data of different urban network databases to build a taxonomy of street feature types. Gomez-Perez et al. (2008) analyze the code and the name of geographic features of the National Geographic Institute of Spain to build a taxonomy of geographic feature types. Lammari et al. (2007) consider that partitioning of a database table on the basis of null values may reveal concept hierarchies. Cerbah (2008) proposes a tool to refine the concept hierarchy based on property representing type values.

2.3.2.4 Based on UML Diagrams

Some works propose a formal ontology design methodology based on UML models (Cranefiled and Purvis 1999; Philippe 2003; Schreiber 2005; IBM 2006; Gasevic et al. 2006; Pinet et al. 2009).

One main advantage of UML is that is taught in many Departments of Universities, and it is widely used, even by non-computer scientists. UML is supported by several tools so designers can use them for describing their diagrams. Users and developers are likely to be familiar with UML notations than traditional formal ontology based languages. For all these reasons, UML could be viewed as a good candidate to model formal ontologies.

There are several common features between UML and formal Ontology-based languages (IBM 2006) but the main drawback of UML is its lack of formal semantics. Some researchers propose a mathematical model for UML (see for instance Breu et al. 1997). The work of Guizzardi (Guizzardi et al. 2002, 2004) concerns the development of different methodological tools (UML profiles, design patterns) in order to build an ontology using UML formally and correctly. Cranefiel and Purvis show how a formal ontology can be built using UML and Object Constraint Language (OCL) (OMG 2006); the concepts are described by UML classes and constraints on concepts are described in OCL (Cranefield et al. 1999).

OCL is a textual language that might overcome the limitation of UML in the future. In the Object Management Group (OMG) specification of OCL (OMG 2006), an annex presents a first version of a formal semantic but currently, this annex does not describe how to make complex reasoning processes within OCL constraints.

An interesting methodology to develop an ontology is to capture (by using UML diagrams) consensual knowledge accepted by the experts. In a second step, the software ontology described in UML can be translated into a formal ontology (RDF, OWL, etc.). Then this produced formal ontology can be enriched in order to offer new possibilities: produce reasoning, reach the requirement of the semantic Web, integrate several database schemas, etc.

For example, the works of Pinet et al. (2006) propose to start modeling a software ontology with a UML class diagram. After that, this UML specification is translated into OWL with Protégé and its UML Storage Backend Plug-In (Protégé). Then, additional specifications are defined with Description Logic in order to produce a formal ontology.

2.4   Conclusion

Ontologies have been used for the last decades for a set of tasks: improving communication between agents (human or software) or reusing data model or knowledge schema. All these tasks deal with interoperability issues and can be applied in different domains. Consequently, ontologies have evolved and several kinds of ontologies have been proposed.

We have presented several visions of ontology types and how to build them. Moreover we have described the main components of each type of ontology. Several examples have been provided in order to help understand the different uses of ontologies.

In the next chapter, we will show which types of system interoperability issues can be resolved by ontologies, and which types of ontologies have been used for this purpose.

References

Astrova, I., Kalja, A.: Automatic transformation of SQL relational databases to OWL ontologies. In: WEBIST, vol. 2, pp. 131–136 (2008)

Aussenac-Gilles, N., Biebow, B., Szulman, S.: Revisiting ontology design: a methodology based on corpus analysis. In: EKAW, Juan-les-Pins, pp. 172–188 (2000)

Bateman, J., Farrar, S.: Towards a generic foundation for spatial ontology. In: Varzi, A.C. (ed.) Formal Ontology in Information Systems: Proceedings of the Third International Conference (FOIS-2004), Laure Vieu Publié par IOS Press (2004)

Borgo, S.: Classifying (medical) ontologies. Tutorial for the Ontology Workshop at the Semantic Mining Summer School (2004)

Borgo, S.: How formal ontology can help civil engineers. In: Teller, J., Lee, J., Roussey, C. (eds.) Ontologies for Urban Development: Interfacing Urban Information Systems. Studies in Computational Intelligence, vol. 61, pp. 143–156. University of Geneva 6,7 Nov 2006. Springer Verlag (2007). ISBN 978-3-540-71975-

Bouattour, O., Halin, G., Bignon, J-C.: A Cooperative model using semantic works dedicated to architectural design. In: Proceedings of the 10ème Conférence – CAADRIA The Association for Computer Aided Architectural Design Research in Asia, New Delhi, 28–30 Avril, 2005, Publication primée: Woung CAADRIA Award 2005, (2005)

Bouattour, O., Halin, G., Bignon, J.-C.: Management system for a virtual cooperative project. In: Proceedings of the eCAADe Conference, Frankfort, Allemagne, Sept 2007

Breu, R., Grosu, R., Huber, F., Rumpe, B., Schwerin, W.: Towards a precise semantics for object-oriented modeling techniques. In: Object-Oriented Technology, ECOOP'97 Workshop Reader (1997)

Buitelaar, P., Cimiano, P., Magnini, B., et al.: Ontology learning from text: an overview. In: Buitelaar, P., Cimiano, P., Magnini, B. (eds.) Ontology Learning from Text: Methods, Evaluation and Applications Frontiers in Artificial Intelligence and Applications Series, vol. 123. IOS Press, Amsterdam (2005)

Buzan, T.: Use your head. BBC Books, (1974)

Caglioni, M., Rabino, G.: Theoretical approach to urban ontology: A contribution from urban system analysis. In: Teller, J., Lee, J., Roussey, C. (eds.) Ontologies for Urban Development: Interfacing Urban Information Systems. Studies in Computational Intelligence, vol. 61, pp. 143–156. University of Geneva 6,7 Nov 2006. Springer Verlag (2007). ISBN 978-3-540-71975-

Cerbah, F.: "Learning highly structured semantic repositories from relational databases - RDBtoOnto tool". In: Proceedings of the 5th European Semantic Web Conference (ESWC 2008), Tenerife, Spain, June 2008

Chaidron, C., Billen, R., Teller, J.: Investigating a bottom-up approach for extracting domain ontologies from urban databases. In: Teller, J., Lee, J., Roussey, C. (eds.) Ontologies for Urban Development: Interfacing Urban Information Systems. Studies in Computational Intelligence, vol. 61, pp. 143–156. University of Geneva 6,7 November 2006. Springer Verlag (2007). ISBN 978-3-540-71975-

Chen, H., Finin, T., Joshi A.: An ontology for context-aware pervasive computing environments. J. Knowl. Eng. Rev. **18**(3), 197–207 (Sept 2003). Cambridge University Press, USA (2003). ISSN:0269-8889

Cranefield, S., Purvis, M.: UML as an ontology modelling language. In: Proceedings of the Workshop on Intelligent Information Integration, 16th International Joint Conference on Artificial Intelligence (IJCAI-99) (1999)

Cranefield, S.: UML and the Semantic Web. In: The International Semantic Web Working Symposium, Palo Alto, (2001)

Ferreira Da Silva, C., Cutting-Decelle, A.-F.: Industrial standards to structure the construction information. COST C21 Technical report no2. Available at http://www.towntology.net/references.php (2005)

Fonseca, F., Câmara, G., Monteiro, A.M.: A framework for measuring the interoperability of geo-ontologies. Spat. Cogn. Comput **6**(4), 307–329 (2006)

Fonseca, F., Davis, C., Camara, G.: Bridging ontologies and conceptual schemas in geographic applications development. Geoinformatica **7**(4), 355–378 (2003)

Fonseca, F., Egenhofer, M., Davis, C., Borges, K.: Ontologies and knowledge sharing in Urban GIS. Comput. Environ. Urban. Syst. **24**(3), 232–251 (2000)

Gandon, F.: Distributed artificial intelligence and knowledge management: Ontologies and multi-agent systems for a corporate semantic web. Scientific Philosopher Doctorate Thesis in Informatics, Defended Thursday the 7th of November 2002, INRIA and University of Nice - Sophia Antipolis, Doctoral School of Sciences and Technologies of Information and Communication, (2002)

Gasevic, D., Djuric, D., Devedzic, V.: Model Driven Architecture and Ontology Development, 328p. Springer-Verlag, Berlin Heidelberg New York (2006).

Camacho-Hübner, E., Golay, F.: Continuity and evolution of ontologies for urban morphological processes. In: Teller, J., Lee, J., Roussey, C. (eds.) Ontologies for Urban Development: Interfacing Urban Information Systems. Studies in Computational Intelligence, vol. 61, pp. 143–156. University of Geneva 6,7 Nov 2006. Springer Verlag (2007). ISBN 978-3-540-71975-

Gómez-Pérez, A., Fernandez-Lopez, M., Corcho, O.: Ontological Engineering with Examples from the Areas of Knowledge Management, e-Commerce and the Semantic Web. First Edition Series: Advanced Information and Knowledge Processing 1st ed. 2004. 2nd printing, 2004, XII, 403 p. 159 illus., Hardcover (2004). ISBN: 978-1-85233-551-9

Gomez-Pérez, A., Ramos Gargantilla, JA., Rodríguez Pascual, A., Vilches Blázquez, LM.: The IGN-E case: Integrating through a hidden ontology Lecture notes in geoinformation and cartography, pp. 417–434 (2008)

Guizzardi, G., Falbo, R.A., Pereira Filho, J.G.: Using objects and Patterns to implement domain ontologies. J. Braz. Comput. Soc. (Special Issue on Software Engineering), **8**(1) (2002)

Guizzardi, G., Wagner, G., Guarino, N., van Sinderen M.: "An Ontologically Well-Founded Profile for UML Conceptual Models", Lecture Notes in Computer Science, vol. 3084, (2004)

IBM: Ontology Definition Metamodel, June 2006

Kaza, N., Hopkins, L.D.: Ontology for land development decisions and plans. In: Teller, J., Lee, J., Roussey, C. (eds.) Ontologies for Urban Development: Interfacing Urban Information Systems. Studies in Computational Intelligence, vol. 61, pp. 143–156. University of Geneva 6,7 Nov 2006. Springer Verlag (2007). ISBN 978-3-540-71975-

Kim, S.-A.: An ontology based learning system for architectural heritage cases. J. Archit. Inst. Korea **21**(10), 97–104 (2005)

Kim, S.-A., Kim, Y.S.: Design process visualizing and review system with architectural concept design ontology. In: International Conference on Engineering Design, ICED 2007, 28–31 Aug 2007. Paris (2007)

Lacasta, J., Nogueras-Iso, J., Zarazaga-Soria, F.J., Muro-Medrano, P.: Generating an urban domain ontology through the merging of cross-domain lexical ontologies. In: Proceedings of Second Towntology Workshop "Ontologies for Urban Development: Conceptual Models for Practitioners," 17, 18 Oct 2007. Castello del Valentino, Turin, Italy (2007)

Lammari, N., Comyn-Wattiau, I., Akoka, J.: Extracting generalization hierarchies from relational databases: A reverse engineering approach. Data. Knowl. Ing. **63**(2), (2007)

Lassila, O., McGuinness, D.: The Role of Frame-Based Representation on the Semantic Web Knowledge Systems Laboratory Report KSL-01-02, Stanford University, 2001; Also appeared as Linköping Electronic Articles in Computer and Information Science, vol. 6, No. 005, Linköping University (2001)

Lee, J., McMeel, D.: "Pre-ontology" considerations for communication in construction. In: Teller, J., Lee, J., Roussey, C. (eds.) Ontologies for Urban Development: Interfacing Urban Information Systems. Studies in Computational Intelligence vol. 61, pp. 143–156. University of Geneva 6,7 Nov 2006. Springer Verlag (2007). ISBN 978-3-540-71975-

Li, M., Du, X-Y., Wang, S.: Learning ontology from relational database. In: Proceedings of International Conference on Machine Learning and Cybernetics. vol. 6, pp. 3410–3415, (2005)

Masolo, C., Borgo, S., Gangemi, A., Guarino, N., Oltramari, A.: WonderWeb DeliverableD18. The WonderWeb Library of Foundational Ontologiesand the DOLCE ontology (final report) (ver. 1.0, 31-12-2003) http://www.loa-cnr.it/Publications.html#Pub2003 (2003)

Mounce, S., Brewster, C., Ashley, R., Hurley, L.: Knowledge management for more sustainable water systems. In: The Proceedings of the Final Conference of the COST ACTION C21 – TOWNTOLOGY Urban Ontologies for an Improved Communication in Urban Civil Engineering Projects. March 2009 Liege, pp. 39–49 (2009)

Nogueras-Iso, J., López, F.J., Lacasta, J., Zarazaga-Soria, F.J., Muro-Medrano, P.R.: Building an Address Gazetteer on top of an Urban Network Ontology. In: Teller, J., Lee, J., Roussey, C. (eds.) Ontologies for Urban Development: Interfacing Urban Information Systems. Studies in Computational Intelligence, vol. 61, pp. 143–156. University of Geneva 6,7 Nov 2006. Springer Verlag (2007). ISBN 978-3-540-71975-

Object Management Group: Unified Modeling Language, version 1.5, Mars 2003 – http://www.omg.org/docs/formal/03-03-01.pdf (2003)

Object Management Group: UML 2.0, OCL specification, May 2006

Philippe, M.: Translations between UML, OWL, KIF and the WebKB-2 Languages (For-Taxonomy, Frame-CG, Formalized English), Technical Report, May/June 2003

Pinet, F., Roussey, C., Brun, T., Vigier, F.: The use of UML as a tool for the formalisation of standards and the design of ontologies in agriculture. In: Advances in Modeling Agricultural Systems, 18 p. Springer, New York (2009).

Pinet, F., Ventadour, P., Brun, T., Papajorgji, P., Roussey, C., Vigier, F.: Using UML for ontology construction: A case study in agriculture. In: The 7th AOS Workshop on Ontology-Based Knowledge Discovery: Using Metadata & Ontologies for Improving Access to Agricultural Information, Bangalore, India, Nov 2006

Protégé.: Standford University – http://protege.standford.edu (2005)

Schreiber, G.: A UML Presentation Syntax for OWL Lite, Technical Report. (2005)

Sowa, J.: Knowledge Representation: Logical, Philosophical and Computational Foundations. Brooke Cole Publishing Co, Pacific Grove (1999).

Sure, Y., Staab, S., Studer, R.: On-To-Knowledge methodology. In: Staab S., Studer R. (eds.) Handbook on Ontologies, chapter 6, pp. 117–132. Springer-Verlag, Berlin Heidelberg New York (2003)

Sure, Y., Studer, R.: OntoKnowledge Project, Deliverable 18: OntoKnowledge Methodology final version, 1999. Available online http://www.ontoknowledge.org/downl/del18.pdf (1999)

Trausan-Matu, S.: A socio-cultural ontology for urban development. In: Teller, J., Lee, J., Roussey, C. (eds.) Ontologies for Urban Development: Interfacing Urban Information Systems. Studies in Computational Intelligence, vol. 61, pp. 143–156. University of Geneva 6,7 Nov 2006. Springer Verlag (2007). ISBN 978-3-540-71975-

Vilches Blázquez, L.M., Bernabé Poveda, M.A., Suárez-Figueroa, M.C., Gómez-Pérez, A., Rodríguez Pascua, A.F.: Towntology & hydrOntology: relationship between urban and hydrographic features in the geographic information domain. In: Teller, J., Lee, J., Roussey, C. (eds.) Ontologies for Urban Development: Interfacing Urban Information Systems. Studies in Computational Intelligence, vol. 61, pp. 143–156. University of Geneva 6,7 November 2006. Springer (2007). ISBN 978-3-540-71975-

Wildemann, T., Salokhe, G., Keizer, J.: Applying New Trends to the Management of Bibliographic Information on Agriculture - http://www.gil.de/publications/zai/archiv/R8_20040003.pdf (2004)

Chapter 3
Ontologies for Interoperability

Catherine Roussey, Francois Pinet, Myoung Ah Kang, and Oscar Corcho

3.1 Introduction

The goal of this chapter is to help readers understand how ontologies can be used to improve interoperability between heterogeneous information systems. We understand *interoperability as the ability of an information system or its components to share information and applications*. In the literature there is not a common agreement on which types of interoperability can be found between heterogeneous systems, but mainly classifications of the different types of heterogeneity that can be found between systems and the levels or layers where this heterogeneity has to be solved or overcome. However, this is not the purpose of this chapter. We will focus on which types of system interoperability can be resolved by ontologies, and which types of ontologies have been normally used for this purpose. About ontology types, we refer to the first ontology classification presented in Chap. 1.

Some of the illustrative examples will be taken from project presentations made in the context of the COST UCE Action C21 (Urban Ontologies for an improved

C. Roussey (✉)
LIRIS, Université de Lyon, France
e-mail: Catherine.Roussey@cemagref.fr

F. Pinet
French Institute for Agricultural and Environmental Engineering, Clermont Ferrand, France
e-mail: Francois.Pinet@cemagref.fr

M.A. Kang
Laboratory of Computer Science, Modelling and System Optimization, Blaise Pascal University, Clermont Ferrand, France

O. Corcho
Departamento de Inteligencia Artificial, Facultad de Informática, Universidad Politécnica de Madrid (UPM), Spain
e-mail: ocorcho@fi.upm.es

G. Falquet et al., *Ontologies in Urban Development Projects*, Advanced Information and Knowledge Processing 1, DOI 10.1007/978-0-85729-724-2_3,
© Springer-Verlag London Limited 2011

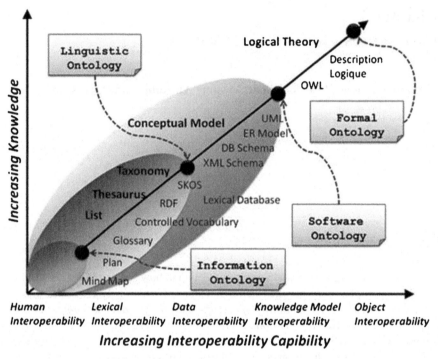

Fig. 3.1 A schematic representation of the different kind of interoperability based on our ontology classification

communication in UCE projects TOWNTOLOGY) or, in general, in the area of Geographic Information Systems (GIS).

As shown in Fig. 3.1, this chapter presents four kind of interoperability: lexical, data, knowledge model and object. (The human interoperability is not presented because these interactions are made only among human). For example, in the first section we provide an analysis of how these ontologies can be used for lexical interoperability in document management systems, followed by section presenting the use of ontology for overcoming differences between heterogeneous databases and knowledge bases. We will analyze their main role is in the context of these systems.

3.2 Lexical Interoperability in Document Management System

In Information Retrieval, users send a query to the system in order to retrieve relevant documents. The goal of linguistic ontologies in this type of system is to normalize the vocabulary used in the document to avoid lexical ambiguity. An example of lexical ambiguity is shown in Fig. 3.2: the green author employs the word "river" in the green document. The red author employs the word "watercourse" in his document to reference the same idea. Hopefully, the linguistic ontology links the terms "river"

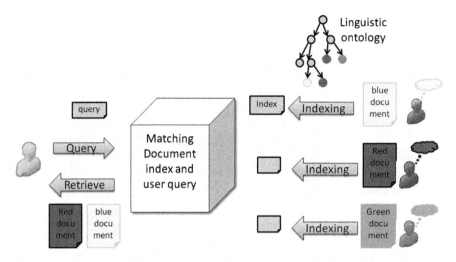

Fig. 3.2 Architecture of an information retrieval system

and "watercourse" to the same concept by using a synonym link. This concept is contained in the green and red document indexes. Indexes contain the description of the document content. Thus document indexes and user queries use the same vocabulary, so the information retrieval system can compare them. Chapter 5 complements this broad description, it explain how multilingual information retrieval system use linguistic ontology.

Linguistic ontologies contain hierarchical links, related links and synonym links between terms. These links could be used during the matching process in order to compute a similarity degree between the document index and the user query. Users build their queries by choosing the appropriate terms in the linguistic ontology. For practical reasons, terms should be defined in the ontology not only by means of a formal definition, if any, but mainly with natural language definitions to explain the referring concept, so that humans can understand them easily. The scope of the linguistic ontology depends on the scope of the corpus of documents: domain, core reference or general.

Semantic Web search engines represent a new trend in Web search engines. In the Semantic Web, users can annotate web pages according to a set of domain, local, core reference, etc., ontologies, what may also include references to linguistic ontologies. Annotation is different to indexing because annotation does not refer to the whole document like indexation. Annotation process associates a piece of data (a part of web page) to its corresponding metadata (a piece of data that describes the web page part). Annotation is composed of RDF triples (subject, property, objet): the subject is a part of web document identified by a URI, the property and the objet (the associated value of the property) is defined inside the linguistic ontology. All the RDF triples and their associated linguistic ontologies compose a graph where leafs are web document parts. Notice that in Fig. 3.3 the same document can be annotated by different users using different linguistic ontologies. This collaborative annotation process can take in charge the large amount of data available on the Web.

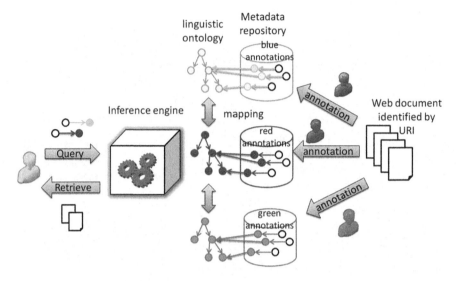

Fig. 3.3 Architecture of Semantic Web search engine

The Semantic Web search engine makes inferences about data and their metadata in order to combine and compare them. Inference mechanisms can be more compli-cated than just a matching process; they can compute new metadata or check them. The final user queries the Semantic Web search engine by using its preferred linguistic ontologies in order to retrieve parts of web pages.

3.2.1   Example: URBAMET Databank

The URBAMET databank is an example of information retrieval system based on a linguistic ontology. The documents search engine is accessible through the URBAMET thesaurus. An analysis of this thesaurus can be found in Chap. 10.

3.2.2   Example: The FAO Case Study of the NEON Project

The "NeOn – Lifecycle support for networked ontologies" project aims at using ontologies for large-scale semantic search engine applications in distributed organi-zations. Indeed, fisheries department has several information and knowledge orga-nization systems describing the world's fisheries and aquaculture. Information resources are available as parts of websites as individual documents, images, data-bases etc. These data sources could be better exploited by bringing together related and relevant information. To reach this goal, a set of fisheries ontologies are devel-oped to provide semantic search information service. The set of fisheries ontologies is composed of: land areas ontology, fishing areas ontology, biological entities ontology, fisheries commodities ontology, vessels ontology, gears ontology and fisheries fact sheets ontology. These ontologies are build by merging and integrating several thesaurus like AGROVOC (AGROVOC), ASFA, RTMS and others fishery glossaries. Indeed these fisheries ontologies are not purely linguistic because they also deal with structured data like database, thus in the NEON project some participants develop a new ontology model merging linguistic ontology model with software and formal ontology model (Montiel et al. 2008).

3.2.3   Example: The GEO Semantic Web Communities of the Italian "Three Lake Region"

The territory of the Italian three lake region has developed a unique urbanism model characterized by combining an historical villas landscape and great naturalistic areas. In order to preserve these landscapes and to promote sustainable tourism, it is necessary to plan urban expansion for a rational use of natural and cultural resources. Sustainable tourism is a multidisciplinary domain dealing with scientific, historical, artistic and economical point of views. This requires integration and sharing of information between a numbers of local actors. (Marcheggiani et al. 2007) propose a Geo Semantic Web community tools based on RDF annotations. Annotations are provided by each local actor to be accessible by all members of their communities. A community of local actors shares the same domains of interest; their centers of interest are described in a domain ontology and the related RDF annotations. Notice that a local actor can belong to several communities. Seven communities are identified: touristic system, municipalities, protected area, guide, police, Bed&Breakfast. The Geo Semantic Web community tools use Google Maps and Google Earth to visualize geographic object. A geographic object could be a point with latitude and longitude coordinate or a more complex geographic object like a polygon. To describe geographic objet the authors used two RDF ontologies the W3C Basic Geo Ontology and the RDFGeom Ontology.

3.3   Data Interoperability Between a Software Chain: Definition of a Data Exchange Format

Software ontology can be used as a data exchange format recognized by different systems. As shown in Fig. 3.4, the output of a blue system stored in this format can become the input of the red or green system. Data exchange format is the result of a lexical and structural agreement between each software company. The structural agreement enables each software to share the same data structure storage. Notice that usually data are stored thanks to an object oriented model. Thus concepts are object classes and instances are objects. The structural agreement is possible only if

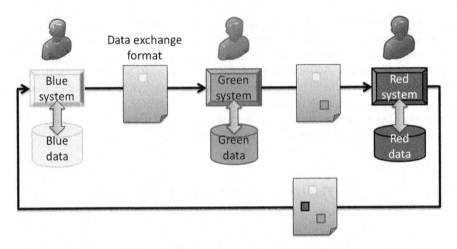

Fig. 3.4 A software chain using a data exchange format

a lexical agreement is reached. The lexical agreement signifies that the same name is used to reference similar classes or property in the different systems. The internal model of each system is not dependant on the data exchange format. That is to say the data associated to an object in the data exchange format, can be stored in several objects inside the blue system. Inversely an object of the blue system can be built by analyzing several objects of the data exchange format. The only constraint about data exchange format is that all the data useful by another system should be defined in the data exchange format. Due to the fact that this ontology is used by different systems, data exchange format should be core reference ontology. Indeed, each system represents a user group task.

3.3.1   Example: Building Information Models

The Aurora is a new university building in Joensuu. During the second phase of the Aurora project, IFC classes are used as data exchange format between several design software: architecture, structure and building services. During the early conceptual stage of the project, several models called Building Information Models (BIM) are build based on IFC classes: 3D Architectural model is build by architect to create space, 3D structural model are used by fabricators and contractors to detail frame structures, The building service design model describes lighting system, the product model estimate the cost of the building process. All of these models exchange data and are associated to specific software with visualization and simulation capabilities. Using BIM and data exchange format improve the communication between stakeholders and the scheduling process. It also improves the cost estimation and the final product quality. For more details, see the case study presented in Chap. 8.

3.3.2   Example: French Data Reference Centre for Water

For example, the French Data Reference Centre for Water (SANDRE in French) is in charge of developing a common language for water data exchange (SANDRE). In France, data related to water and hydrology are issued from thousands of organizations and public services. The SANDRE's priorities are to make compatible and homogeneous data definitions between producers, users and databanks. For example, some themes considered by SANDRE are: groundwater, hygrometry, etc. SANDRE proposed "a common language concerning data involved in the French Water Information System. Specific terms relevant to water data are clearly defined and data exchange specifications are also produced to fulfill the communication needs between partners involved in the field of water" (SANDRE). One of the SANDRE's goals is to define, at a national level, a common vocabulary concerning the field of water (SANDRE's common language). To fulfill this task, data models have been developed. They are associated to data dictionaries that gather all the definitions of data relevant to a topic concerning water. XML-based exchange formats have been also proposed. These XML format could be considered as software ontology focused on Water community, thus it also defined a core reference ontology about water.

3.3.3   Example: Farm Information Management Project

The French standard proposed by the FIM project (GIEA in French; Pinet et al. 2009) describes a large number of concepts related to farms. The final goal of the standard is to provide more complete data interchange formats in order to facilitate and to improve interoperability between information systems of the French Farms (GIEA).

The first step of the project was to carry out an inventory of the various previous standardization initiatives. Then, different terms, concepts and their relationships have been identified for different main fields of Farm activities (land management, agricultural infrastructures and buildings etc.). An important part of the FIM project consists in integrating and enhancing the definition of concepts, and work on standardization already initiated by the various partners. The monitoring of these approaches and the participation in various work groups and their corresponding project committees are therefore fully integrated in the project.

A software ontology has been chosen to formalize the proposed standard. All the members of the project can propose new concepts to the developed ontology. Data interchange formats are also proposed on the basis of the vocabularies and the concepts of the ontology. The ontology is represented by UML class diagrams. UML has been chosen to model the ontology because the participants of the FIM project are familiar with UML.

Fig. 3.5 Ontologies used
during the development of
information system

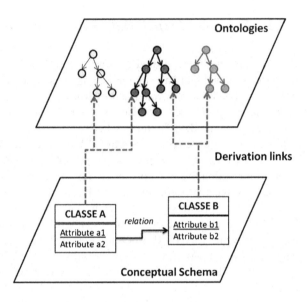

3.4   Knowledge Model Interoperability for Life Cycle System (Object Type Interoperability)

This kind of interoperability is proposed by Fonseca (Fonseca et al. 2000). The goal is
not to exchange directly data or to query heterogeneous data source but to focus on how
to design, implement or update easily an information system by using set of ontologies.
Ontologies become an engineering artifact which is a component of the information
system development. Thus reusing data or knowledge may decrease cost of developing GIS project, and may improve the quality of the development process. Most
part of ontologies used in this kind of interoperability system are software and core
reference ontologies. Moreover all the systems design with the same ontologies
will interoperate more easily because they are based on the same assumption about
physical world perception. The use of ontology, translated into an active geographic
information system component leads to what Fonseca call Ontology-Driven
Geographic Information Systems (ODGIS) (Fig. 3.5).

3.4.1   Example: ODGIS

Software Ontology can be a description of a generic knowledge model in order to
develop new specific knowledge model dedicated to particular software able to solve
a particular domain task. Each specific knowledge model based on this generic model
will be easily mapped to another one which is also a specialization of the generic
knowledge model. This type of system development based on generic knowledge
model is called Ontology Driven Information System (ODIS) (Guarino 1998).

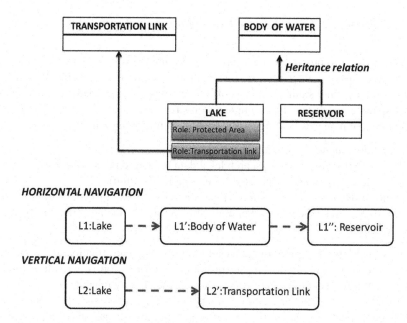

Fig. 3.6 Two examples of navigation between objects

Several software ontologies can be used to control the system development: domain ontology, task ontology, core reference ontology or foundational ontology like CityGML, geometric ontology, spatial reference system ontology or GML.

(Fonseca et al. 2000) propose an extension of this ODIS called Ontology Driven Geographic Information Systems (ODGIS). ODGIS are built using software components derived from various ontologies. These software components are classes that can be used to develop new applications (Fonseca et al. 2000, 2002). The mapping of multiple ontologies to the system classes is achieved through object-oriented techniques using multiple inheritances. ODGIS employs user classes that are derived through multiple inheritances from various formal ontologies to solve schematic heterogeneity. Thus a single geographic object supports multiple views; that is to say that each view is an object role containing an instance of a different parent class. The problem of the different levels of detail was approached by the introduction of a navigation mechanism that allows an object (the implementation of an ontology entity) to change its class by generalization or specialization. See for example Fig. 3.6, the object L1 instance of the class Lake, can be change to the new object L1', instance of the class Body of water. L1' has less detail than L1 but it could be change to the new object L1" instance of reservoir class. This type of change is a vertical navigation along the hierarchic classification of user classes. Another operation called role extraction enables horizontal navigation (Fonseca et al. 2002). An object role can be automatically transformed into a new instance, acting as an independent object. Therefore, the new instance can be matched to an object associated with another entity in a different ontology. As shown in Fig. 3.6, the object L2' instance of Transportation link class, is created from the role transportation link of the objet L2 instance of Lake class.

3.4.2   Example: User Adapted Interface Development

Metral et al. (2007a) propose to use a core reference ontology to develop automatically several user specific interfaces of information system. User specific interfaces enable to access only suitable sources of information using an adapted vocabulary. A user specific interface is for example a web site.

This system manages heterogeneous sources of information like:

- Textual documents: regulation, legal text.
- GIS : cartographic system to search legal data related to parcel for example.
- Master and local plans (maps used for urban planification).
- 3D city models are used to simulate the impact of urban project or to promote this project. 3D model are communication tool that do not contains textual information.

The goal of this system is to gather all the sources of information and to adapt their presentation according to a user profile. All information is not suitable to a group of user: for example legal texts are not adapted to city inhabitants.

Thus, this system contains a core reference ontology untitled OUPP. OUPP is a global schema integrating in a common representation all the object representations, found in sources of information. An object, for example the railway station of the Lyon city, is an instance of a OUPP concept: railway station. Each source of information is linked to the instances they describe by an annotation link. Two types of annotation link exist: conceptual annotation link and instance link.

Each user group viewpoint is represented by a local ontology. Local ontology is a selection of dedicated OUPP concepts with the appropriate terminology. In this system only the linguistic part of OUPP is used. More precisely, a local concept is linked to a OUPP concept by semantic relations: equivalent relation or specialization/generalization one.

Thus thanks to the matching between local ontology and the core one, the system is able to compute all the sources of information suitable for a user group and build automatically the user adapted interface of the system (Fig. 3.7).

3.4.3   Example: MDA

(Cutting Decelle et al. 2006) presents an approach of software development known as Model Driven Architecture (MDA). MDA focuses on models (or conceptual schema) and models transformations as the primary steps in the development process. MDA prescribes three kinds of models:

- The Computational Independent Model (CIM) focuses on the environment and the requirement of the system.
- The Platform Independent Model (PIM) specifies the operation of the system independently of the platform that supports it.

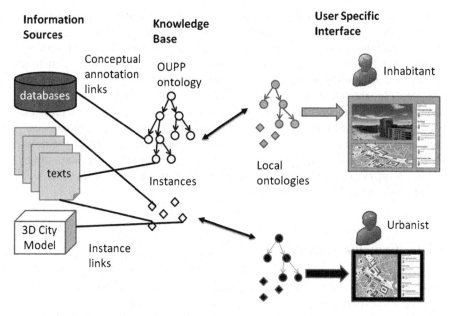

Fig. 3.7 Ontology based user specific interface

- The Platform Specific Model (PSM) focuses on the detail of the use of a specific platform by a system.

Model transformation is composed of a set of transformation rules, which specify the way a part of one model can be used to create a part of another model.

Thus, system development follows the different steps: the design of the CIM, the transformation of the CIM to PIM, the choice of the platform and the transformation of the PIM to PSM.

MDA approach allows different applications to be integrated by explicit relations between their models, thus enabling the integration, the interoperability and the evolution of supporting system.

Core Reference ontologies can be used to annotate part of the models between different applications. So, mapping between models will easily be identified.

3.5   Object Interoperability: A Global System Related to Heterogeneous Local Systems

This type of system interoperability enables several heterogeneous systems to have a common user interface for querying. The global system is composed of a core ontology.

The goal of this core ontology is to unify and gather the different representations of real objects or phenomenon stored in each local system. The specific domain model of each local system is represented by a local ontology. This local ontology can be a specification of the core one. A wrapper is a system that abstracts data from a data source and transforms them into the common model defined in the core ontology. Wrappers play the role of a translator between the local ontology and the core one. Thanks to these wrappers, the mediator is able to identify each different representations of the same real object stored in a data source. Thus the mediator can query each local data source by using the associated wrapper and gather all the result. Mediator decides how to access each data sources and in which order, normally by making a query planning step. Moreover in this type of architecture, the local system is still available for local users.

3.5.1   Example: Forum

Another project named FORUM proposes mediation architectures to facilitate the access to different French environmental data sources (FORUM). In France, environmental data are handled by a large number of stakeholders for different purposes: evaluate the environmental quality, find the better place for a new infrastructure, evaluate the impacts of a human activity, etc. Mediation architectures can be used to solve the problem of accessing these heterogeneous data.

The user query is based on a core reference ontology about environment (e.g. a global schema). The global system usually needs to access several data sources to answer the user query. Thus, the user query is rewritten in several queries by the global system; each one is dedicated to extract the needed information from a data source.

3.5.2   Example IGN-E Case : The Phenomen Ontology

The National Geographic Institute of Spain (IGN-E) has in charge to manage four cartographic databases that correspond to different scale: (1:25,000), (1:50,000), (1:200,000) and (1:1,000,000). These databases present a great heterogeneity due to the difference of the information sources used to build them. IGN-E wants to integrate all these four databases in order to facilitate their maintenance and to build a common features catalogue. (Gomez-Pérez et al. 2008) propose to build a domain ontology called PhenomenOntology able to query several cartographic databases. The goal of the PhenomenOntology is to link each databases in order to query simultaneously heterogeneous databases and to keep their structure. First the PhenomenOntology is built to contain all the features types stored in each databases. Secondly, as shown in Fig. 3.8: a global system able to manage local heterogeneous system.

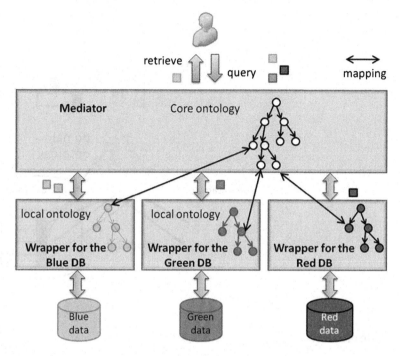

Fig. 3.8 A global system able to manage local heterogeneous system

Figure 3.9, each instance is linked to a features type by a mapping. This is a simplification of the global system presented in Fig. 3.8. This simplification is possible because all the databases share a common point of view of the domain.

3.5.3 Example: Integration of 3D City Models and Air Quality Models

In Chap. 7 of this book Metral and Cutting-Decelle propose to use a core reference ontology called OUPP to integrate CityGML, a 3D city model, with an air quality model. CityGML is used to visualize 3D elements and the air quality model is able to compute flow pollution. The integration of these two models enables to visualize air pollution flow in a 3D city model. CityGML and the air quality model are represented by two domain ontologies. The goal of the core reference ontology OUPP is to map equivalent concept belonging to each domain ontology. The mapping should specify how the transformation of a 3D attribute into an air quality one. Metral et al. (2007b) focuses on the extraction of street canyon, a very important air quality component, from the 3D city model.

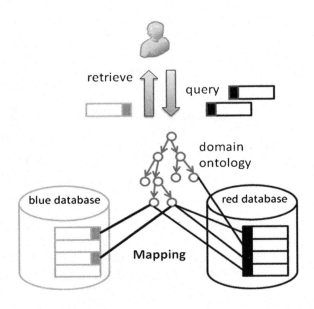

Fig. 3.9 The IGN-E case of heterogeneous databases

3.6   Conclusion

Ontologies have been used for the last decades for a set of tasks, one of which is focused on achieving interoperability between heterogeneous systems. We have presented a new vision of interoperability issues and how different type of ontology can be used in the task of interoperability.

Our description is not exhaustive, and other types of interoperability could be found, but our aims are to show that for each type of interoperability there are different approaches to be taken into account. This survey is useful when approaching an interoperability problem and having to select the resources to be used for solve it. In the next chapters you will find some more detailed descriptions about ontology usage and construction.

References

AGROVOC: A Multilingual Agricultural Thesaurus. ftp://ftp.fao.org/gi/gil/gilws/aims/references/flyers/agrovoc_en.pdf

Cutting Decelle, A.F., Bourey, J.P., Grangel, R., Young, R.I.M.: Ontology based communications through model driven tools: the MDA approach feasibility of the approach in urban engineering projects. In: Teller, J., Lee, J., Roussey, C. (eds.) Ontologies for Urban Development: Interfacing Urban Information Systems. Studies in Computational Intelligence 61, University of Geneva 6, 7 Nov 2006, pp. 143–156. Springer, Berlin/Hiedelberg (2007). ISBN 978-3-540-71975-

Fonseca, F., Egenhofer, M., Davis, C., Borges, K.: Ontologies and knowledge sharing in urban GIS. Comput. Environ. Urban Systemsx **24**(3), 232–251 (2000)

Fonseca, F., Egenhofer, M., Davis, C., Câmara, G.: Semantic granularity in ontology-driven geographic information systems. AMAI Ann. Math. Artif. Intell Spec Iss Spatial Temp. Granul. **36**(1–2), 121–151 (2002)

FORUM Project Web Site: http://www.lirmm.fr/FORUM/

GIEA (FIM) Web site: http://www.projetgiea.fr

Gomez-Pérez, A., Ramos Gargantilla, J.A., Rodríguez Pascual, A., Vilches Blázquez, L.M.: The IGN-E Case: Integrating Through a Hidden Ontology. Lecture Notes in Geoinformation and Cartography, pp. 417–434. Springer, Berlin/Heidelberg (2008)

Guarino, N.: Formal ontology and information systems. In: Guarino, N. (ed.) Formal Ontology in Information Systems, Proceedings of FOIS'98, Trento, Italy, 6–8 June 1998, pp. 3–15. IOS Press, Amsterdam (1998)

Marcheggiani, E., Nucci, M., Tummarello, G., Morbidoni, C.: Geo semantic web communities for rational use of landscape resources. In: Proceedings of the 2nd Cost Action C21 – Towntology Workshop Ontologies for Urban Development: Conceptual Models for Practitioners, Turin, Oct 2007

Metral, C., Falquet, G., Karatzas, K.: Ontologies for the integration of air quality models and 3D city models. In: Proceedings of the 2nd Cost Action C21 – Towntology Workshop Ontologies for Urban Development: Conceptual Models for Practitioners, Turin, Oct 2007 (2007a)

Métral, C., Falquet, G., Vonlanthen, M.: An ontology-based system for urban planning communication. In: Teller, J., Lee, J., Roussey, C. (eds.) Ontologies for Urban Development: Interfacing Urban Information Systems. Studies in Computational Intelligence 61, University of Geneva 6, 7 Nov 2006, pp. 143–156. Springer, Berlin/Heidelberg (2007b). ISBN 978-3-540-71975-

Montiel-Ponsoda, E., Aguado de Cea, G., Gómez-Pérez, A., Peters, W.: Modelling multilinguality in ontologies. Poster at Coling Conference, Manchester

Pinet, F., Roussey, C., Brun, T., Vigier, F.: The use of UML as a tool for the formalisation of standards and the design of ontologies in agriculture. In: Advances in Modeling Agricultural Systems, 18 pp. Springer, New York (2009)

SANDRE: SANDRE Web site. http://sandre.eaufrance.fr/rubrique.php3?id_rubrique=60&lang=en

Chapter 4
Ontology Alignment in the Urban Domain

Sylvie Calabretto

4.1 Introduction

Concepts in the domain of Urban Civil Engineering are often categorized and described using ontologies. Such ontologies may be designed independently by domain experts who have a minimal communication or no communication between them. As a result, similar concepts may be described differently and their categorization may result in heterogeneous ontologies.

More and more ontology-based urban systems are being built in different countries. However, most of the language-processing oriented ontologies that have been built so far have English or another language as basis. Since there is a growing need for multilingual ontologies, it is natural to ask for multilingual ontology alignment and viewpoint confrontation.

In this chapter, we first introduce several justifications for heterogeneity and give illustrations on urban problems. We then give some definitions on ontology matching and alignment, and some elements on ontology alignment approaches. Then we propose an overview of ontology alignment in urban or GIS domain and of viewpoint confrontation systems. Finally, we present the Hyppodamos tool as a solution for multilingual ontology alignment.

4.2 Heterogeneity in Urban Problems

Heterogeneity does not lie solely in the differences between goals of the applications according to which they have been designed or in the expression formalisms in which they have been encoded. They have been different classifications to types

S. Calabretto (✉)
Institut National des Sciences Appliquées de Lyon (INSA-Lyon), France
e-mail: sylvie.calabretto@insa-lyon.fr

G. Falquet et al., *Ontologies in Urban Development Projects*, Advanced Information and Knowledge Processing 1, DOI 10.1007/978-0-85729-724-2_4,
© Springer-Verlag London Limited 2011

of heterogeneity: syntactic heterogeneity, terminological heterogeneity, conceptual heterogeneity and semiotic heterogeneity. Usually, several types of heterogeneity occur together. The terminological heterogeneity occurs due to the variations in names when referring to the same entities in different ontologies.

4.2.1 Syntactic Heterogeneity

Syntactic heterogeneity occurs when two ontologies are not expressed in the same ontology language. This happens when two ontologies are modelled by using different knowledge representation formalisms, for instance OWL and F-logic. A solution to this heterogeneity consists in establishing equivalences between constructs of different languages. But this is not always possible. For instance if a language is more expressive than another one, not all F-logic expressions can be translated to OWL.

4.2.2 Terminological Heterogeneity

The terminological heterogeneity occurs due to the variations in names when referring to the same entities in different ontologies. This can be caused by the use of different natural languages, e.g. Paper vs. Articulo, different technical sublanguages, e.g. Paper vs. Memo, or the use of synonyms, e.g., Paper vs. Article. The Fig. 4.1 is an example in the urban domain. It is based on the glossary of urban, regional and environmental planning terms established in 2004 by Calderon and Ventura (Fig. 4.2).

4.2.3 Conceptual Heterogeneity

Conceptual heterogeneity stands for the differences in modelling the same domain of interest. This type of heterogeneity is also called semantic heterogeneity in Euzenat (2001) or logical mismatch in Klein (2001). This can happen because of the use of different axioms for defining concepts or because of the use of totally different concepts (geometry axiomatised with points as primitive objects or with spheres as primitive objects). Benerecetti et al. (2001) identifies three different reasons for conceptual heterogeneity to hold: difference in coverage, difference in granularity and difference in perspective.

4.2.4 Semiotic Heterogeneity

Semiotic heterogeneity is also called pragmatic heterogeneity in Bouquet et al. (2004). This heterogeneity is concerned with how entities are interpreted by people.

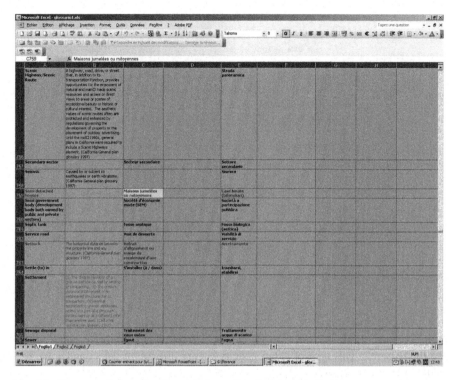

Fig. 4.1 Glossary of urban planning terms in english, french and italian languages

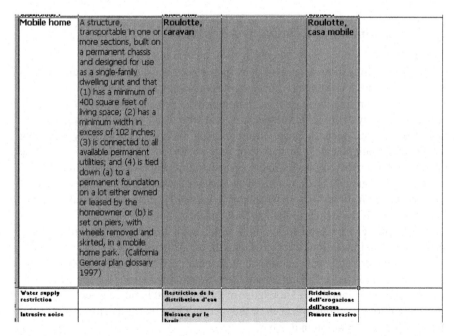

Fig. 4.2 Glossary with focus on mobile home term (caravane in french and casa mobile in italian)

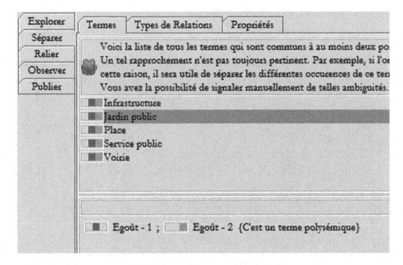

Fig. 4.3 Example of semiotic heterogeneity

In the example of Fig. 4.3, the term "Egoût" is interpreted differently by the Expert 1 and the Expert 2. This type of heterogeneity is very difficult to detect and solve by a computer.

4.2.5   Terminology in Ontology Alignment

Ontology matching aims at finding correspondences between semantically related entities of different ontologies. These correspondences may stand for equivalence as well as other relations, such as consequence, subsumption, or disjointness, between ontology entities. Ontology entities, in turn, usually denote the named entities of ontologies, such as classes, properties or individuals. Ontology matching results, called alignments, can thus express with various degrees of precision the relations between the ontologies under consideration (Euzenat and Shvaiko 2007).

Ontology alignment is a set of correspondences between two or more (in case of multiple matching) ontologies (by analogy with molecular sequence alignment). The alignment is the output of the matching process.

Alignments can be used for various tasks, such as ontology merging, query answering, data translation or for browsing the semantic web.

Ontology merging is the creation of a new ontology from two, possibly overlapping, source ontologies. The initial ontologies remain unaltered. The merged ontology is supposed to contain the knowledge of the initial ontologies, e.g., consequences of each ontology are consequences of the merge. This concept is closely related to that of schema integration in databases.

4.2.6 Ontology Alignment Approaches

The ontology alignment problem can be expressed as: in How to find the relationships that hold between the entities represented in different taxonomies?

We can identify two approaches (Nogueras-Iso et al. 2006) for the ontology construction: manual and automated ontology construction.

In the manual approach, we use the matching of terms (names and acronyms) between the different taxonomies. We can consider three categories of matches:

- Exact match
- Partial match: one concept is broader or narrower No match
- Provisional match: taxonomy errors (homonyms) imply erroneous matches

The automated approaches are used because manual mappings are time consuming and because some mappings may not be successful (content creators have not assigned the correct feature type). Two main approaches have been discussed in the literature: one which exploits the abstract data (nodes) represented by its names (lexical methods) and another which exploits the relationships (edges) between the various classes that form the structure of the ontology, (structural methods). Consequently, some of these techniques attempt to compare text strings that describe the entities in the ontologies (terminology-based ontology alignment) while others calculate the similarity measures between entities taking into account the structure of their corresponding ontologies (structural ontology alignment).

4.2.7 Overview of Ontology Alignment Tools

The state of the art of ontology alignment methodologies was recently surveyed by Euzenat and Shvaiko (2007). Previously, Rahm and Bernstein surveyed schema matching in databases (Rahm and Bernstein 2001).

In this section, we cover ontology and alignment tools even if most of them do not focus specifically on the urban domain. A notable exception is offered by Fonseca et al. (2002). They introduce an ontology-driven geographic information system (ODGIS), which is used to drive the creation of ontologies that will enable the integration of geospatial data.

Chimaera (McGuinness et al. 2000) is a software tool developed by the KSL group at Stanford, which provides tools for merging ontologies and checking the correctness of ontologies. Chimaera is web-based. Its graphical user interface supports a set of commands accessible via spring-loaded menus as well as drag and drop editing. The interface displays the knowledge base being edited and allows for users to check an automated merging procedure by highlighting the classes that require the user's attention. The authors of Chimeara consider the task of merging two ontologies to be one of combining two or more ontologies that may use different vocabularies and may have overlapping content. The major two tasks are to (1) to coalesce two semantically identical terms from different ontologies so that they are referred to by the same name in the resulting ontology, and (2) to identify terms that should be related by subsumption, disjointness, or instance relationships and provide support for introducing those relationships.

COMA++ (Aumueller et al. 2005) is a schema and ontology mapping tool, which is in many ways similar to our own mapping tool. However, both tools have been developed independently. COMA++ supports an iterative and automatic matching of ontology components and multiple matching algorithms. COMA++ supports multiple ontology and schema formats such as OWL, XSD, and XML.

The MAFRA toolkit is a mapping framework for distributed ontologies which adopts an open architecture in which concept mappings are realized through semantic bridges. A semantic bridge is a module that transforms source ontology instances into target ontology instances manually defined. The MAFRA toolkit supports a graphical user interface that provides domain experts with functionalities that are needed for the specification of semantic bridges. In the MAFRA toolkit, the ontologies are represented as graphs and in particular cases as trees using the Touch Graph library (http://www.touchgraph.com).

Falcon-AO (Jian et al. 2005) is an automatic ontology alignment tool that uses linguistic and graph matching techniques. It attempts to align ontologies using linguistic similarity between two entities relying on their names, labels, comments and other descriptive information. Falcon-AO relies on a graph matcher, which measures the structural similarity between the graphs that represent the ontologies.

Clio (Hernández et al. 2001) is a graphical tool used for the semi-automatically mapping of relational and XML schemas. In contrast, our mapping tool is mainly intended to match ontologies and therefore supports the mapping of XML and OWL/RDFS ontologies represented in XML, RDFS, OWL, or N3 (Berners-Lee et al. 2005). Using Clio, the user loads a source schema and a target schema and establishes connections between objects in both schemas graphically. Such connections are referred to as value correspondences, which express how one or more objects in the source schema are transformed into a target value. Clio has a mapping engine that incrementally produces database (SQL) queries that realize the mappings implied by the correspondences. The AgreementMaker generates a document that shows the mappings between concepts and can be used in a variety of ways, including in generating database queries.

MapOnto (An et al. 2005), which is inspired by Clio, is a research prototype for mapping between a database schema and an ontology as well as between two different database schemas. MapOnto works in an interactive and semi-automatic manner, taking input from the user for creating simple attribute-to-attribute correspondence and allowing the user to select a set of logical formulas that can be used to establish correspondences between related attributes. These logical formulas are generated by the tool using knowledge embedded in the ontologies. These logical formulas are ordered to suggest to the user the most reasonable mapping between the two models. MapOnto supports a graphical interface, which is based on Protégé (Gennari et al. 2003). Unlike our tool, the correspondences between attributes are not represented by lines in the interface, but as logical formulas displayed in a separate pane.

Cruz et al. (2007) have proposed an integration framework, in geospatial domain, to facilitate access to the information that is contained in distributed and heterogeneous databases (Cruz et al. 2002). Their approach relies on the alignment of ontologies. When such mappings have been established, we say that the two ontologies are aligned or matched. They consider two different architectures: a centralized architecture and a peer-to-peer (P2P) architecture. In the former architecture, there is a global ontology. Each distributed ontology is aligned with the global ontology. As a consequence, a query expressed in terms of the concepts of the global ontology can be translated into a query to one of the distributed or local databases using the mappings that are established during the alignment process. In the latter architecture, a query to a source peer can be translated into a query to a target peer, provided that the ontologies of the two peers have been aligned. Whichever the architecture, querying can be easily extended to new databases, and therefore to new regions.

Nogueras-Iso et al. (2000) use URBISOC, a thesaurus focused on Spanish terminology for Town Planning, developed by the CINDOC/CSIC institute (Centre for Scientific Information and Documentation / Spanish National Research Council). The proposition is made through the IDEZar Project (collaboration agreement signed in March 2004 between the City Council and the University of Zaragoza). The Objective of the project is the development of a local SDI for Zaragoza, to facilitate, increase and coordinate the use of spatial data by the Council and to develop applications for the citizens and to provide them with access to public sector information. Formal Concept Analysis (FCA) approach is used (it enables the extraction of a hierarchy of concepts from the feature instances contained in the source repositories) and seems to be more flexible: it allows dynamic building of the ontology (at least, a draft), it doesn't need to define the concepts, it just need to observe the data that exists. They have also created a domain specific ontology that facilitates the interoperability (synchronization, update and merge) of the separate repositories.

4.2.7.1 Overview of Viewpoints Confrontation Systems

For the purpose of confrontation, we defined the notion of opinion-viewpoint as opposed to the notion of viewpoint which is an emerging paradigm in Computer Science and especially in Information Systems Design (that is, a view angle on an entity). An opinion-viewpoint is a dynamic, non-consensual theory which is expressed on a domain for the purpose of sharing. It can be easily found in Sciences in the process of theory elaboration, and, to give an immediate example, this paper for instance is an opinion-viewpoint.Very few existing systems include confrontation of viewpoints in their functionalities. Indeed, allowing confrontation of viewpoints implies that the notion of viewpoint is well defined. Viewpoints-based systems, such as Bénel et al. (2001, 2002, 2006), Porphyry (2004) and Zaher et al. (2006), allow some form of confrontation. Porphyry especially includes a graph filtering system that shows, when several viewpoints are considered, which of them contain a given resource (Fig. 4.4).

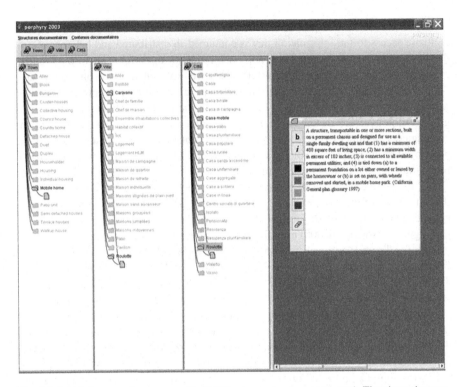

Fig. 4.4 In this first test, the terms are "in flat" (no hyponyms or meronyms). The viewpoints are the three languages. The shared documentary entities are the definitions in one or another language [NB: Look at the terms appearing as synonyms in a same language]

The reason why confrontation is not included in the current approaches of collective work is that the same software is generally used by small communities that do not necessarily wish to share their research work (Ribière and Dieng 2002). Confrontation can only be envisaged either as an inner functionality that works within a single community, or as a general tool that works only on published work.

Generating inventiveness through confrontation is a difficult task in a digital environment. There are three issues that we had to deal with. First of all: confrontation by digital computation. At this level of expertise, when even terminology can vary from an expert to another, any algorithm is overtaken by the complexity of the semantics that is involved in the process. It is important to limit the bias introduced by inaccurate matching algorithms. Therefore, we planned the environment as being used by the experts themselves, and the algorithms as being mere tools to test on the subject of study_validating or refusing their result. The second issue comes right from the solution of the first one: if the experts are supposed to control the environment, it is important to build it such as they can use it without being very proficient with the computer. We have thus kept the GUI as simple as possible, limiting the number of options and merging all algorithms into three options: exhaustive search,

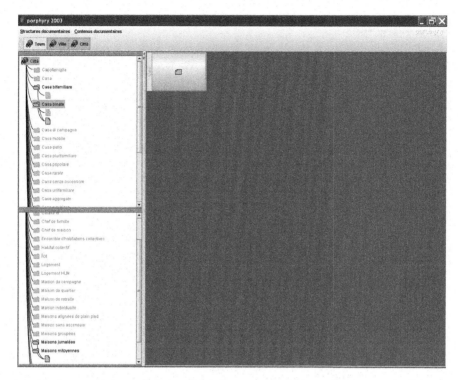

Fig. 4.5 Revealing of a little bit complex overlapping of terms and definitions

quick search and immediate search (since the algorithms merely propose their result, *search* is the most adapted term for what they do from the expert's viewpoint).

The third issue is at the level of data and representation. Digital processing, especially when it comes to matching things, implies that some graph structure will be used. Expressing a urban viewpoint as a graph can also induce a bias. We do not express viewpoints ourselves (at the moment), so we use the solutions taken by whatever source we have for them. For instance, Porphyry uses a representation that puts little constraint in the formalism, arguing that when experts in humanities are involved, interpretation is more important that formalness.

In the following, we show how we have used Porphyry for modelling the glossary of urban, regional and environmental planning terms established in 2004 by Calderon and Ventura (Figs. 4.5 and 4.6).

4.2.7.2   The Hyppodamos Tool

The goal of the Hyppodamos environment (Gesche et al. 2006, 2007; Gesche 2008; Berdier et al. 2008) is to allow an expert to confront and to align several ontologies on compatible subjects. We do not limit ourselves to a single formalism, thus we

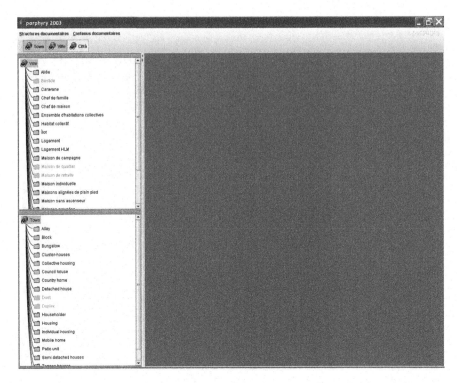

Fig. 4.6 Revealing of untranslatable terms from french towards english and conversely

created a generic formalism to allow the import from the formalisms used by the software that already allow the expression of viewpoints (Fig. 4.7) (Towntology for instance). We are not limited to a single media either (for now, we use text and images that are the main means of knowledge representation), nor to a single language (however, the expert actually doing the confrontation must still be able to understand what he is working on).

The environment itself is organized according to the computer-aided paradigm: it provides a place where the viewpoints can be imported (a virtual desk), and a set of tools that allow either an automated or a manual processing on them. These tools can be used at any moment, in any state of the viewpoints (Fig. 4.8). Viewpoints are thus never overwritten, instead a save file is issued linking to them.

There are five actions that we expect an expert to use while confronting. Three of them have been included in the environment, and the remaining two have to do with building the graphs (which we assume is already done). They are:

- Observation: the main, even though almost passive activity of the expert is to watch the viewpoints, study them and observe the effects of the other actions on them.

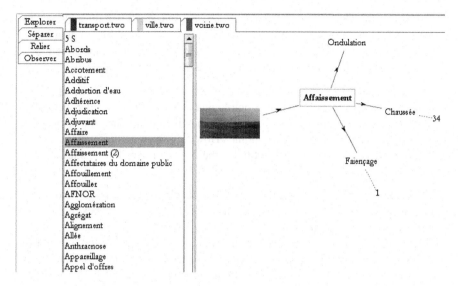

Fig. 4.7 A viewpoint in urban domain

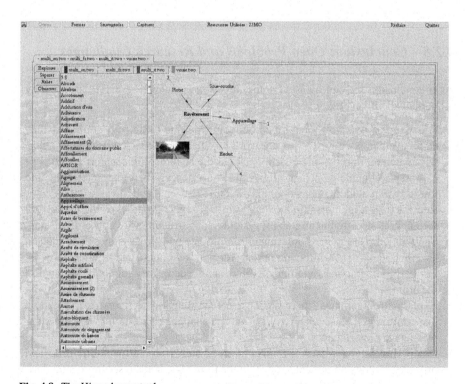

Fig. 4.8 The Hippodamos tool

- Extraction and Organization: the actions involved in graph building. Interesting patterns have to be extracted from the raw viewpoints (for example a digital paper, or the mind of the expert) and they must be organized within a graph structure.
- Connection and Dissociation between patterns of different viewpoints.

Ontology matching only involves a single action, connection. Its aim is to find matches between patterns of matched ontologies, in order to allow interoperability most of the time. The algorithms we took from this domain have the same goal, finding any relation between the viewpoints. However, since we deal with an expert/ machine partnership where the expert holds the power of decision, this task had to be split in two. Indeed:

1. When identical names are used for different meanings in several points of view, they must be dissociated (it was, for instance, the case of Thebes, a name of many cities in the antique world).
2. Whenever one of the matching algorithms points out that some terms could be connected, and it is not the case, it is also useful to explicitly dissociate them. These dissociations are not only correcting some error of a matching algorithm. Most of the time, they carry just as much sense as most connections. Among the experts using Porphyry especially, terminology can be as much a stake as diverging interpretations on a given subject.

4.2.8 Conclusion: Open Problems and Research Challenges

As a conclusion we can mention some directions in which research on ontology alignment should evolve.

- Foundations: Available model-theoretic semantics are sufficiently similar, so they could eventually converge. Recent work on categorical characterisation of ontology matching raised some questions about the statement in categorical terms of expressive alignments, which go beyond equivalence. Therefore, interesting and useful work could be pursued in this direction (Euzenat and Shvaiko 2007).
- Representing alignments: In the long term, we expect progress on the framework for integrating different alignment systems. Infrastructures are now still missing. Such an infrastructure should match ontologies and process the alignment on specified data. Therefore, alignment formats and metadata become crucial. Furthermore, graphical alignment editors are needed. They should be easy to use for ordinary users.
- Explaining alignments: there are only a few matching systems that provide a justification of their results. Explanation is a challenge for ontology alignment as well as user interfaces.
- Processing alignments: Currently, many systems are rather monolithic and provide ontology alignment at once. In the future, we hope to see more modularisation and also more alignment processors to be developed.

References

An, Y., Borgida, A., Mylopoulos, J.: Inferring complex semantic mappings between relational tables and ontologies from simple correspondences. In: OTM Confederated International Conferences (Part II). Lecture Notes in Computer Science, vol. 3761, pp. 1152–1169. Springer, Berlin (2005)

Aumueller, D., Do, H.H., Massmann, S., Rahm, E.: Schema and ontology matching with COMA++. In: ACM SIGMOD International Conference on Management of Data, pp. 906–908. ACM Press, New York (2005)

Bénel, A., Egyed-Zsigmond, E., Prié, Y., Calabretto, S., Mille, A.: Truth in the digital library: from ontological to hermeneutical systems. In: Proceedings of the Fifth European Conference on Research and Advanced Technology for Digital Libraries, Darmstadt, September 4–9, 2001. Lecture Notes in Computer Science, Vol 2163, pp. 366–377. Springer-Verlag, Berlin (2001)

Bénel, A., Calabretto, S., Iacovella, A., Pinon, J.M.: Porphyry 2001: semantics for scholarly publications retrieval. In: Proceedings of the Thirteenth International Symposium on Methodologies for Intelligent Systems, Lyon, June 26–29, 2002. Lecture Notes in Artificial Intelligence, Vol, 2366, pp. 351–361. Springer-Verlag, Berlin (2002)

Bénel, A., Iacovella, A., Calabretto, S.: Porphyry and Steatite: software layers for sense makers in humantities. In: Proceedings of the Workshop on Indexing and Knowledge in Human Sciences, Nantes, June 26–28, 2006, pp. 72–75 (2006)

Benerecetti, P., et al.: On the dimensions of context dependence: partially, approximation and perspective. In Proc. 3rd International and Interdisciplinarity Conference on Modeling and Using Context (CONTEXT), vol 2116 of LNCS, pp. 59–72, Dundee (UK) (2001)

Berdier, C., Calabretto, S., Caplat, G., Gesche, S.: Managing heterogeneity in urban ontologies. In: 3rd Workshop of COST Action C21: Construction of Multilingual Ontologies for Urban Civil Engineering Projects, Octobre 2008, Zaragoza, Espagne (2008)

Berners-Lee, T., Connolly, D., Prud'homeaux, E., Scharf, Y.: Experience with N3 rules. In: W3C Workshop on Rule Languages for Interoperability, Washington, D.C (2005)

Bouquet, P. et al.: D2.2.1 Specification of a common framework for characterizing alignment, knowledge Web (FP6-507482), http://knowledgeweb.semanticweb.org/semanticportal/deliverablesD2.2.1v1.pdf (2004)

Cruz, I.F., Rajendran, A., Sunna, W., Wiegand, N.: Handling semantic heterogeneities agreements. In: Tenth International ACM GIS Symposium, pp. 168–174. ACM, New York (2002)

Cruz, I.F., Sunna, W., Makar, N., Bathala, S.: A visual tool for ontology alignment to enable geospatial interoperability. J. Vis. Lang.Comput. 18(3), 230–254 (2007)

Euzenat, J.: Towards a principled approach to semantic interoperability. In: Proc. IJCAI Workshop Ontologies and Information Sharing, Seatle (WA US), pp. 19–25, (2001)

Euzenat, J., Shvaiko, P.: Ontology Matching. Springer, Heidelberg (2007)

Fonseca, F.T., Egenhofer, M.J., Davis, C.A., Câmara, G.: Semantic granularity in ontology-driven geographic information systems. Ann. Math. Artif. Intell. 36(1–2), 121–151 (2002)

Gennari, J.H., Musen, M.A., Fergerson, R.W., Grosso, W.E., Crubézy, M., Eriksson, H., Noy, N.F., Tu, S.W.: The evolution of protégé: an environment for knowledge-based systems development. Int. J. Hum. Comput. Stud. 58(1), 89–123 (2003)

Gesche, S.: Exploitation de l'hétérogénéité entre points de vue-opinion. In: Actes du XXVème congrès INFORSID, INFORSID'2008, Fontainebleau, France, 27–30 mai 2008, pp. 101–116 (2008)

Gesche, S., Calabretto, S., Caplat, G.: Un modèle pour la Confrontation d'opinions numérisées sous Porphyry. In: Colloque International sur le Document Electronique, CIDE'2006, Fribourg, Suisse, 18–22 septembre 2006, pp. 253–267 (2006)

Gesche, S., Caplat, G., Calabretto, S.: Managing difference of opinion in semantic structures. In: International Workshop On Semantically Aware Document Processing and Indexing held in cooperation with ACM SIGWEB, SADPI'07, Montpellier, France, may 21–22, 2007, pp. 79–86 (2007)

Hernández, M.A., Miller, R.J., Haas, L.M.: Clio: a semi-automatic tool for schema mapping. In: ACM SIGMOD International Conference on Management of Data, p. 607 (2001)

Jian, N., Hu, W., Cheng, G., Qu, Y., Falcon, A.O.: Aligning ontologies with Falcon. In: K-CAP 2005 Workshop on Integrating Ontologies, CEUR Workshop Proceedings 156, Banff, Canada (2005)

Klein, M.: Combining and relating ontologies: an analysis of problems and solutions. In: Proc. IJCAI Workshop Ontologies and Information Sharing, Seatle (WA US)(2001)

McGuinness, D.L., Fikes, R., Rice, J., Wilder, S.: An environment for merging and testing large ontologies. In: Seventh International Conference on Principles of Knowledge Representation and Reasoning (KR 2000), Colorado, pp. 483–493 (2000)

Nogueras-Iso, J., López, F.J., Lacasta, J., Zarazaga-Soria, F.J., Muro-Medrano, P.R.: Building an address gazetteer on top of an urban network ontology. 1st Workshop of COST Action C21: "Ontologies for Urban Development: Interfacing Urban Information Systems", Geneva, 6–7 November 2006 (2006)

Porphyry.: Porphyry Project. http://www.porphyry.org (2004). Accessed 4 Feb 2010

Rahm, E., Bernstein, P.A.: A survey of approaches to automatic schema matching. VLDB J. **10** (4), 334–350 (2001)

Ribière, M., Dieng, R.: A viewpoint model for cooperative building of an ontology. 10th International Conference in Conceptual Structures. LNAI, vol. 2393, pp. 220–234. Springer, Heidelberg (2002)

Zaher, H., Cahier, J.P., Zacklad, M.: The Agoræ / Hypertopic approach. In: Harzallah, M., Charlet, J., Aussenac-Gilles, N. (eds.) Proceedings of Indexing and Knowledge in Human Sciences, Nantes (2006)

Chapter 5
Ontologies and Multilingualism

Gilles Falquet and Jacques Guyot

5.1 Introduction: Ontologies and Natural Languages

The definition of an ontology as a specification of a conceptualization of a domain is independent of the terminology used in a particular natural language to describe this domain. In fact we can make a clear distinction between the conceptual structure of a domain and the way the concepts are designated by terms in a natural language. This view is exemplified in ontology specification languages such as OWL in which there is no connection with terms or texts in natural language, except for comments. In such a language, an ontology designer can arbitrarily define new concepts that do not correspond to any term in an existing language.

So why do we need to consider natural languages when building ontologies? There are multiple answers to this question, some of which are highly practical while others have a more theoretical background.

5.1.1 Theoretical Connections

On the theoretical side one can first observe that the lexicon of each natural language provides a conceptualization of the world. Most of the lexical forms, in particular nouns, designate a family of individuals that form a concept (e.g. dog, road, computer, ...).

G. Falquet (✉) • J. Guyot
Centre universitaire d'informatique, University of Geneva, Route de Drize 7,
CH-1227 Carouge, Switzerland
e-mail: Gilles.Falquet@cui.unige.ch; guyot@cui.unige.ch

G. Falquet et al., *Ontologies in Urban Development Projects*, Advanced Information
and Knowledge Processing 1, DOI 10.1007/978-0-85729-724-2_5,
© Springer-Verlag London Limited 2011

This designation can of course be ambiguous in presence of polysemous forms like *bank* or *table*. The world's conceptualization generated by a language's lexicon is usually represented in lexical ontologies like WordNet, that are often used as a basis or skeleton for building more specific or formal ontologies. They are also of great help for many practical applications like synonym removal, word sense disambiguation, query expansion in information retrieval, etc.

Another theoretical connection between ontologies and natural languages originates in the non-circularity of definitions. It is usually desirable to avoid circular definitions in formal ontologies. But the only way to avoid circularity is to admit that some concepts, called primitive or basic, are not defined within the ontology. Then, the only way to know what these concepts are is either to name them according to a well-known natural language term or to describe them with words. For instance, the CityGML model, in its *Water Bodies* sub-model refers to water body classes such as lake, river, ditch, bayou, etc., that are not defined in the model. This is acceptable because the purpose of this ontology is to describe urban objects and these descriptions do not require extremely precise definitions for concepts that are on the border of the domain. In this case, the linguistic form, like *sea*, is associated to a consensual meaning that is considered as sufficient.

Finally, linguistic forms are the only way to anchor an ontology in a real domain. An ontology whose concepts and relations identifiers are purely arbitrary strings of characters (C419, C2001, icl, pof, ...) would hardly be considered a conceptualization of some domain. At some point there must be a link between the "internal" concept identifiers and some known concept of the domain. This is where linguistic forms play an important role.

5.1.2   Practical Connections

Ontology designers must base their work on solid foundations, usually provided by domain specific information sources such as dictionaries, reference texts, legal texts, and many other types of documents. These documents, except for pictures, are expressed in some natural language. Moreover, in every specialized domain of human activity, a specific terminology has emerged to easily and unambiguously designate the frequently used concepts. Because specialists of the domain have learned to work with these concepts, it is quite clear that any usable ontology should be consistent with this terminology and the conceptualization it induces.

Similarly, from the ontology designer point of view it is certainly more convenient to work with concept names that exist in the natural language, even if the concept meaning in the ontology differs from its usual sense in everyday language. At some point the designer may also be led to create new concepts, acting as a terminologist, here again it is often suitable to name these concepts with (combinations of) existing linguistic forms.

5.1.3 Multilingualism

When working in a multilingual environment, the above-mentioned connections between an ontology and a natural language must be extended to several natural languages (Collier et al. 2006). This may occurs is several circumstances, for instance

– An ontology may serve as a common reference for an international community of users. In such a situation users generally prefer to accessing the ontology in their own language; they also need to find equivalent terms in other languages, e.g. for translation purpose.
– In ontology driven user interfaces, such as guided interactive information retrieval systems, the user will certainly be more efficient in her own language.
– In semantic indexing of large multilingual text corpuses (see Sect. 5.3 below) it is necessary to know the lexical form corresponding to a concept in all the considered languages
– The information sources required to build an ontology may exist only in some languages therefore the development process must take into account several languages (to avoid the reductionist approach consisting in translating all into a single target language)
– When an ontology needs to be localized, i.e. adapted to a particular language and culture, the ontological work should be carried out in several languages

Each one of these situations poses challenges of which we will explore some in the remaining of this chapter. We will first study the representation issues (how to take into account multiple languages when building ontologies), then, we will show how ontologies, connected to multilingual lexicons, can enhance information indexing and retrieval in a multilingual context.

5.1.4 Ontologies and Point of Views

In a context where different point of views must be taken into account, it can be useful to consider each point of view as a different language. For instance, it is well known that domain specialists have developed specific vocabularies to exchange information in a precise and non-ambiguous way. As a consequence, when a human activity spans several domains, the involved actors may experience communication problems due to this diversity of vocabularies. This can typically occur in urbanism related activities, such as urban planning, where urban engineers, architects, politicians, transportation engineers, or citizen organizations participate in decision processes. Since each one of these groups possesses its own vocabulary and conceptualization of the world, improving communication between them cannot rely on the development of a single "monolingual" ontology. In fact, we are confronted with a situation that is similar to multilingualism or multiculturalism. In particular, the "near synonym" problem frequently arises as well as differences in definitions of the same concept.

5.2 Approaches to Multilingualism in Ontologies

5.2.1 The Basic Concept-Centric Approach

This approach is based on the idea that most of the domain concepts exists in all the considered cultures. In other words, concepts are universal while their linguistic representation is culture-specific. Admitting this hypothesis, multilingualism can be supported by first building a "universal" ontology and then associating linguistic information to each concept.

The OWL ontology language proposes a basic mechanism to handle linguistic information in the form of *annotation properties*. An annotation property is a kind of meta-data attached to a concept. Its value is a string together with a language tag. In OWL knowledge bases the rdfs:label property is typically used to provide the linguistic form of a concept in different languages. Figure 5.1 shows the forms for the concept *Piéton* in French, English, and Italian (in the Protégé ontology editor).

Many existing ontologies are based on this approach. For instance, the Unified Medical Language System (UMLS) (National Library of Medicine 2009) is comprised of a set of concept identifiers (over one million) associated to terms originating from sources vocabularies from 18 different languages.

The concept-centric approach is well suited for normative terminologies, e.g. for ensuring that the same term is always translated in the same way in all the official documents issued by an organization. In a sense, these ontologies are similar to multilingual thesauri, the aim of which is mostly to define a controlled vocabulary. The main disadvantages of this approach are

1. The lexical information attached to a concept is limited to a character string, so there is no possibility to define relationships between lexical forms or to build sophisticated lexical structures.
2. The lexical forms (labels) are strictly equivalent, i.e. each label of a concept is supposed to designate exactly this concept. This can be true for very specialized domains but that is rarely the case for wider domains. For instance, the usual translation of the French word *fauteuil* (armchair) into Italian is *poltrona* but their meanings are slightly different (a *poltrona* is necessarily perceived as comfortable which is not the case for *fauteuil*). If it is necessary to be really precise

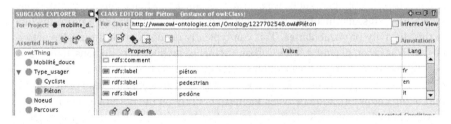

Fig. 5.1 Lexical forms attached to the Pieton concept in three different languages (in the protégé ontology editor)

then one must create two different concepts and use (invent) new terms to designate them in the language in which there is no direct lexicalization for them.

5.2.2 Concept-Centric with Structured Linguistic Elements

A more sophisticated version of this concept-centric approach can be obtained by considering à three-level model where concepts, terms, and forms are represented.

The conceptual level is intended to represent the concepts (or meanings) and their definitions. It is comprised of ontological elements such as concepts, semantic relations, properties, individuals. Formulae or texts express the concept definitions and domain axioms.

The terminological level is made of terms, which are associations between concepts and lexical forms. For instance the chemical term *acid* associates the linguistic form acid to the concept defined as *a compound which donates a hydrogen ion to another compound in a reaction*. Terms may be interrelated through terminological relations such as antonymy.

The lexical level represents the forms, which are character strings used in written language. These forms may be connected through lexical relationships such as plural or other inflectional variants. Moreover, additional relations and categories may be defined: variants, notes, context, etc.

There is, for instance, a proposal to re-implement the AGROVOC multilingual thesaurus in OWL with such a structure (Lauser et al. 2002, 2006; Soergel et al. 2006). In this case the ontology has two main concepts: *domain_concept* and *lexicalization*. All the domain concepts are subconcepts of *domain_concept*, while terms are instances of *lexicalization*, and forms are (string) properties of terms. Terms may have properties like *has synonym* or *has translation* that link them to other terms.

The multilingual support proposed in the Neon project (Montiel-Ponsoda et al. 2008) extend this approach by proposing a sophisticated structure to represent lexical information and to link this information to ontological element of the OWL language (class, property, individual, ...). The aim of this model is to fully localize an ontology, so that an ontology engineer or a user can work in his or her language. This is why every ontological element must have a localized lexical form.

The sophistication of the terminological level remedies the problem of strict equivalence of terms that exists in the basic concept-centric approach. Indeed, it becomes possible to associate weights to the links between terms and concepts, to indicate preferred terms, etc.

5.2.3 Interconnection and Alignment Approach

Instead of considering a unique ontology that represents the domain conceptualization, it is possible to maintain individual ontologies, corresponding to multiple views of the domain, and establish equivalence or similarity links between their concepts.

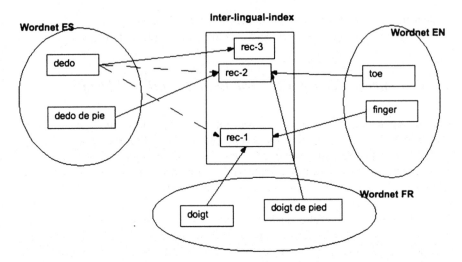

Fig. 5.2 Interconnection records between synsets of different wordnets. *Solid lines* represent EQ_SYNONYM relations, *dashed lines* represent EQ_HAS_HYPONYM relations

If the concepts correspond to terms in different natural languages, this is a mean to keep the different conceptualizations of the world and not to impose a unique view. This is particularly useful for lexical ontologies that are bound to their source language.

The creators of the EuroWordnet initiative have taken this approach to interconnect Wordnet ontologies developed for different languages. Their interconnection model is based on a so-called "inter-lingual index" (ILI). The ILI is a set of ILI records that are intended to connect equivalent concepts. All the concepts belonging to different ontologies that are linked to the same ILI record are considered as equivalent, as shown on Fig. 5.2. However, as mentioned for the previous approaches, the equivalence notion is often too restrictive. It often happens that a term in one language has no exact equivalent in another one. To address this issue the ILI has been extended in two ways:

1. The initial set of ILI records, which was directly drawn from the English Wordnet (i.e. there was a one to one correspondence between ILI records and English synsets) has been extended with new records that represent specific concepts of other languages. For instance, the Spanish word *dedo*, which means finger or toe, has no corresponding term in English. Thus a new ILI-record for dedo must be created.
2. Different kinds of relations between a synset and an ILI-record have been introduced (Peters et al. 1998):

   EQ_NEAR_SYNONYM when a sysnset matches multiple ILI-records.
   EQ_HAS_HYPONYM when a synset is more general than all available ILI-records.
   EQ_HAS_HYPERNYM when a synset can only be connected to more specific ILI-records.

This interconnection approach preserves the conceptual structure of each ontology. However, it requires a very precise and tedious work, carried out by terminologists, to establish the interlinking structure.

When the ontologies are more formal it becomes possible to automate the interconnection phase by applying concept similarity measures, see for instance Rodriguez and Egenhofer (2003) or ontology alignment techniques such as the one proposed by Li et al. (2006). These methods are based on structural comparisons of the concept definitions (how they are related to other concepts and where they are in the concept hierarchy) and on textual comparison of the comment, glosses, or terms associated to the concepts (with the help of multilingual dictionaries). They are appropriate for providing a first alignment of the ontologies, which must be followed by a human revision phase to improve the quality of the alignment.

5.3   Applications of Multilingual Ontologies

5.3.1   Finding and Checking Translations

When working in a very specialized domain, human translators and terminologists usually don't find term translations in existing multilingual dictionaries or thesauri. In addition, they must ensure that the terms they use really have the intended meaning. Multilingual ontologies made of aligned or partially aligned monolingual ontologies may be of great help in such situations.

For instance, Falquet and Mottaz (2000) propose a semi-automated technique to find the best candidate translations for a term. Given two monolingual ontologies A and B, the first phase consists in explicitly aligning the basic concepts of both ontologies, i.e. those concepts that are not explicitly defined in their ontology. Generally these basic concepts are not central in the domain and so deciding if two such concepts are equivalent or have subconcept relation is relatively straightforward. For instance, an urban ontology may refer to the concepts *color*, *air*, or *tree* without defining them explicitly. Figure 5.3 shows two concept definitions (for *armoire* in a

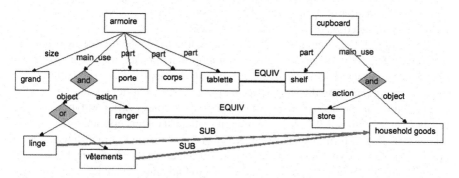

Fig. 5.3 Two concept definitions with aligned basic concepts

French ontology and *cupboard* in an English ontology) together with the aligned basic concepts they refer to. The second phase makes use of these basic equivalences to compare the definitions of defined concepts. It computes an edit distance between a definition *a* in A and a definition *b* in B by counting the number of change operations needed to transform *a* into a definition *a'* that is equivalent to *b*. The candidate translations for a concept are the concepts of the other ontology with the most similar (closest) definitions.

5.3.2   Multilingual Information Retrieval

Multilingual information retrieval (MLIR) consists in finding the most relevant document for a user need, considering that

1. the information need is expressed by a set of keywords or key phrases or sentences in the user's own languages
2. the document corpus contains documents written in different natural languages

MLRI has become more and more important with the advent of new communication technologies that enable users to access remote information sources. In many occurrences, these sources may contain documents that are not written in the user's preferred language but in some other language the user understands or for which he or she can afford a translation. MLRI is also crucial in international organizations that often have several working languages or that produce translated versions of their documents.

A classical approach for solving MLIR requests proceeds in three steps:

1. automatically translate the query into all the supported languages;
2. match each translated query to the documents written in the same language (applying standard monolingual IR techniques);
3. merge the result sets (ordered lists of documents) to produce a single ranked list of relevant documents.

This last phase is particularly difficult because merging ranked sets cannot be carried out by a simple comparison of the relevance values (Reference) since they have been computed on different sets of documents.

With a multilingual ontology it becomes possible to handle the MLIR problem differently. The basic idea is to replace each term that appears in a document or in the query by a concept identifier. Then it is possible to apply mono-lingual IR techniques, simply replacing the word space by the concept identifier space.

Depending on the degree of sophistication of the ontology different types of processing can be achieved. The strict minimum is a flat list of concepts identifiers, each one with its lexical form in each language, this is in fact a kind of multilingual lexicon. Experiments have shown that this can be sufficient to provide acceptable results (Guyot et al. 2006). In addition, it is much easier to find multilingual lexicons (lists of words together with their translation) than fully formalized multilingual ontologies.

It is however clear that a more sophisticated multilingual ontology, with a multiple lexicalisations for each concept should improve the quality of the indexing process.

If a multilingual ontology with semantic relations (in particular *subconcept* links) is available then the ontology can serve to enhance the retrieval process in several ways:

Disambiguation. Although experiments have shown that disambiguation is less crucial than can be thought at first, it is obvious that indexing an ambiguous form (e.g. *table*) with the correct concept is always suitable. There exist several disambiguation algorithms that are based on the inspection of related terms in the ontology. For instance, if the words *chair* and *eat* are found near *table* in the text, this will indicate that the correct sense for table is probably *a piece of furniture having a smooth flat top ...*, because this sense is close (in terms of semantic path) to senses for *chair* and *eat* in the ontology.

Reasoning. The matching process may take advantage of semantic relations determine that documents that do not match the query at the keyword level are nevertheless relevant. For instance, if the query is the set of keyword Q = {*bird, car*}, a document containing the words *sparrow* and *limousine* should be considered as relevant because the corresponding concepts are subsumed by *bird* and *car*. Other semantic relations such as *is_part_of* may also be used to enhance the matching process, depending on the context.

Interactive search. Interactive search techniques, such as faceted search, propose to build the user query by navigating within (subsets of) the domain ontology. By following semantic links the user should be able to discover the concepts that best fit her information needs and then access the documents that are indexed by these concepts. Since the interface must display the linguistic forms that denote concepts, not internal concept identifiers, it is clear that these techniques work only with ontolgies that have a (multilingual) lexical layer.

5.3.3 Semantic Annotation of Documents

The next generation of search engine should rely on semantic web techniques such as semantic annotation of documents. A semantic annotation, in its simplest form, is a list of concepts belonging to a domain ontology. The concepts associated to a document indicate what the document is about. This is similar to the semantic indexing process describe here-above. In this case the syntactic structure of the sentences is lost. In fact, this approach considers documents as bags of concepts and cannot rely on deeper semantic information.

A more precise kind of annotation consists in semantic graphs, for instance RDF graphs. In this case the graph nodes correspond to individuals that are concept instances and the labeled edges represent semantic relations between these individuals. The graph is thus a (partial) representation of the semantics of the document.

Terminologically rich and multilingual ontologies play a key role to enable semantic annotation.

1. They serve as references for labeling the graph nodes (with concept identifiers) and the graph edges (with relation identifiers).
2. Automatically annotating large collections of documents requires natural language processing tools (in particular parsers) to recognize the lexical forms corresponding to concepts and concept instances. These tools must be provided with adequate lexical information.
3. Natural language processing tools can take advantage of ontological knowledge to solve syntax analysis problems. For instance, ambiguous sentences may be disambiguated if some domain knowledge is available.

5.4 Conclusion

There exist natural and unavoidable connections between ontologies and natural languages. With the exceptions of ontologies that are used in fully automated processes that do not communicate with human users and do not access textual data, most ontologies must supply terminological information. This is particularly true when they are intended for multilingual context of use. We have seen that there are three main approaches to equip ontologies with multilingual terminological information: from simple concept labels to sophisticated terminological/lexical structures or ontology alignment techniques.

Multilingual ontologies certainly have an important role in knowledge engineering, in particular for applications that must deal with formalized knowledge *and* knowledge expressed in natural languages. We have presented three such applications: translation checking, multilingual information retrieval and the semantic annotation of documents.

Bibliography

Collier, N., Kawazoe, A., Jin, L., Shigematsu, M., Dien, D., Barrero, R., Takeuchi, K., Kawtrakul, A.: A multilingual ontology for infectious disease outbreak surveillance: rationale, design and challenges. Lang. Resour. Eval. **40**, 405–413 (2006)

Falquet, G., Mottaz Jiang, C.L.: Conflict resolution in the collaborative design of terminological knowledge Bases. In Proc. EKAW 2000 (International Conference on Knowledge Engineering and Knowledge Management), Lecture Notes in Computer Science.. Springer-Verlag, Berlin (2000)

Guyot, J., Radhouani, S., Falquet, G.: Conceptual indexing for multilingual information retrieval. In: Peters, C., et al. (eds.) Accessing Multilingual Information Repositories: 6th Workshop of the Cross-Language Evaluation Forum, CLEF 2005, Vienna, Austria, Revised Selected Papers. Lecture Notes in Computer Science, vol 4022, Springer, Berlin (2006)

Kerremans, K., Temmerman, R., Tummers, J.:Representing multilingual and culture-specific knowledge in a VAT regulatory ontology: support from the termontography method. Proc. Workshop on Regulatory Ontologies and the Modelling of Complaint Regulations (WORM CoRe; Catana, Italy), Lecture Notes in Computer Science, Springer-Verlag, Berlin (2003)

Lauser, B., Wildemann, T., Poulos, A., Fisseha, F., Keizer, J., Katz, S.: A Comprehensive framework for building multilingual domain ontologies: creating a prototype biosecurity ontology. Proc. DC-2002 Metadata for e-Communities: Supporting Diversity and Convergence, Florence (2002)

Lauser, B., Sini, M., Liang, A., Keizer, J., Katz, S.: From AGROVOC to the agricultural ontology service / concept server an OWL model for creating ontologies in the agricultural domain. Proc International Conference on Dublin Core and Metadata Applications, Manzanillo, Colima, Mexico (2006)

Li, Y., Li, J., Zhang, D., Tang, J.: Result of ontology alignment with rimom at oaei'06. In Proc. of the International Workshop on Ontology Matching (OM- 2006), Nov. 5, 2006, Athens, Georgia, USA (2006)

Montiel-Ponsoda, E., Aguado de Cea, G., Gómez-Pérez, A., Peters, W.: Modelling multilinguality in ontologies. Coling 2008: Proceedings of the 22nd International Conference on Computational Linguistics, Manchester (2008)

National Library of Medicine. The Unified Medical Language System (UMLS). http://www.nlm. nih.gov/research/umls/online_learning/OVR_001.htm (2009). Retrieved on 18 Feb 2009

Peters, W., Vossen, P., Díez-Orzas, P., Adriaens, G.: Cross-linguistic alignment of wordnets with an inter-lingual-index. Comput. Humanit. 32, 221–251 (1998)

Rodriguez, M.A., Egenhofer, M.J.: Determining semantic similarity among entity classes. IEEE Trans. Knowl. Data Eng. 15, 442–456 (2003)

Soergel, D., Lauser, B., Liang, A., Fisseha, F., Keizer, J., Katz, S.: Reengineering thesauri for new applications: the AGROVOC Example. Journal of digital information, 4(4). Retrieved July 4, 2011, from http://journals.tdl.org/jodi/article/view/112 (2006)

Part II
Ontologies in the Urban Domain

Chapter 6
Ontologies in the Geographic Information Sector

Roland Billen, Javier Nogueras-Iso, F. Javier López-Pellicer, and Luis M. Vilches-Blázquez

6.1 Introduction

Geographical information (GI) or geoinformation describes phenomena associated directly or indirectly with a location (coordinates systems, address systems...) with respect to the Earth's surface. Such phenomena can be either spatially discrete (represented by geometric primitives like points, lines, regions, etc.) such as a municipality, a road axis, etc. or spatially continuous (represented by interpolation on an image grid for example) such as terrain's elevation, pollution diffusion, etc. GI is created by manipulating geographic data (or geospatial data) in a computerized system. Geospatial data can be acquired by different means: topographic survey, remote sensing, aerial photographs, GPS, laserscan, and all other types of sensors or survey techniques. Traditionally, these data are the core component of Geographic Information Systems (GIS), which is the term commonly used to refer to the software packages that allow to capture, store, check, integrate, manipulate, analyze and display them.

Geographic information is therefore used in a wide variety of domains; indeed, in any application dealing with spatial or geographical frame of reference. Typical applications are land registration, hydrology, cadastre, land evaluation, planning or environmental observation. The link between urbanism applications and GI domain is obvious as most of information treated in urban applications is indeed GI (maps or spatial databases including information about buildings, networks, terrain, etc.).

R. Billen (✉)
Geomatics Unit, University of Liege, Belgium
e-mail: rbillen@ulg.ac.be

J. Nogueras-Iso • F.J. López-Pellicer
Computer Science and Systems Engineering Department, University of Zaragoza, Spain
e-mail: jnog@unizar.es; fjlopez@unizar.es

L.M. Vilches-Blázquez
Ontology Engineering Group, Universidad Politécnica de Madrid, Spain
e-mail: lmvilches@fi.upm.es

G. Falquet et al., *Ontologies in Urban Development Projects*, Advanced Information and Knowledge Processing 1, DOI 10.1007/978-0-85729-724-2_6,
© Springer-Verlag London Limited 2011

Therefore, it is reasonable to depict the use of ontologies in the GI sector in the framework of the Towntology project.

The potential of GI as an instrument to facilitate decision-making and resource management in diverse areas (e.g., natural resources, facilities, cadastre or agriculture, urban planning) of government or private sectors has led to the evolution of GIS into the broader concept of *Spatial Data Infrastructure* (SDI). According to the Global Spatial Data Infrastructure Association Cookbook (Nebert 2004), "the term Spatial Data Infrastructure is often used to denote the relevant base collection of technologies, policies and institutional arrangements that facilitate the availability of and access to spatial data". The European Committee for Standardization (CEN) defines the SDI concept as a platform-neutral and implementation neutral technological infrastructure for geospatial data and services, based upon non-proprietary standards and specifications (CEN 2006).

From the previous definitions of SDI it can be derived that one of the main objectives of SDIs is to make the work with geospatial data more efficient (McKee 2000; Nebert 2004), avoiding problems that occur with conventional GIS technology and geographic data sets. Bernard et al. (2004) remarks that there are two major problems with traditional GIS stand-alone applications: first, data sets exist in a plethora of different data formats (datasets in different formats often have to be converted in order to be used in a different system); and second, these data are often not (sufficiently) documented (it is difficult or even impossible for outside users to discover data sets and to assess whether a given data set is useful for their tasks). In other words, what these authors are meaning is the inability of isolate GIS tools to deal with interoperability issues in the current context where GI must be shared between online systems. As mentioned by Egenhofer (1999) with respect to GI interoperability, "the goal of interoperating GISs is to achieve an automated process that will allow to use data and software services across the boundaries that their collectors and designers envisioned".

Going a bit further with GI interoperability issues, the main obstacle for the interoperation of systems is the heterogeneity in data and services managed by these systems. In order to determine whether two systems are heterogeneous, one must analyze their different features and this yields different types of heterogeneity as well as different types of inteoperability levels. A commonly made distinction is that between syntactic (solving syntactic heterogeneity) and semantic interoperability (solving semantic heterogeneity) (Kolodziej 2003). The syntactic interoperability is concerned with the technical level, i.e. it refers to the ability for a system or components of a system to provide information portability and inter-application as well as cooperative process control. It comprises intercommunication at communication level protocol, hardware, software, and data compatibility layers. The semantic interoperability, in contrast, deals with the domain knowledge necessary for informatics services to "understand" each other's intentions and capabilities.

In order to overcome interoperability problems, GI standards have been developed by organizations and standardization bodies such as the Open Geospatial Consortium (OGC) or ISO/TC211 (ISO technical committee for geographic information and geomatics). The use of GI standards has gradually eliminated many of the difficulties resulting from incompatibility of data structure and syntax but it is not enough to solve completely the problems derived from semantic heterogeneity. According to Bishr (1998), semantic heterogeneity is defined as the consequence of different conceptualizations of a real world fact. Because of different perspectives on the same real world facts, there may not be a common base of definitions of the underlying facts between two disciplines (domains). Derived from these different perspectives, Bishr distinguishes two main subtypes of semantic heterogeneity: cognitive heterogeneity and naming heterogeneity. Cognitive heterogeneity occurs when the same term is used in different domains for representing different concepts. On the other hand, naming heterogeneity occurs when the same real world facts are understood in the same way but are named differently.

Semantic interoperability problems arise in different scenarios of GI interoperability, ranging from discovery and retrieval of GI to the integration of data from different sources. For instance, in the case of GI discovery, though there are standardized interfaces for catalogue services operations (e.g., OGC Catalogue services specifications), the conformance to the specifications does not prevent from having GI catalogues with semantic heterogeneity problems. Catalogue implementations based on simple word-matching between user queries and metadata holdings suffer from typical naming and cognitive heterogeneities in the form of synonymy and homonymy problems respectively (Bernard et al. 2004). And as reported in Sect. 6.3, similar problems of semantic heterogeneity occur in the case of GI retrieval or integration of data from different sources.

The objective of this chapter will be the study of GI ontologies as a possible approach to facilitate semantic interoperability and overcome the problem of semantic heterogeneity. The explicit definition of knowledge by means of ontologies is commonly used as a mechanism to understand and solve the semantic heterogeneity arisen when interoperating between two systems (Wache et al. 2001). Defining, building and using ontologies have become a key research topic in Geographical Information Sciences (GISc). A lot of work has been dedicated to the definition of geographical ontologies and to the use of them in practical applications.

Apart from this introduction section about GI, SDIs and interoperability issues, the remaining parts of this chapter are structured as follows. Sect. 6.2 describes the features of geographical information related ontologies. After, we focus on the role of ontologies to facilitate GI interoperability (Sect. 6.3). Sect. 6.4 presents three study cases discussing ontology design methodologies and ontology's uses in the geographical information context. Finally, Sect. 6.5 gathers conclusions, and Sect. 6.6 points out open problems and research perspectives.

6.2   Ontologies in GI

In the GI sector, and more especially in spatial database community, the term ontology is often associated to (Yeung and Hall 2007):

- A *concept* of using formally and explicitly defined terminology and vocabulary to describe real world features or phenomena associated with a specific discipline, domain or application.

- A *systematic collection and specification* of spatial entities, their properties and relations, which are commonly stored in a hierarchical structure and shared by users in a particular discipline or domain.
- An emerging *approach* to designing spatial database systems that has several advantages over conventional methods of systems development, including:
  - Allowing the establishment of correspondence and interrelation among different domains of spatial entities and relations.
  - Contributing to create better information systems by improving communication between systems developers, managers and users.
  - Enabling a user-centred approach to systems development.
  - Providing the underlying concept and technology for interoperable database systems.
  - Designing spatial databases from a perspective beyond the map metaphor that views the real world as independent layers of information that can be combined and overlaid.

Let's put aside for now the spatial database design approach and focus on the first two aspects. As seen in Chap. 2, ontologies can be implemented using various ontological languages (e.g., RDF/S[1] or OWL[2]) and can be managed using specific tools (e.g., Protegé[3]). Ontologies can also be recorded graphically using entity-relationship or UML diagrams. As stated by (Yeung and Hall 2007) and deeply discussed by Fonseca et al. (2002, 2003), the process of ontology building and documentation is comparable to database conceptual data modelling because both processes aim to identify and define real world features and determine their relationships. However, although the processes are similar, the end products are not the same. While the purpose of a conceptual schema is to describe the intended database structure at a high level of abstraction, an ontology represents a consensual agreement on the meanings of and relations between the vocabulary of terms used to represent data. There is not necessarily direct correspondence between the structure of an ontology and the structure of the database as it is represented by a conceptual database model. This point is illustrated in the case study 2 in Sect. 6.4.2.

As discussed in Chap. 2, ontologies can be obtained through top-down, bottom-up or middle out approaches. Just recall that a top-down approach builds ontology from upper level ontologies, bottom-up extract ontology from implemented systems, and middle out approach is a combination of the two others. Case study 1 (Sect. 6.4.1) is an example of top-down approach when case study 2 (Sect. 6.4.2) is a bottom-up case.

Generally speaking, Ontologies are created by consensus among the experts of data pertaining to a particular domain. These experts are sometimes collectively referred to as an *information community*, using a series of ontology building activities

---

[1] Resource Description Framework (RDF), see Manola and Miller (2004).

[2] Web Ontology Language (OWL), see McGuinness and van Harmelen (2004).

[3] http://protege.stanford.edu/

(Medina-Nieto 2003). These activities include extraction from existing database schemas (in the case of bottom-up approaches) and a formal data modelling process, called *semantic modelling*, that focuses on identifying and defining relevant terms. In the ontology building processes, it is often necessary to solicit the help of subject matter experts to ensure accuracy and precision of definitions.

Ontology as an approach to database design and implementation serves several useful purposes. The ability of ontologies to provide unambiguous meanings of and structured relationships among the terminology used to describe the real world makes them a useful tool to address the problem of semantic heterogeneity in database design and application, but it is also a crucial medium of communication by providing precise notions that can be used to describe an application domain. It also provides the means to help define the semantics of database fields in a clear and unambiguous manner.

When focusing on semantic heterogeneity and interoperability, the greatest value of ontology is its role in supporting database interoperation strategies by means of query translation and schema integration. Query translation is the process of translating or mapping heterogeneous field names used in different data sets to an ontology in order to query them simultaneously using a single operation, for example by one SQL statement. Schema integration, on the other hand, makes use of the concept of ontology to combine the schemas of individual data sources into one global schema. The next section focuses on the specific roles of ontologies for resolving problems resulting from semantic heterogeneity.

6.3   Ontologies as a Way to Solve Interoperability Issues

This section reviews the state of the art in the use of ontologies in three typical GI interoperability scenarios. Firstly, Sect. 6.3.1 describes the use of ontologies to help in the discovery and retrieval of GI resources. Secondly, after GI resources are available, Sect. 6.3.2 presents how ontologies can contribute to solve the problems involved in data integration from heterogeneous sources. Thirdly, Sect. 6.3.3 describes the role of ontologies as the conceptual model that guides the design and development of information systems in the GI context.

6.3.1   Ontology-Based Discovery and Retrieval of Geographic Information

Discovering and retrieving geographic information is obviously one of the main goals of developing interoperable systems, and by extension of SDIs. It is also crucial to discover suitable geoprocessing services to handle these data. Conventionally, discovery and retrieval for geographic information and geoprocessing services is carried through based on keywords. However, keywords are not always sufficient to find exactly suitable geographic information because they lack semantics, there are ambiguities in natural language and inference mechanisms cannot be applied. The emergence of ontology provides possibility to enhance discovery and retrieval; it solves problems of semantic heterogeneity between user's search and description of geographic information in SDI.

SDIs provide catalogue services for discovering appropriate data and services for a specific task. Searches in these catalogues are currently mainly based on string-matching keywords with metadata entries (Lutz 2005). Keyword-based search can have low recall if different terminology is used and/or low precision if terms are homonymous or because of their limited possibilities to express complex queries (Bernstein and Klein 2002 cited by Lutz 2005). A way to overcome these limitations is to use ontologies to improve matching processes.

For instance, Bernard et al. (2004) describe the architecture of an ontology based discovery and retrieval system of geographical information. In this system, different Web Feature Services are described with metadata which includes a reference to an application ontology that describes the feature types in terms of a shared domain ontology. The user queries are processed as follows: the user states their queries in terms of the shared domain ontology; then the system expands the user query restrictions with the names of the stored features. Lutz and Klien (2006) show the evolution of the previous system. This latter version defines a query language and provides a user interface that helps users to formulate queries using a well-known domain vocabulary. In this system, the names of the elements of the Geography Markup Language – GML (see Sect. 6.3.2) returned by the Web Feature Services are mapped to a shared vocabulary that is used to expand the user queries using a Description Logic reasoner.

Other works in this line are the ones proposed by Hübner et al. (2004) and Navarrete (2006). The first one describes an ontology based reasoning system that allows integrating heterogeneous geographical information by resolving structural, syntactic and semantic heterogeneities. The query system supports the specification of queries of the type *concept@location in time*. The user selects a set of registered domain-specific application ontologies (in the thematic, spatial, and temporal domains) based on a common vocabulary and use them to select search terms that are expanded by selecting all equivalences and subconcepts (for the thematic search term), spatially related place names (for the spatial search term), and relevant time periods (for temporal ones). The second one provides a framework to represent semantic relations among the concepts from different datasets of a repository. The system is based on a high level ontology constructed by merging the knowledge provided by the datasets of the repository that describe in a precise and formal way the content of the repository. This ontology is then used to define semantic services or queries that enable agents find and integrate thematic information. It specifically focuses on finding datasets containing information on a particular theme (including theme subclasses if they are considered of interest); translating the content of a dataset to another compatible vocabulary; and integrating heterogeneous content from different datasets.

With respect to the discovery and retrieval of geographic information services, similar approaches based on ontology-based descriptions of queries and service advertisements can be adopted. By using ontologies to enrich services' description, their semantics become machine-interpretable, and users are enabled to pose concise and expressive queries. Furthermore, logical reasoning can be used to discover implicit relationships between search terms and service descriptions. Lutz (2005) proposes ontology-based descriptions of operations consisting of a semantic signature, which contains Description Logics (DL) concepts (instead of datatypes) to represent inputs and outputs, and a specification of pre- and postconditions in First Order Logic (FOL). The operation descriptions and the associated ontologies occur at two levels: At the domain level, they describe the generic operations of the domain and thus provide a shared vocabulary (preferentially related to existing standards or agreements within the domain rather than designed from scratch, e.g. the 19100 series of ISO standards published by ISO/TC 211), on which, at the application level, service providers (or requesters) can base the descriptions of (or queries for) a particular operation.

6.3.2   Data Integration in Heterogeneous Spatial Databases

Geographic applications are an example of the need to bring data integration to a big scale. This is the case for the studies of weather, environment, sustained development, terrain use (ground use), mobile applications and more. Semantic understanding is necessary to discover and extract the essential information into a structure suitable for integration from the sources of data. Researchers show the need to focus on a specific domain to achieve the main goal of semantic understanding.

Ontologies define semantics independently of data representation and reflect the relevance of data without accessing them. Such a high-level description of the semantics of geographic information provides more and new means for comparing and integrating spatial data. In addition, ontologies enable knowledge reuse by semantically describing data that were derived from consensus reached by different GIS communities.

Kashyap and Sheth (1996) present a semantic taxonomy to demonstrate semantic similarities between two objects and related this to a structural taxonomy. At present days, intelligent integration has been applied to heterogeneous database integration. From artificial intelligence world often it is achieve by means agents or mediators that provide intermediary services by linking data resources and application programs.

Within the SDI context, several ontologies have been built in last years with the purpose of facilitating integration of data. Some of them are the following:

- *Ontology for Geography Markup Language*[4] provides an ontology-based representation of the Geography Markup Language(GML) version 3.0 using OWL as

---

[4] http://efe.ege.edu.tr/~unalir/MK/gml30.owl

ontology language. GML is an OGC specification for the encoding and exchange of GI. The motivation for defining this ontology, developed at the Drexel University in 2004, was to define a core ontology that could be reused and extended in other ontologies for specific application domains.

• *Geospatial Resource Description Framework* (GRDF) (Alam et al. 2008) is another OWL ontology whose concepts and properties extend also the definitions found in GML. The purpose of this ontology is to define an expressive language in the geospatial domain making profit of the advantages provided by Web semantic languages.

• *OntoSensor* (Russomanno et al. 2005) is an ontology based on the IEEE Suggested Upper Merged Ontology (SUMO)[5], which is a top-level ontology defining general concepts and associations. The purpose of OntoSensor is to provide an ontological perspective of SensorML, the language specified by OGC to represent sensor data collected from remote dispositives. SensorML is also a language derived from GML.

6.3.3   Ontology-Driven Geographic Information Systems

Ontology has been proposed to play a central role in information system's life cycle, leading to ontology-driven information systems (ODIS) (Guarino 1998). In this case the ontology drives all aspects and components of the system. In ODIS the ontology is called application ontology and it is a specialization of a domain ontology and a task ontology (Guarino 1998). The difference between ontology-driven and other types of information systems is that the ontology is made explicit before the information system is even designed. As explained by Fonseca (2007), using an ontology during the development stage enables designers to practice a higher level of knowledge reuse than is usually the case in software engineering. The use of a common vocabulary across heterogeneous software platforms provides for the reuse and sharing of the application domain knowledge. Thus, designers can focus on the structure on the domain instead of being overly concerned with implementation details. Developing and using ontologies should be a prerequisite to conceptual modeling, ontologies being by definition broader than conceptual schemas. At run time, an ontology may enable the communication between software agents or be used to support information integration. Complementary information on ODIS can be found in Chap. 2.

The approach of Fonseca is also connected with a recent approach to software engineering that is called Model Driven Engineering (MDE) or Model Driven Development (MDD). MDD focuses on models as the primary artefact in the development process, with transformations as the primary operation on models. This new

---

[5] http://www.ontologyportal.org/

approach allows to concentrate the efforts on modelling system functionalities, instead of platform specific details. The successive application of model transformations facilitate the conversion of the original model (based on systems functionality) into a platform-specific application. Grangel et al. (2007) describe the main issues for the adoption of this MDD approach within the urban domain.

6.4   Practical Case Studies

The last section will present three particular case studies on ontology design method-ologies and ontology's uses within the GI context. The first two concern a top-down ontology design approach applied to hydrology (*core reference and formal ontology*) and a bottom-up ontology design approach applied in the case of urban spatial data-base reengineering project (*local and software ontology*), respectively. The third case concerns the use of ontologies for the semantic annotation of geocoding services in the field of urban management systems (*domain and formal ontology*).

6.4.1   Development of a Domain Ontology to Facilitate Interoperability in the Context of Hydrography

The first case study of the three above mentioned is a project launched by the Spanish National Geographic Institute (IGN-E) to facilitate the semantic harmoni-zation of hydrographic information among data producers at different levels (national, regional and local). IGN-E developed a common reference model by means of a core reference ontology, called *hydrOntology*.

hydrOntology is an ontology that follows a top-down development approach. Its main goal is to harmonize heterogeneous information sources coming from diverse cartographic agencies and other international resources.

Initially, this ontology was created as a local ontology to establish mappings between different IGN-E data sources (feature catalogues, gazetteers, etc.). Its purpose was to serve as a harmonization framework among Spanish cartographic producers. Later, the ontology evolved into a global domain ontology, and now it attempts to cover most of the hydrographical features found in a map. The final version of this ontology was finished in the mid-2008.

The statistical data (metrics) and its different taxonomic relations provide an overview of the *hydrOntology* characteristics. *hydrOntology* has 150 classes, 34 object properties, 66 data properties and 256 axioms. Some examples of the four taxonomic relations defined in the Frame Ontology (Farquahr et al. 1997) and the OKBC Ontology (Chaudhri et al. 1998), namely, Subclasses, Disjoint-Decomposition, Exhaustive-Decomposition and Partitions, have been imple-mented in the ontology. Further details are shown in Vilches-Blázquez et al. (2007). The ontology documentation is exhaustive, thus, definitions and their definition sources can be found in each concept (class). The ontology has an important amount of labels with alternative names (synonyms) as well as concept and synonym provenances.

In order to develop this ontology following a top-down approach, more than 20 different knowledge models (feature catalogues of IGN-E, the Water Framework European Directive, the Alexandria Digital Library, the UNESCO Thesaurus, Getty Thesaurus, GeoNames, FACC codes, EuroGlobalMap, EuroRegionalMap, EuroGeonames, different Spanish Gazetteers and many others) have been consulted; additionally, some integration problems of geographic information and several structuring criteria (Vilches-Blázquez et al. 2007) have been considered. The aim was to cover most of the existing GI sources for building an exhaustive core reference ontology. Thus, the ontology contains 150 relevant concepts related to hydrography (e.g. river, reservoir, lake, channel, and others).

Regarding methodological issues, *hydrOntology* was built following METHONTOLOGY, a widely-used ontology building methodology. This methodology emphasises the reuse of existing domain and upper-level ontologies and proposes to use, for formalisation purposes, a set of intermediate representations that can be later transformed automatically into different formal languages. A detailed description of this methodology can be found in Gómez-Pérez et al. (2003).

hydrOntology has been developed according to the ontology design principles proposed by Gruber (1995) and Arpírez et al. (1998). Some of its most important characteristics are that the concept names (classes) are sufficiently explanatory and rightly written. Each class groups only one concept and, therefore, classes in brackets and/or with links ("and", "or") are avoided. According to some naming conventions, each class is written with a capital letter at the beginning of each word, while object and data properties are written with lower case letters.

With respect to databases, it should be added that this project handles various information databases, both Spanish and European. These databases are created at different scales (from 1:1,000,000 to 1:5,000) and come from diverse institutions or producers. A common component of these databases is that all sources have hydrographical information related to Spanish geographical feature instances.

As commented before, this project handles two European databases (EuroGlobalMap, and EuroRegionalMap), and four Spanish databases that belong to IGN-E. The Spanish databases have information at different scales; of the four Spanish databases, two are Numerical Cartographic Databases (Numerical Topographic Database (BTN25) and Numerical Cartographic Database (BCN200)), and two are gazetteers (Conciso Gazetteer and National Geographic Gazetteer). Finally, with regard to the local databases, the project employs two, one developed by a local producer (Cartographic Institute of Andalusia) and other, by a thematic producer (Hydrographical Confederation of Ebro River).

Within this context of databases, semantic understanding is achieved by setting wrappers between *hydrOntology* and various databases with R2O language (Barrasa et al. 2004). The wrappers, which are still in progress, build and improve relationships between features (from ontology) and instances (from databases). An overview of this work is shown in Fig. 6.1.

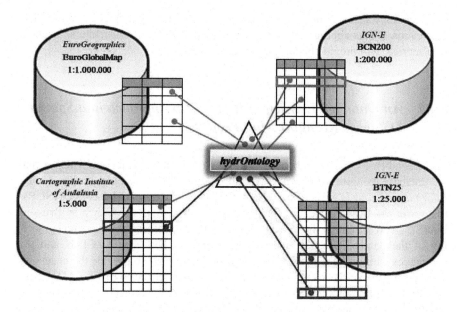

Fig. 6.1 An overview of wrappers between *hydrOntology* and databases

Fig. 6.2 Hybrid approach of *hydrOntology* (Inspired by Wache et al. 2001)

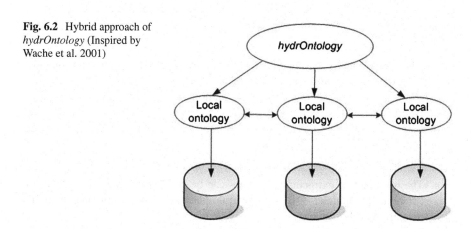

Once *hydrOntology* is consolidated as a harmonization framework for the community of GI producers, the second phase will involve a complex integration framework of databases and ontologies. An overview of this integration approach is shown in Fig. 6.2. This approach is related to the hybrid approach proposed in Wache et al. (2001). In the hybrid approach, *hydrOntology* will provide the global shared vocabulary and each producer (European, regional and local) will have a local ontology that sets mappings with the global ontology and its databases. The application of this approach to the Spanish Spatial Data Infrastructure's gazetteer web service[6] will provide better and richer answers.

6.4.2 An Ontology Extraction Bottom-Up Approach in a Spatial Database Reengineering Project

The second case concerns a bottom-up ontology extraction approach within a spatial database reengineering project (Chaidron et al. 2007). In Belgium, the *Centre Informatique pour la Région Bruxelloise* (CIRB) manages spatial databases (SDBs) that cover the Brussels Region. This particular set of SDBs is known as Brussels UrbIS 2 ©. At the end of the nineties, it became obvious that a complete reengineering of the databases was needed. A collaboration between the CIRB and the Geomatics Unit of the University of Liege started in 1998 to provide the necessary support to achieve the reengineering process of part of the SDB (the ADM base containing 33 classes and 830,000 instances mostly related to geographical administrative information), i.e. bringing the DB to its second operational version.

The objective was to create *a posteriori* a feature catalogue and conceptual data models. One of the first step was the (re)-definition of *local software ontologies* of the original database (Fonseca et al. 2003). In order to fulfil project's objective, a bottom-up ontology extraction approach has been adopted. It can be divided in several steps (Fig. 6.3):

1. The first step consists in analysing the existing database documentations and then extracting a draft version of the ontologies. Local ontologies can be extracted from data catalogues or data dictionaries and semantic nets can be derived from CDMs (examples of extraction are presented below). The derived ontology should be expressed in an ontology-language like KIF or OWL, or even in UML.
2. At this stage, two options are possible depending on DB designer collaboration.

    a. The relevance of extracted ontologies can be checked by comparing them to the related populated DB. Final ontologies can be then obtained and the extraction process ends.
    b. If it is possible, the next step is to submit the draft ontologies to the DB designers. An important issue at this stage is to ensure that both "teams" use the same language, the same concepts. A definition is provided for each concept. This definition includes a textual description as well as a formal expression of its relations with other concepts (IS A, part of and possible topological relations).

---

[6] http://www.idee.es/gazetteerIGN/indexLayout.jsp?PAGELANGUAGE=EN

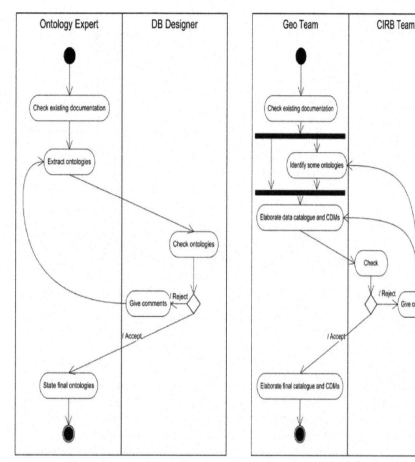

Proposed bottom-up approach   *Its practical application in the*
   (UML Activity diagram)   *project (UML Activity diagram)*

Fig. 6.3 A theoretical bottom-up approach and its practical application (Chaidron et al. 2007)

3. Remarks formulated by the DB designers must be included in the ontologies
   extraction process and new ontologies have to be provided until final acceptance.

Some difficulties occurred during practical application of this approach. First,
the existing documentation was incomplete and non-standardised; specific relational
schemes, a simple data list, data acquisition specifications (for photogrammetric
and land surveying measurements). As a result, only some hierarchic and thematic
links have been deduced from this documentation. Then, the DB designers failed at
the beginning to validate the draft outputs. Tools and methods to formalize their
knowledge had to be provided to them and more especially a common *spatial
language*. For this purpose we have used first a "natural" language expressed within

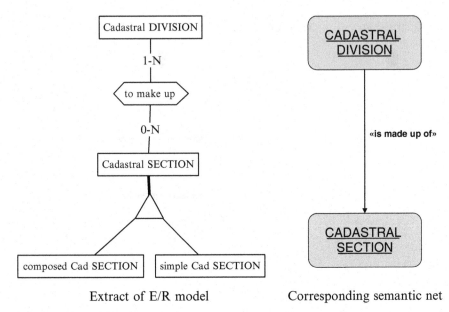

Extract of E/R model   Corresponding semantic net

Fig. 6.4 An extract of Urbis2© E/R model and its corresponding semantic net (Chaidron et al. 2007)

and Entity / Relationship (E/R) formalism, and later we adopted a more specialized *geo-formalism* (i.e. CONGOO formalism, Chaidron et al. 2007).

One of the most important aspects of the submission / acceptation process was the establishment of objects spatial properties: object representation and spatial relationships between objects. By identifying spatial (topological) relationships between objects, this stage revealed object's definition inconsistencies. It appeared to be the most crucial element of the extraction approach (see Chaidron et al. 2007 for further details).

As presented in Fig. 6.3, the practical application of the bottom-up approach was slightly different to the theoretical approach as the expected outputs were feature catalogue and CDMs when full documented ontologies were not. Deriving a semantic from the reengineering E/R model is possible. However, such CDM are not ontologies because it has been designed for a specific information system, describing the contents of a specific database, i.e. the specifications of one possible "world" (Bishr and Kuhn 2000; Fonseca et al. 2003). That means that we would have to operate an intermediate step to build a kind of semantic net (Fig. 6.4); a richer model (global-transposable-sharable) than the database conceptual schema, capturing the semantics of information in a formal way, and usable as a possible way for data integration (Morocho et al. 2003).

This study clarifies the role of ontologies in SDB's design and reengineering. If the ontology level is necessary for DB's design (and interoperability) (Frank 1997; Smith and Mark 1998), related ontologies are not always formalized.

Therefore, local SDB ontologies are usually hidden in SDBs and associated documentations (feature catalogues and CDMs). In this case, it is possible to extract them from the documentation by applying a bottom-up approach. This process could be improved by a good collaboration with DB's original designer when the DB is poorly documented.

From our experience, extracting local ontologies (and associated objects definitions) implies a very good knowledge of spatial relationships between DB's objects; we believe that a comprehensive analysis of spatial relationships between instances should be the first stage of local ontologies extraction.

6.4.3   Enabling Geolocating via Ontologies

The third case concerns the use of ontologies for the semantic annotation of geocoding services in a system that integrates different geocoding services. This use case, described in detail in Florczyk et al. (2009), deals with the geocoding of urban addresses using different geocoding services such as a local council geocoding service, a national cadastre geocoding service and a national gazetteer service. Ontologies are used here to solve the semantic heterogeneity between the results retrieved from the different services in terms of address organization.

In Spain, the Zaragoza city council launched its local SDI in 2004 named IDEZar. This SDI has been created in collaboration with the University of Zaragoza (Lopez-Pellicer et al. 2006). IDEZar has as a mandatory requirement the implementation of new geocoding services because many urban related datasets were only georeferenced with street addresses. Two use cases were defined: an on-line geocoder in the SDI web portal to geocode input text addresses and a batch geocoder for large files containing address names.

Urban management systems need geocoding functionality support to enable the assignation of geographic coordinates to location description such as "about 100 m south of a park, and near a coffee shop". Usually, available geocoding services work on absolute locations and are not appropriate for this kind of task (Hutchinson and Veenendall 2005) and should be enhanced with other services such as a point of interest (POI) service. A system that integrates several geocoding services and other similar would join the functionality of them to provide a location (e.g. the geocoded results of an environment geocoder and a POI geocoder are applied to constrain the query to a third geocoder). However, this approach introduces a high level of complexity in the use of services and data integration. Domain ontologies such as an administrative units ontology (Lopez-Pellicer et al. 2008) might help to fuse the data models. However, the key issue here is the selection of the geocoder services applied to solve the user query.

The service description is composed of a description of the geocoder data model based on domain ontologies, such as an administrative units ontology, and a set of service attributes. Florczyk et al. (2009) distinguish the following attributes for the geocoding service description: coverage, content type, spatial object type,

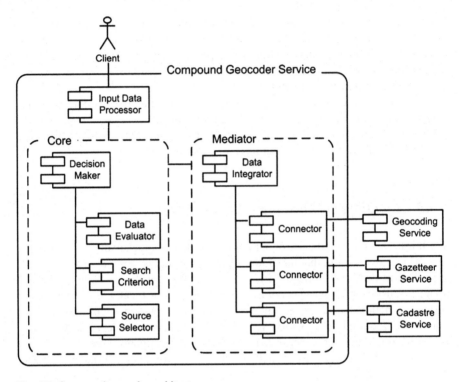

Fig. 6.5 Compound geocoder architecture

result accuracy, reliability, precision and granularity. Some of them are linked to an appropriate ontology. For example, coverage, that defines the data location area, is linked to a concept provided by the appropriate administrative unit ontology.

The architecture of the geocoder integration service consists of the following components (see Fig. 6.5):

1. The first component consists of an **input data processor** that is responsible for pre-processing of input data that uses the typical geocoding strategies.
2. The decision maker is the core component. It hides the process of service selection and the evaluation of the query results.
3. The **mediator** component that contains:

   a. Pluggable service connector responsible of the invocation to service providers.
   b. Data integration component that hides the mapping process.

The adequate description of each service with the help of domain ontologies determines the behaviour of the whole system mainly because the service characteristics are clues for service selection. For example, the administrative unit ontology plays a fundamental role in service selection. This ontology is responsible for defining the relations among the administrative units that provide the basis for source selection according to the correlation between the query constraints and the service coverage. Also, when data from different sources should be integrated in a response, ontologies are applied. For example, the administrative unit ontology helps to build an extensible data model suitable for the representation of the spatial data relationship in the context of administrative units that is used to merge administrative units found in each response.

This approach was applied to the two geocoding use cases defined in IDEZar. The first was implemented as a part of the system in charge of advertising (through the IDEZar web portal) daily incidents on the urban network. The application georeferences input addresses from forms and returns a list of proposals that are visualized on the associated map. The compound geocoder builds the list of proposals according to an internal ranking based on text comparison, the street type correspondence if available, and, above all, the characteristics of each source geocoding service. The second case is a batch geocoder tool for large CSV (Comma-separated values) files containing address names. The logic of the tool is highly configurable as a result of the characteristics of the chosen architecture.

This experience shows that the usefulness of ontologies in service description and selection in the field of urban management systems. Selecting the best service is a hard task that might be leveraged with the use of service descriptions annotated with semantic descriptions. However, today service descriptions lack these descriptions. Moreover, data and data model behind these services fail to have a semantic description. Defining ontologies and processes to automatically create these descriptions from services should be the first stage of the use of ontologies for integrating services.

6.5   Conclusions

This chapter has presented roles, types, uses and design processes of ontologies within the Geographic Information sector. One has focused on solving interoperability issues which is especially crucial when dealing with SDIs. The use of ontologies in three typical GI interoperability scenarios have been presented; discovery and retrieval of GI, data integration in heterogeneous spatial databases and development of GIS. In all of these cases, the heterogeneous nature of GI (syntax and semantic) makes the use of ontologies especially important.

Then, three real cases discussing ontology design methodologies and ontology's uses in the GI context have been presented. The first two concerns respectively a top-down ontology design approach applied to hydrology and a bottom-up ontology design approach applied in the case of urban spatial database reengineering project. The third case concerns the use of ontologies for the semantic annotation of geocoding services in the field of urban management systems.

The use of ontologies is growing in the GI community; it is a consequence of development of SDIs and of global services needing various types of GI. Ontologies play a central role in system development, information retrieval and data integration.

Knowing that urban information is often of spatial or geographical nature, it is necessary to consider GI ontologies and their uses when approaching urban ontologies context.

6.6 Open Problems and Research Challenges

Beside general research issues such as the evaluation of ontologies quality (Guarino and Welty 2004), there are some specific research challenges for the GI community (Albrecht et al. 2008; Bucella et al. 2009).

As already mentioned by Mark et al. (2004), there is a need to continue to develop geo-ontologies. Indeed, although the use of ontologies in the GI sector is widely discussed (mainly in academia), there are rather few ontologies on geographic relations and processes. It appears that we are short of ontologies of geographic processes and ontologies are much easier translated into a database schema than into process model. A practical ontology of process that is both proven to be formally correct and at the same time well enough developed to reach to the level of real world applications is still missing (Albrecht et al. 2008). Additionally, a huge work has still to be done to cover concepts such as spatial relations, vagueness or geo-object's changes. It is also rather clear that due to the strong interaction between space and time, spatio-temporal ontologies are a key issue for further model integration.

Further to the need for more geo-ontologies, some authors have also pointed out some technical development needs. For example, Albrecht et al. (2008) raise the issue that moving from static GIS repositories to GIS-based process modelling systems requires the development of reusable libraries of process specifications. They also identify a rather important technical drawback which is that current ontology editors are far from allowing a straightforward connection to GIS; there is usually a long way towards linking original geospatial ontology development with the creation of professional GIS database schemata.

Finally, another future challenge is to ensure integration with other domain ontologies (construction, historical, etc.), which are notably crucial in the urban context.

References

Alam, A., Khan, L. Thuraisingham, B.: Geospatial Resource Description Framework (GRDF) and security constructs. In: IEEE 24th International Conference on Data Engineering Workshop, ICDEW 2008, pp. 475–481 (2008)

Albrecht, J., Derman, B., Ramasubramanian, L.: Geoontology tools: the missing link. Trans. GIS 12(4), 49–424 (2008)

Arpírez, J.C., Gómez-Pérez, A., Lozano, A., Pinto, H.S.: (ONTO)2Agent: An ontology-based WWW broker to select ontologies. In: Gómez-Pérez, A., Benjamins, RV. (eds.) ECAI'98

Workshop on Applications of Ontologies and Problem-Solving Methods, Brighton, United Kingdom, pp. 16–24 (1998)

Barrasa Rodríguez, J., Corcho, O., Gómez-Pérez, A.: R$_2$O, an extensible and semantically based database-to-ontology mapping language. In: Bussler, C., Tannen, V. (eds.) Second Workshop on Semantic Web and Databases (SWDB'04), Toronto, Canada (2004)

Bernard, L., Einspanier, U., Haubrock, S., Hübner, S., Klien, E., Kuhn, W., Lessing, R., Lutz, M., Visser, U.: Ontology-based discovery and retrieval of geographic information in spatial data infrastructures. Geotechnologien Science Report No. 4 (2004)

Bernstein, A., Klein, M.: Towards high-precision service retrieval. In: Horrocks I., Hendler J.(eds.) The Semantic Web–First International Semantic Web Conference (ISWC 2002), pp. 84–101. Springer, Sardinia(2002)

Bishr, Y.: Overcoming the semantic and other barriers to GIS interoperability. Int. J. Geogr. Inf. Sci. **12**(4), 299–314 (1998)

Bishr, Y., Kuhn, W.: Ontology-based modelling of geospatial information. In: Third AGILE Conference on Geographic Information Science, Helsinki (2000)

Bucella, A., Cechich, A., Fillottrani, P.: Ontology-driven geographic information integration: a survey of current approaches. Comput. Geosci. **35**, 710–723 (2009)

Chaidron, C., Billen, R., Teller, J.: Investigating a bottom-up approach for extracting ontologies from urban databases. In: Teller, J., Lee, J., Roussey, C. (eds.) Ontologies for Urban Development, Studies in Computational Intelligence, vol. 61, pp. 131–141. Springer, Berlin/ Heidelberg (2007)

Chaudhri, V.K., Farquhar, A., Fikes, R., Karp, P.D., Rice, J.P.: Open knowledge base connectivity 2.0.3. Technical Report KSL-98-06, Knowledge Systems Laboratory, Stanford, http://www. ai.sri.com/okbc/okbc-2-0-3.pdf (1998)

Egenhofer, M.: Interoperability: theory and concepts. In: Goodchild, M., Egenhofer, M., Fegeas, R., Kottman, C. (eds.) Interoperating Geographic Information Systems, pp. 1–4. Kluwer Academic, Norwell (1999)

European Committee for Standardization (CEN). Geographic information – standards, specifica- tions, technical reports and guidelines, required to implement spatial data infrastructures, CEN/ TR 15449, (2006)

Farquhar, A., Fikes, R., Rice, J.: The ontolingua server: A tool for collaborative ontology construc- tion. Int. J. Hum. Comput. Stud. **46**(6), 707–727 (1997)

Florczyk, A.J., Lopez-Pellicer, F.J., Rioja, R., Nogueras-Iso, J., Zarazaga-Soria, F.J.: Enabling geolocating via ontologies. In: Teller, J., Cutting-Decelle, A.F., Billen, R. (eds.) Urban Ontologies for an Improved Communication in Urban Development Projects (Proceedings of the Final Conference of the COST Action C21 – Towntology: Urban Ontologies for an Improved Communication In Urban Development Projects, Liège, 9&10 March 2009), pp. 85–94. Les Editions de l'université de Liège (2009)

Fonseca, F.: The double role of ontologies in information science research. J. Am. Soc. Inf. Sci. Technol. **58**(6), 786–793 (2007)

Fonseca, F., Davis, C., Câmara, G.: Bridging ontologies and conceptual schemas in geographic information integration. GeoInformatica **7**(4), 355–378 (2003)

Fonseca, F., Egenhofer, M., Agouris, P., Câmara, C.: Using ontologies for integrated geographic information systems. Trans. GIS **6**(3), 231–257 (2002)

Frank, A.: Spatial Ontology. In: Stock, O. (ed.) Spatial and Temporal Reasoning, pp. 135–153. Academic Publisher, Dordrecht (1997)

Gómez-Pérez, A., Fernández-López, M., Corcho, O.: Ontological Engineering. Springer, London (2003)

Grangel, R., Metral, C., Cutting-Decelle, A., Bourey, J., Young, R.: Ontology based communica- tions through model driven tools: feasibility of the MDA Approach in Urban Engineering. In: Ontologies for Urban Development, vol. 61 of Studies in Computational Intelligence, pp. 181–196. Springer, Berlin/Heidelberg (2007)

Gruber, T.R.: Toward principles for the design of ontologies used for knowledge sharing. Int. J. Hum. Comput. Stud. **43**(5–6), 907–928 (1995)

Guarino, N.: Formal ontology in information systems. In: 1st International Conference on Formal Ontology in Information Systems (FOIS'98), pp. 3–15. IOS Press, Amsterdam (1998)

Guarino, N., Welty, C.: An overview of ontoClean. In: Staab, S., Studer, R. (eds.) Handbook on Ontologies, pp. 151–172. Springer, Berlin/ Heidelberg (2004)

Hübner, S., Spittel, R., Visser, U., Vogele, T.: Ontology-based search for interactive digital maps. IEEE Intell. Syst. **19**(3), 80–86 (2004)

Hutchinson, M., Veenendall, B.: Towards using intelligence to move from geocoding to geolocating. In: Proceedings of the 7th Annual URISA GIS in Addressing Conference, Austin (2005)

Kashyap, V., Sheth, A.: Semantic and schematic similarities between object in databases: a context-based approach. VLDB **5**, 276–304 (1996)

Kolodziej, K. (ed.): Open GIS Web Map Server Cookbook. Version: 1.0.1. Stage: Draft. Open Geospatial Consortium Inc (Open GIS Consortium Inc), OGC Document Number 03-050r1 (2003)

López-Pellicer, F.J., Álvarez, P., Lacasta, J., Muro-Medrano, P.R.: IDEZar: procesos, herramientasy modelos urbanos aplicados a la integración de datos municipales procedentes de fuentes heterogéneas. In: Avances en las Infraestructuras de Datos Espaciales. Treballs d'ínformàtica i tecnologia, pp. 105–113. Universidad Jaime I de Castellón, Castelló de la Plana (2006)

López-Pellicer, F.J., Florczyk, A.J., Lacasta, J., Zarazaga-Soria, F.J., Muro-Medrano, P.R.: Administrative units, an ontological perspective. Lect. Notes Comput. Sci. LNCS **5232**, 354–363 (2008)

Lutz, M., Klien, E.: Ontology-based retrieval of geographic information. IJGIS **20**(3), 233–260 (2006)

Lutz, M.: Ontology-based service discovery in spatial data infrastructures. In: Workshop on Geographic Information Retrieval (GIR 2005), Bremen, Germany, ACM Press, New York (2005)

Manola, F., Miller, E.: RDF Primer W3C Recommendation 10 Feb 2004. http://www.w3.org/TR/rdf-primer/ (2004)

Mark, D., Smith, B., Egenhofer, M., Hirtle, S.: Ontological foundations for geographic information science. In: McMaster, R., Usery, L. (eds.) A Research Agenda for Geographic Information Science, pp. 335–350. CRC Press, Boca Raton (2004)

McGuinness, D.L., van Harmelen, F.: OWL: Web Ontology Language Overview (W3C Recommendation 10 Feb 2004). http://www.w3.org/TR/owl-features/ (2004)

McKee, L.: Who wants a GDI? In: Groot, R., McLaughlin, J. (eds.) Geospatial Data Infrastructure - Concepts, cases, and good practice, pp. 13–24. Oxford University Press, New York (2000)

Medina-Nieto, M.A.: An overview of ontologies, technical report. Center for Research in Information and Automation Technologies, Interactive and Cooperative Technologies Lab, Universitad de las Américas Puebla, Mexico (2003)

Morocho, V., Pérez-Vidal, L., Saltor, F.: Semantic integration on spatial databases. In: Proceeding of VIII Jornadas de Ingenieria del Software y Bases de Datos, Alicante, pp. 603–612 (2003)

Navarrete, A.: Semantic integration of thematic geographic information in a multimedia context, Ph. D. thesis, Universidad Pompeu Fabra (2006)

Nebert, D. (ed.): Developing Spatial Data Infrastructures: The SDI Cookbook v.2.0, Global Spatial Data Infrastructure (GSDI). Available from: http://www.gsdi.org (2004)

Russomanno, D.J., Kothari, C., Thomas, O.: Building a sensor ontology: a practical approach leveraging ISO and OGC models. In: Proceeding 2005 International Conference on Artificial Intelligence, Las Vegas , NV, pp. 637–643(2005)

Smith, B., Mark, D.: Ontology and geographic kinds. In: Poiker, T., Chrisman,N. (eds.) Proceedings of the Tenth International Symposium on Spatial Data Handling, pp. 308–320. Simon Fraser University, Burnaby (1998)

Vilches-Blázquez, L.M., Bernabé-Poveda, M.A., Suárez-Figueroa, M.C., Gómez-Pérez, A., Rodríguez-Pascual, A.F.: Towntology & hydrOntology: relationship between urban and hydrographic features in the geographic information domain. In: Ontologies for Urban Development. Studies in Computational Intelligence, vol. 61, pp. 73–84. Springer, Berlin/Heidelberg (2007)

Wache, H., Vögele, T., Visser, U., Stuckenschmidt, H., Schuster, G., Neumann, H., Hübner, S.: Ontology-based integration of information — A survey of existing approaches. In: IJCAI-01 Workshop: Ontologies and Information Sharing, Seattle, WA, pp 108–117 (2001)

Yeung, A.K.W., Hall, G.B.: Spatial database systems. Design, Implementation and Project Management. Springer, Dordrecht (The Netherlands) (2007)

Chapter 7
Ontologies for Interconnecting Urban Models

Claudine Métral and Anne-Françoise Cutting-Decelle

7.1 Introduction

Various accurate urban models have been developed and are used in the urban field, to perform for example air quality calculation, building energy consumption or traffic simulation. 3D city models representing the structure of a city in three dimensions are special urban models issued from 3D GIS (3 Dimensional Geographic Information Systems). The use of urban models, particularly 3D city models, is increasing in urban planning. The consequence of an integrated approach in urban planning is the use of different models, most of the time in an interconnected way able to simulate the urban issues together with their inter-relations.

In the first part of the chapter, we will present our needs and expectations in terms of urban information: modelling and interconnection of the information. An important issue related to the representation of urban information is then discussed: the comparison of the role of conceptual schemas and ontologies, since strong links do exist between the two approaches. The chapter then analyses three ontology-based approaches in relation with urban modelling. The interconnection of urban models through ontologies is described in the last part of the chapter and examples are given on the basis of real case studies.

C. Métral (✉)
Centre universitaire d'informatique, Switzerland
e-mail: Claudine.Metral@unige.ch

A.-F. Cutting-Decelle
CODATA France and Ecole Centrale Paris/LGI, Grande Voie des Vignes,
F-92295 Châtenay-Malabry, France
e-mail: afcd@skynet.be

G. Falquet et al., *Ontologies in Urban Development Projects*, Advanced Information
and Knowledge Processing 1, DOI 10.1007/978-0-85729-724-2_7,
© Springer-Verlag London Limited 2011

7.2 Urban Information: Modeling and Interconnection Issues

Urban models have a long history beginning in the 1960s. Since this period, the term urban model has usually been related to simplifications and abstractions of real cities, in contrast to its earlier usage referring to ideal cities (Foot 1981). Today, accurate models can be used to perform, for example, urban simulations (Waddell et al. 2008), building energy consumption (Jones et al. 2000), water quality calculation (Kianirad et al 2006) or air quality estimation (Moussiopoulos et al. 2006).

3D numerical models generally come from the CAD (Computer-Aided Design) field or from the GIS field as for 3D city models. In the first case they usually have no functionality beyond display while, in the latter case, they can be associated with spatial queries. In fact 3D models are named mock-ups while the term urban models usually refer to dynamic models. According to Foot (1981), urban models:

- are used to evaluate the effects of changes in relation to certain land-use activities (such as residential or industrial development), transport network, etc.
- mainly relate to spatial aspects of the urban system although they attempt to estimate the spatial consequences of changes in non-spatial variables.

Air quality models, for example, are associated with complex processes taking into account many parameters related to pollutant sources, prevailing wind, or the configuration of the streets and buildings.

According to the point of view and the purpose, the same reality can give rise to different models: for example a physical or a numerical mock-up, an information model associated with geo-data or a mathematical model of in-play processes represented through differential equations, as shown on the Fig. 7.1 below (issued from a personal discussion with Professor François Golay from EPFL-Switzerland).

If urban models can be seen as decision-making tools, they most of the time relate to one domain at the same time, such as transportation, air quality or building energy consumption, or to the physical aspects of the city as in 3D city models. Urban models could benefit from data being directly available within 3D city models while providing results which could, in return, be used and visualised through city models. As urban issues are interrelated in the real world, the interconnection of urban models can be considered as reflecting the reality more precisely. They also allow urban actors to explore the city and to plan it (prior to acting on it) in a more global way.

On the basis of case studies related to the urban field, this chapter will explain how domain ontologies can provide a robust and reusable method to interconnect urban models.

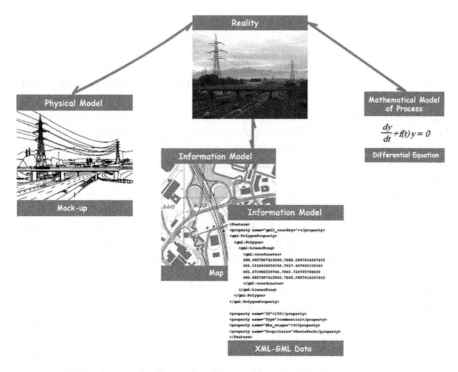

Fig. 7.1 Different models of different types for the same reality

7.3   Urban Information: Ontologies or Conceptual Schemas?

Fonseca et al. (2003) provides a good analysis of the differences between ontologies and conceptual schemas. In the traditional systems modeling approach, the modeler is required to capture a user's view of the real world in a formal conceptual model. In doing so, the modeler follows an established paradigm, such as object-orientation or entity-relational, that is chosen in terms of the available programming environment. Such an approach forces the modeler to mentally map concepts acquired from the real world to instances of abstractions available in his paradigm of choice. This mapping is done informally and in an ad-hoc fashion, thereby introducing inconsistencies and inaccuracies that inevitably lead to conflicts between the user's concepts and the abstractions captured by the conceptual model. The basic reason for these conflicts is the lack of an initial agreement between user and modeler on the concepts of the real world. Such an agreement could be established by means of an ontology, which is a shared conceptualisation of an application domain. If the ontology, based on the user's view of the world, is previously generated and formalised so that it can be used in the development process, such conflicts would be less likely to happen.

On the other hand, the consolidation of concepts and knowledge represented by a conceptual schema can be useful in the initial steps of ontology construction.

Studies have been performed in the geographic domain which is closely related to the urban domain. Thus, following Anselin (1989) and Egenhofer (1993), the author asks a good question, about the specificity of the geographic and urban world: "What is special about spatial?". To adequately represent the geographic world, we must have computer representations capable of not only capturing descriptive attributes about its concepts, but also capable of describing the geometrical and positional components of these concepts. These representations also need to capture the spatial and temporal relationships between instances of these concepts. For example, in order to represent a public transportation system, the application ontology must contain concepts such as street, neighborhood, bus stop, and timetable. The computer representation of the transportation system has to recognize relationships such as "this bus line crosses these neighborhoods", "there is a bus stop near the corner of these streets" and "the bus stops at this location at 1:00 pm". Unlike the case of conventional information systems, most of these spatial and temporal relationships are not explicitly represented in a GIS, and can often be deduced using geographic functions.

In the past few years, since ontologies have gained the attention of the GIS research community (Smith and Mark 1998, 1999, 2001; Smith 1998; Mark 1993; Frank 1997, 2001; Fonseca and Egenhofer 1999; Bittner and Winter 1999; Câmara et al. 2000; (Rodríguez et al. 1999), many researchers have asked themselves whether ontologies were actually the well-known conceptual data modeling techniques in disguise (Winter 2001). Guarino (1998) advises against using ontology as just a fancy name denoting the result of activities like conceptual analysis and domain modelling.

Fikes and Farquhar (1999) consider that ontologies can be used as building block components of conceptual schemas. Fonseca et al. (2003) agrees with Cui et al (2002) in that there is a main difference between an ontology and a conceptual schema: they are built with different purposes. While an ontology describes a specific domain, a conceptual schema is created to describe the contents of a database. Bishr and Kuhn (2000) consider that an ontology is external to information systems and is a specification of possible worlds, while a conceptual schema is internal to information systems and is chosen as the specification of one possible world.

Ontologies are semantically richer than database conceptual schemas, and thus closer to the user's cognitive model. Conceptual schemas are built to organize what is going to be stored in a database, and then are used to document it. An ontology represents concepts in the real world. For instance, a reservoir can be represented differently in diverse databases, but the concept is only one, at least from one community's point of view. This point of view is expressed in the ontology that this community has specified. For instance, a reservoir is a reservoir, regardless of whether it is represented, for the purposes of an information system, by an aerial photograph, a polygon, or a digital terrain model. A conceptual schema that intends to capture all the peculiarities of geographic data should specify differently each of the three representations.

For the same author, this debate on the differences between ontologies and conceptual schemas was partially motivated by the lack of practice in the use of ontologies for real-world problem solving, along with the scarcity of consistent ontologies. In fact, the theory on the use of ontologies is being developed with the broader intention of providing a basis for knowledge consolidation and exchange, a goal that is far beyond the capabilities of current data modelling tools and techniques. Generally speaking, conceptual schemas correspond to a certain level of knowledge formalisation, even though they discard a number of concepts and ideas about which the data modeler and the user have agreed upon. On the other way, ontologies facilitate the integration, in the model, of background knowledge about the entire information systems development process. In this chapter, and in order to keep a track of this background knowledge, we will work on ontology-based approaches and on an interconnection of models based on ontologies.

7.4   Interconnection of Urban Models Through Ontologies

An ontology-based approach for interconnecting urban models is described in the following sections of this chapter. The general methodology can be summarized in two main steps:

– represent as ontologies (i.e. represent formally the underlying knowledge of) the resources to integrate or interconnect.
– interconnect these ontologies, what is generally not a trivial task as one has to fill in the semantic gap between the source ontologies.

The following sections present the approach, on the basis of real case studies. A first part explains the way of creating the ontologies while the second part focuses on the articulation between the resulting ontologies.

7.5   Creation of the Ontologies

In this section, we will briefly describe some domain ontologies related to urban models, with their main features and specificities.

7.5.1   Ontology of CityGML

CityGML is an open information model for the representation and exchange of virtual 3D city models on an international level (OGC 08–007 2008). CityGML defines the most relevant features in cities and regional models with respect to their geometrical, topological, semantical, and appearance properties such as:

– the terrain (named as Relief Feature),
– the coverage by land use objects (named as Land Use),

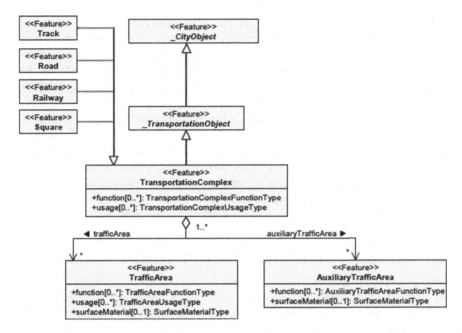

Fig. 7.2 Part of the UML diagram of the transportation feature of CityGML

– transportation (both graph structures and 3D surface data),
– vegetation (solitary objects, areas and volumes, with vegetation classification),
– water objects (volumes and surfaces),
– sites, in particular buildings (bridge, tunnel, excavation or embankment in the future),
– City Furniture (for fixed object such as traffic lights, traffic signs, benches or bus stops).

CityGML has been defined as classes and relations in UML, the Unified Modeling Language (UML). Figure 7.2 shows a part of the UML diagram of CityGML.

As we can see, a `TransportationComplex` is a particular kind of `TransportationObject` (which is itself a particular kind of `CityObject`) and is subdivided thematically into `TrafficArea` (representing the areas used for the traffic of cars, trains, public transport, airplanes, bicycles or pedestrians) and `AuxiliaryTrafficArea` (associated with grass for example). In fact, a `TransportationComplex` is composed of `TrafficAreas` and `AuxiliaryTrafficAreas`.

Defining the ontology of CityGML is thus relatively easy:

– UML classes will be translated into concepts;
– associations/roles will be translated into semantic relations;

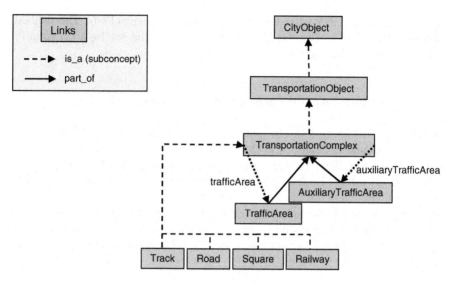

Fig. 7.3 Part of the ontology of the transportation feature of CityGML

- association cardinalities will be expressed as restrictions relatively to relations;
- aggregation/composition will be expressed as "part of" links;
- generalisation will be expressed as "is a" links (with the meaning of subconcept);
- UML class attributes will be translated either into concept attributes or into relations between concepts.

Figure 7.3 below shows this UML diagram (without the part corresponding to the geometry) in an ontological form.

Here are some examples to illustrate the way according which class attributes have been translated:

- function as a relation between TransportationComplex and Transportation-ComplexFunctionType itself defined as a concept;
- surfaceMaterial also as a relation between the concepts TrafficArea and TrafficSurfaceMaterialType but with the following restriction: a TrafficArea has at most one TrafficSurfaceMaterialType.

7.5.2   Ontology of Urban Planning Process OUPP

The ontology of urban planning process (OUPP) is still under development at the University of Geneva. In this paper we describe the part of OUPP related to soft mobility aspects. To define this ontology we have used the method proposed by

Uschold and King (1995) extended by Uschold and Grüninger (1996). This method is composed of four phases: (1) identify the purpose of the ontology, (2) build it, (3) evaluate it, (4) document it.

7.5.2.1 Identification of the Purpose and the Scope of the Ontology

In this phase we have to define the purpose of the ontology.

In our case and as described in (Métral et al 2009b) the purpose is to promote such a way of travelling. The legal aspects (which are important to urban planners or politicians) will not be described in this paper in order to focus on some aspects such as the duration of travelling for a kind of user (as these aspects seem questioning to many potential users) or the appealing character of some paths (promenades, for example, and particularly promenades through parks). So the relevant terms to be put in the ontology include: `Duration` (of a travel), `Type_of_user` (`Cyclist`, `Pedestrian`, etc.).

7.5.2.2 Construction of the Ontology

This phase is broken down into three parts: ontology capture, ontology coding and integration of existing ontologies (if any) into the current one.

Ontology Capture

This means identify key-concepts and relationships that will represent the knowledge of the domain of interest, then define them precisely and unambiguously. The knowledge can originate from experts of the domain, text mining, meta-data of databases, etc. In this case study, various documents and data related to soft mobility were mainly used.

The knowledge thus extracted has to be structured. Textual definitions have to be defined by referring to other terms and including notions such as class, relation, etc. To perform this task, Uschold and Grüninger (1996) recommend the middle-out strategy, namely identifying first the core of basic terms, then specifying and generalizing them as required. In this case study, what has been identified first includes:

- `Type_of_user` which is a class;
- `Duration` which is a class and is defined by a `Value` for a particular `Type_of_user` and a particular `Section`.

Then, the top and the bottom concepts of these core concepts were defined:

- the bottom concepts of `Type_of_user` are `Cyclist` and `Pedestrian`;
- a `Section` is ended by a `Junction` at each extremity and is part of a `Route`.

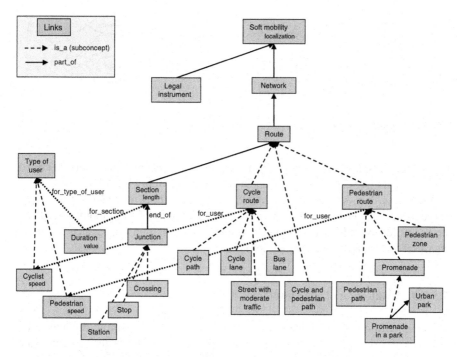

Fig. 7.4 Part of OUPP related to soft mobility aspects

Then the different kinds of Routes (Cycle_route, Pedestrian_route, etc.) and the different kinds of Junctions (Crossing, Stop, etc.) were defined.

Ontology Coding

As quoted by (Gómez-Pérez et al. 2004) this phase means (a) committing to basic terms that will be used to specify the classes, relations, entities and (b) writing the code in a formal representation language. The Fig. 7.4 below shows as a graph the ontology defined for representing soft mobility aspects within OUPP.

Integration of Existing Ontologies (If Any)

This optional phase deals with the identification of ontologies that already exist in the domain and their evaluation in order to be able to say to which extent they can (or cannot) be reused. This phase can be achieved in parallel with the previous phases.

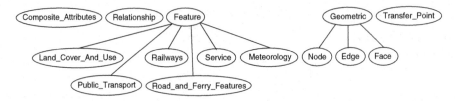

Fig. 7.5 Basic classes in OTN

In our case study, an Ontology for Transportation Systems (OTN) was identified (Lorenz et al 2005). The main classes in OTN are shown in Fig. 7.5 above:

OTN describes various transportation aspects but nothing related to soft mobility. So re-using OTN is not pertinent for creating an ontology of soft mobility but it can be useful for extending this ontology to other transportation issues such as public transport for example (see next section).

7.5.2.3   Evaluation of the Ontology

This evaluation has to be made in a pragmatic way to determine the adequacy between the ontology and the concerned application. The criteria include the following: consistency, completeness, concision (no redundancy, good degree of granularity), etc.

As this case study aims at defining an ontology-based model for promoting soft mobility for the inhabitants, the evaluation phase should include usability tests with end-users.

7.5.2.4   Documentation of the Ontology

This documentation can differ according to the type and purpose of the ontology. It means producing definitions (formal, non formal) to specify the meaning of the terms of the ontology, giving examples, etc. It can also include naming conventions such as the use of upper or lowercase letters to name the terms.

In this case study the names of the classes begin with uppercase letters while the names of the properties begin with lowercase letters. Furthermore a knowledge base composed of the source documents associated with the ontology is on-going.

7.5.3   Ontology of Air Quality Model

Air quality models are important tools to study, understand and predict air pollution levels. One of the main air quality problems at the scale of the city is related to the street canyons retaining pollutants. That is while our case study focuses on street canyon models.

Many street canyon models have been defined. While most of them are two-dimensional models such as (Baik and Kim 1999), (Huang et al 2000), there exists some three-dimensional models such as (Kim and Baik 2004), (Santiago et al 2007). Although different, these models show some common characteristics.

Their input parameters are:

– the pollutant source characteristics (source location, emitted product, etc.)
– the meteorological conditions, mainly the prevailing wind conditions (speed, direction related to the street canyon, etc.) but also, to some extent, the thermal conditions (solar heating)
– the street canyon geometry, in particular its aspect ratios such as height-to-width ratio, height-to-height ratio or its orientation with respect to the ambient wind.

Their output parameters are:

– a flow mainly characterized by its vortices (associated to an intensity, a rotation direction, a location, etc.)
– a pollutant dispersion distribution.

An ontology has been defined according to the same method as for OUPP. The Fig. 7.6 below shows it in a graph form.

All those ontologies have been coded into OWL using the Protégé editor.

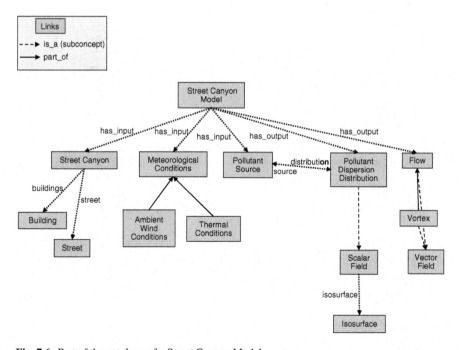

Fig. 7.6 Part of the ontology of a Street Canyon Model

7.6   Interconnection of the Ontologies

In the simplest cases concepts of the two ontologies can be directly connected together while more complex cases require an articulation or a link between the two ontologies.

7.6.1   Simple Case: Direct Interconnection

The direct interconnection of ontologies can be done either through an equivalence link or through an inclusion link. Figure 7.7 below shows such an example of a direct interconnection.

The concept Route of OUPP is similar to the concept Route of OTN. The only difference relies on the context: soft   mobility for OUPP and public

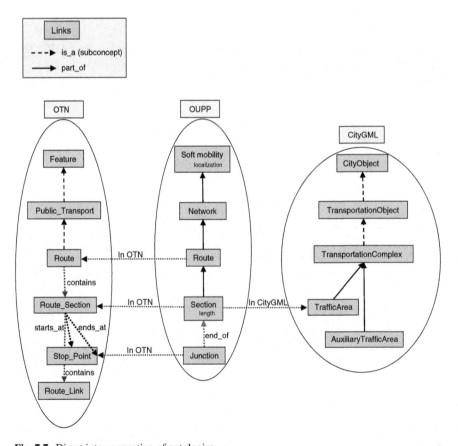

Fig. 7.7 Direct interconnection of ontologies

transport for OTN. The concepts Section (OUPP) and Route_Section (OTN) are also similar: the difference here is that a Route_Section is oriented while a Section is not. A Junction (OUPP) is also similar to a Stop_Point (OTN) while being more general. Similarly, a Section (OUPP) is similar to a TrafficArea (CityGML) which is more general as it is related to all kinds of transport. As features of CityGML are related to a geometry, these interconnections make possible the representation within 3D city models of the instances associated with the concepts of OUPP or OTN.

7.6.2 Complex Case: Interconnection Through an Articulation or Mediator Ontology

Some approaches such as (Mitra et al 2000) propose the construction of articulation ontologies where articulation rules (implications between concepts of the two ontologies) describe the semantic relationships between the two source ontologies. These articulation rules are generated using a semi-automatic articulation engine with the help of a domain expert then translated into yield concepts in an articulation ontology and semantic implication edges between the articulation ontology and the source ontologies. The authors also propose functional rules that are intended to normalize values expressed in different systems of measurement. Other approaches such as (Métral et al 2008) extend the previous approach by defining a mediator ontology containing either interconnection concepts that may have different types of semantic links with the source ontologies, or true concepts that may not exist in the source ontologies. These approaches can support sophisticated interconnection patterns between urban ontologies, and formally define them. In addition, they are particularly suited to ontologies that are developed and maintained independently, as this is usually the case for urban ontologies.

As an illustration of this method, we will present here the interconnection of an air quality (AQ) model with CityGML (CGML), which is a complex interconnection involving computations and aggregations. Here are the main phases to define this interconnection:

A concept instance in an ontology corresponds to a set of concept instances in the other one. For example a Street_Canyon in AQ exists only if, in CGML, there is a Road bordered by Buildings in a particular configuration:

```
OUPP:Street_Canyon
     in_AQ                   a AQ:Street_Canyon
     street         a CGML:Road
     buildings_1    a set of CGML:Building
     buildings_2    a set of CGML:Building
```

where buildings_1 and buildings_2 refer to the set of buildings that border the street on both sides.

Furthermore, these `buildings` must be continuously aligned:

```
for all s in OUPP:Street_Canyon
  for all x in s.buildings_1
    borders(x,s.street)
  and for all y in s.buildings_2
    borders(y,s.street)
  and continuously_aligned (s.buildings_1)
  and continuously_aligned (s.buildings_2)
```

where `borders` and `continuously_aligned` are geometric predicates.

In addition, the properties of concepts in AQ can be computed from the properties of concepts that exist in CGML.

For example, the `height-to-height ratio` of a `Street_Canyon` in AQ can be computed from the properties defined in CGML and by defining a function named `average_height`:

```
for all s in OUPP:Street Canyon
  s.in_AQ.height-to-height_ratio=
  average_height(s.buildings_2)/
    average_height(s.buildings_1)
```

where:
`in_AQ=a AQ:Street Canyon`
`average_height` is a geometric predicate
`buildings_2` and `buildings_1` refer respectively to the buildings on the windward side and the buildings on the leeward side of the canyon.

Figure 7.8 below shows an illustration of this complex interconnection pattern.

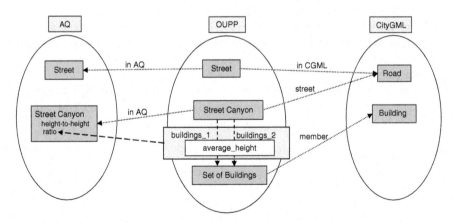

Fig. 7.8 Interconnection of ontologies performed through a mediator ontology

7.7 Open Problems and Research Challenges

Despite the significant number of research activities in this domain, a number of problems still remain open – thus creating important challenges in terms of research opportunities.

Among the open issues, we can mention:

- the big diversity of languages, formalisms, methodologies and tools that can be used to express and to formalise ontologies, most of them being neither equivalent, nor even compatible (see the COST TU0801 project wiki : http://isis.unige.ch/semcity/);
- numerous research papers refer to ontologies, either specific to a domain, or else more generic ; some of them are data ontologies, others are process ontologies. However most of the ontologies mentioned in those papers cannot directly be used for interconnection purposes, since the concepts developed remain theoretical and abstract, and the ontologies often kept at a basic level of description;
- the interconnections between models can be difficult to set up into details, in particular when correspondences between concepts are not one-to-one or else when the interpretation of the terms used is ambiguous. The expression of instance matching and adaptation can also be difficult to perform;
- in the urban field we can have, in both ontologies, similar concepts referring to the same real object but with different geometrical representations (plane representations, 3D, B-REP, CSG, …) or when different representation scales are used without being explicitly mentioned.

Based on the previous issues, several research themes can be proposed, among which we will mention – without any attempt to sort them out between more theoretical or more applied topics:

- the elaboration of real ontologies relevant to the domains of urbanism, urban planning and urban management, fully documented and formalised;
- a comparison of ontology tools based on the development of urban ontologies, thus enabling the user to find out the tools that are more suited to the urban sector. This comparison can also help to highlight or to define the tool functionalities that are really useful for the urban domain;
- the development of domain-specific ontological languages, in particular of graphical languages able to visualise the geometrical aspects of the concepts;
- the development of tools facilitating the measure of the geometric heterogeneity, thus leading to better and more reliable alignment processes specific to urban ontologies;
- an analysis of the paradigm of data ontologies, process ontologies, domain ontologies and foundational ontologies, with their domain of interest, their benefits/ drawbacks and the best use that can be made for each of them in an urban project – which of them is the most suited to the kind of use that is planned.

7.8   Conclusion and Perspectives

Integrating or interconnecting urban data or information is a crucial problem, even when focusing on a single issue. A disaster management, a flood for example, requires information not only about the levels of water but also about the height of terrain and of city objects (buildings, tunnels, bridges, etc.) in order to determine which objects are affected and to which extent. These data and information can originate from different services of the same city or from different neighbouring cities but have to be interpreted, inter-related or integrated in order to manage the disaster in a global way.

After a short comparison of conceptual model-based and ontology-based approaches, an ontology-based approach has been described to interconnect urban models and information. With such interconnections it is now possible to:

- promote soft mobility by users: indeed, with the interconnection of CityGML, OUPP and OTN, it is possible to visualize in 3 dimensions soft mobility routes or routes accessible partly by foot and partly with public transportation systems;
- compute the duration of a particular route for a type of user (see (Métral et al 2009a));
- visualize within 3D city models based on CityGML the pollution induced by vehicle traffic in street canyons;
- identify the best positioning of a sidewalk or a cycle path, for example;
- visualize within 3D city models based on CityGML the decrease of pollution induced by the travelling of n vehicles replaced by soft mobility travelling.

As this methodology is not related to one kind of model, it can be used for multiple interconnections of urban models, for example transportation or building energy consumption models.

It is the first step towards what can be called semantically enriched 3D city models (based on CityGML) with an improved semantics and thus an improved adequacy to urban planning purpose (see (TU0801 2008)).

References

Anselin, L.: What is special about spatial data? Alternative perspectives on spatial data analysis. NCGIA, Santa Barbara (1989)

Baik, J.-J., Kim, J.-J.: A numerical study of flow and pollutant dispersion characteristics in urban street canyons. J. Appl. Meteorol. **38**(11), 1576–1589 (1999)

Bishr, Y.A., Kuhn, W.: Ontology-based modelling of geospatial information. In: AGILE Conference on Geographic Information Science, Helsinki, 2000

Bittner, T., Winter, S.: On ontology in image analysis in integrated spatial databases. In: Agouris, P., Stefanidis, A. (eds.) Integrated spatial databases. Digital Images and GIS. Lecture Notes in Computer Science, vol. 1737, pp. 168–191. Springer, Berlin (1999)

Câmara, G., Monteiro, A., Paiva, J., Souza, R.: Action-driven ontologies of the geographical space: beyond the field-object debate. In: GIScience 2000, First International Conference on Geographic Information Science, Savannah, 2000

Cui, Z., Jones, D., O'Brien, P.: Semantic B2B integration. Issues in ontology based applications. ACM SIGMOD Rec. Web Edn. **31**(1), 43–48 (2002)

Egenhofer, M.: What's special about spatial? Database requirements for vehicle navigation in geographic space. SIGMOD Rec. **22**, 398–402 (1993)

Fikes, R., Farquhar, A.: Distributed repositories of highly expressive reusable ontologies. IEEE Intell. Syst. **14**, 73–79 (1999)

Fonseca, F., Egenhofer, M.: Ontology-driven geographic information systems. In: 7th ACM Symposium on Advances in Geographic Information Systems, Kansas City, 1999

Fonseca, F., Davis, C., Camara, G.: Bridging ontologies and conceptual schemas in geographic applications development. Geoinformatica **7**(4), 355–378 (2003)

Foot, D.: Operational urban models: an introduction. Taylor & Francis, London (1981)

Frank, A.: Spatial ontology. In: Stock, O. (ed.) Spatial and temporal reasoning, pp. 135–153. Kluwer, Dordrecht (1997)

Frank, A.: Tiers of ontology and consistency constraints in geographical information systems. Int. J. Geogr. Inf. Sci. **15**, 667–678 (2001)

Gómez-Pérez, A., Fernández-López, M., Corcho, O.: Ontological engineering. Springer, London (2004)

Guarino, N.: Formal ontology and information systems. In: Guarino, N. (ed.) Formal ontology in information systems, pp. 3–15. IOS Press, Amsterdam (1998)

Huang, H., Akutsu, Y., Arai, M., Tamura, M.: A two-dimensional air quality model in an urban street canyon: evaluation and sensitivity analysis. Atmos. Environ. **34**(5), 689–698 (10) (2000)

Jones, P., Williams, J., Lannon, S.: Planning for a sustainable city: an energy and environmental prediction model. J. Environ. Plann. Manage. **43**(6), 855–872 (2000)

Kianirad, E., Bedoya, D., Ghosh, I., McGarvey, K., Novotny, V.: Review of watershed ecological models. Technical report no 7, Center for Urban Environmental Studies, Northeastern University, Boston. www.coe.neu.edu/environment/DOCUMENTS/TR-7-Review%20of%20 Watershed%20Ecological%20Models.pdf (2006). Accessed 31 Jan 2011

Kim, J.-J., Baik, J.-J.: A numerical study of the effects of ambient wind direction on flow and dispersion in urban street canyons using the RNG k–e turbulence model. Atmos. Environ. **38**(19), 3039–3048 (2004)

Lorenz, B., Ohlbach, H.J., Yang, L.: Ontology of transportation networks. In: Lorenz, B. (ed.) Deliverables of the project REWERSE (Reasoning on the Web with Rules and Semantics), REWERSE-DEL-2005-A1-D4. EU FP6 Network of Excellence (NoE). http://rewerse.net/ deliverables/m18/a1-d4.pdf (2005). Accessed 31 Jan 2011

Mark, D.: Toward a theoretical framework for geographic entity types. In: Franck, A., Campari, I. (eds.) Spatial information theory. Lectures notes in computer science, vol. 716, pp. 270–283. Springer, Berlin (1993)

Métral, C., Falquet, G., Karatsas, K.: Ontologies for the integration of air quality models and 3D city models. In: Teller, J., Tweed, C., Rabino, G. (eds.) Conceptual models for urban practitioners, pp. 27–42. Società Editrice Esculapio, Bologna (2008)

Métral, C., Billen, R., Cutting-Decelle, A.-F., Van Ruymbeke, M.: Ontology-based models for improving the interoperability of 3D urban information. In: Teller, J., Cutting-Decelle, A.-F., Billen, R. (eds.) Urban ontologies for an improved communication in urban development projects, pp. 69–83. Les Editions de l'Université de Liège, Liège (2009a)

Métral, C., Falquet, G., Cutting-Decelle, A-F.: Towards semantically enriched 3D city models: an ontology-based approach. In: Kolbe TH, Zhang H, Zlatanova S (eds.) Academic Track of GeoWeb 2009 – Cityscapes, International Archives of Photogrammetry, Remote Sensing and Spatial Information Sciences (ISPRS), vol. XXXVIII-3-4/C3, Vancouver (2009b)

Mitra, P., Wiederhold, G., Kersten, M.: A graph-oriented model for articulation of ontology inter-dependencies. In: Proceedings of Conference on Extending Database Technology 2000 (EDBT'2000), Konstanz (2000)

Moussiopoulos, N., Berge, E., Bøhler, T., de Leeuw, F., Grønskei, K.E., Mylona, S., Tombrou, M.: Ambient air quality, pollutant dispersion and transport models. Report of the European Topic Centre on Air Quality, prepared under the supervision of G. Kielland, Project Manager, European Environment Agency, Copenhagen (2006)

OGC 08-007r1: OpenGIS city geography markup language (CityGML) encoding standard. In: Gröger, G., Kolbe, T.H., Czerwinski, A., Nagel, C. (eds.) Open Geospatial Consortium. www.opengeospatial.org/standards/citygml (2008). Accessed 31 Jan 2011

Rodríguez, A., Egenhofer, M., Rugg, R.: Assessing semantic similarity among geospatial feature class definitions. In: Vckovski, A., Brassel, K., Schek, H.-J. (eds.) Interoperating Geographic Information Systems – Second International Conference, INTEROP'99. Lecture Notes in Computer Science, vol. 1, pp. 1–16. Springer, Berlin (1999)

Santiago, J.L., Martilli, A., Martin, F.: CFD simulation of airflow over a regular array of cubes, Part I: Three-dimensional simulation of the flow and validation with wind-tunnel measurements. Bound. -Lay. Meteorol. **122**(3), 609–634 (26) (2007)

Smith, B.: An introduction to ontology. In: Peuquet, D., Smith, B., Brogaard, B. (eds.) The ontology of fields, pp. 10–14. National Center for Geographic Information and Analysis, Santa Barbara (1998)

Smith, B., Mark, D.: Ontology and geographic kinds. In: International Symposium on Spatial Data Handling, Vancouver 1998

Smith, B., Mark, D.: Ontology with human subjects testing: an empirical investigation of geographic categories. Am. J. Econ. Sociol. **58**, 245–272 (1999)

Smith, B., Mark, D.: Geographical categories: an ontological investigation. Int. J. Geogr. Inf. Sci. **15**, 591–612 (2001)

TU0801: Semantic enrichment of 3D city models for sustainable urban development. Memorandum of Understanding (MoU). http://w3.cost.esf.org/index.php?id=240&action_number=TU0801 (2008). Accessed 31 Jan 2011

UML-Unified Modeling Language, UML Resource Page. http://www.uml.org/. Accessed 31 Jan 2011

Uschold, M., Grüninger, M.: Ontologies: principles, methods and applications. Knowl. Eng. Rev. **11**(2), 93–155 (1996)

Uschold, M., King, M.: Towards a methodology for building ontologies. In: Skuce, D. (ed.) IJCAI'95 Workshop on Basic Ontological Issues in Knowledge Sharing, Montreal, pp. 6.1–6.10 (1995)

Waddell, P., Wang, L., Liu, X.: UrbanSim: an evolving planning support system for evolving communities. Preprint of paper forthcoming. In: Brail, R. (ed.) Planning support system. Lincoln Institute for Land Policy, Cambridge (2008)

Winter, S.: Ontology: buzzword or paradigm shift in GI science? Int. J. Geogr. Inf. Sci. **15**(7), 587–590 (2001)

Chapter 8
Call for LOD – Linking Scales and Providers Through Digital Spatial Representations

Anssi Joutsiniemi, Jarmo Laitinen, and Juho Malmi

8.1 Introduction

This article provides insight into linkages of data within a common spatial ontology over different scales, that are not obvious from the perspective of software interoperability. The aim of text is to stress the importance of the data usage and potentials that open up when large amounts of digital representations comes available. *The focus is on industry standards of three scales of spatial design and the potential added value of their data as a by-product of ordinary usage.* Samples are chosen to promote the idea that the intelligent usage of standards is far more important and far reaching than the original aim of the standardising.

A. Joutsiniemi
Institute of Urban Planning and Design, School of Architecture, Faculty of Built Environment, Tampere University of Technology, Finland
e-mail: anssi.joutsiniemi@tut.fi

J. Laitinen
ICT in Construction, Department of Civil Engineering, Faculty of Built Environment, Tampere University of Technology, Finland
e-mail: jarmo.laitinen@tut.fi

J. Malmi
Virtual Building Laboratory, Department of Civil Engineering, Faculty of Built Environment, Tampere University of Technology, Finland
e-mail: juho.malmi@tut.fi

G. Falquet et al., *Ontologies in Urban Development Projects*, Advanced Information and Knowledge Processing 1, DOI 10.1007/978-0-85729-724-2_8, © Springer-Verlag London Limited 2011

8.2   Industry Standards of Various Scales

The most general form of standardising can be found in standards of X3D.[1] Like its precursor, VRML (Virtual Reality Modelling Language), its main usage is to simulate the real-time 3-dimensional computer graphics especially through the World Wide Web. Due to its open XML syntax and ability to encode various dialectics of VRML, NURB geometry, H-anim and various external events, X3D has sometimes been used as an interchange format between other software. The difficulty of adopting a single standard or a single future scenario, either in urban development or in computer systems, stems from the absence of players to manage, maintain or finance the imagined big picture. Examples are chosen to show how these intermediate steps are converging from the strategies of multiple players.

For convenience we define three scales, or levels of detail (LOD), which also divide software into families according to their usage (i.e. GIS, CAD, CAM) and their common data formats. The largest, roughly above the unit size of 10^2 m is called *urban scale*. The smallest, roughly within extents of 10^0 m is in turn called *product scale*. Finally the intermediate scale sizing on average 10^1 m is called *building scale*. A brief, and hardly comprehensive, introductory selection of currently available standards in this scale framework could be as follow.

8.2.1   Urban Scale

– GML (Geography Markup Language) is a rich XML based language schema defined by the Open Geospatial Consortium (OGC, OGCE in Europe) for geographic modelling and data interchange. There are several OGC approved GML application schemas whose idea is to implement GML in specific areas of interest. For instance one of these, CityGML, is intended to represent a working semantic information model for cities and landscapes.
– KML (Keyhole Markup Language) (OGC 2008) is a lightweight XML based language schema used primarily by Google Earth and Google Maps. KML specifies only the very basic set of features commonly used in 3D GIS with the possibility to call data from network resources or to point to network resources. In addition it can call geometry described by a COLLADA (.dae) file and offers ways to specify custom schema features. Among other things, these features enable placing other information models inside a KML file (e.g. a full GML model), which provides for one to one data exchange with agreed standards, while others may still use the 3d and geographical information provided by the standard KML.

---

[1]Currently competing alternatives for X3D are formats such as U3D and COLLADA.

8.2.2   Building Scale

- IFC (Industry Foundation Classes) is a comprehensive schema for building industry information model defined by the International Alliance for Interoperability (IAI). IFC aims to ease and standardize data exchange and management at all stages of a building project. That is to say from early planning via building management all the way to eventual demolition. Currently the ready to use IFC-schema struggles with lacking implementations of data exchange use cases. IAI seems not to encourage separate implementations with smaller scope of data exchange such as what we see on the geographic side by OGC.
- IFG – (IFC for GIS) extended IFC schema. IFC format only supports one geographically correct location (IFCsite) point. The purpose of IFG is to address this issue by introducing entities that provide for Cartesian – Geodetic coordinate transformations. Furthermore it enhances IFCs' geographic data capabilities, with the aim to enable IFC – GML transfers.

8.2.3   Product Scale

- Geometric Description Language (GDL)[2] is a trademark of Graphisoft R&D zrt. It is the programming language used to control their main product ArchiCAD. GDL is widely utilized by ArchiCAD users and architecture related manufacturers to create parametric objects for use in ArchiCAD. Despite its proprietary nature GDL is well documented and third party use is encouraged. Graphisoft has a tradition of publishing interfaces to ease GDL data transfer to other formats and CAD systems.
- Design Web Format (DWF) is an open[3] distribution and communication format by AutoDesk (AutoCAD provider). The purpose of this format is to transfer design information and design content to users in highly compressed form over the web. The characteristics of DWF focusing on page description and 3D models are in fact very similar to any 'digital paper' formats, say for example, Adobe's Portable Document Format (PDF) developed from the early 1980s PostScript (PS) page description language.

When observing the data structures available for coding physical objects and their interaction into a formal representation, we see a clear pattern. The least common denominator of these chosen standards is that all of them are able to store data in the form of nested spatial descriptions and their alphanumeric properties. Ontologies, in the general sense of formal representation, are therefore found in two levels of interoperability in these standards: First in the *specifications level*, where the common geometrical characteristics of entities and their geographical reference

---

[2] Proprietary format of Graphisoft (ArchiCAD provider).
[3] The specification can be downloaded as part of the Autodesk® DWF™ Toolkit.

system is defined (using a core reference ontology of geometrical object) and, second, in *view definitions level*. We shall take a closer look at these basic distinctions that open up some major issues of interoperability as a whole.

8.3 Interoperability

The organizations developing various standards have a tendency to work towards considerably broad, all-inclusive presentations of their subjects. In data management this paves a path for nearly universal all inclusive file formats. This approach of carefully detailed standardization process is commonly found in the old expert systems tradition. Intuitively this means breaking the unimaginable field of possibilities into atoms and classifying each piece of information that may potentially exist. At first sight this seems the best way to guarantee universal interoperability. But does the solution really lie in carefully designed file format schemas, where each piece of information and its relation to the processes in which it is generated or used? All this worked perfectly in an ideal, reductionist and somewhat closed universe.

Since the data stored in digital information systems and data warehouses has proven to be more and more valuable if properly collected, managed and made extensively exchangeable. Case is therefore an essential requirement of computer systems. In general it is an issue of how diverse systems and organizations achieve their skills for working in a common ground. More technically speaking we refer to the definition of the Institute of Electrical and Electronics Engineers, which defines interoperability as an "ability of two or more systems or components to exchange information and to use the information that has been exchanged." (IEEE 1990) (Fig. 8.1)

Hietanen (2006) stressed the importance of different levels of interoperability and ordered them in an Interoperability Pyramid. A characteristic of the pyramid is that the number of people involved increases (Fig. 8.2) while the level of interoperability

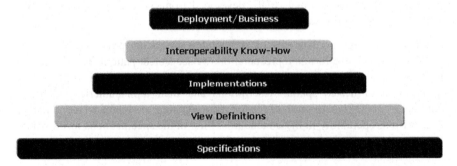

Fig. 8.1 Interoperability pyramid (Adapted from Hietanen 2006). The size of a block indicates the required ontological skills necessary for development work. This can be seen as supply or opportunity side of ontology development

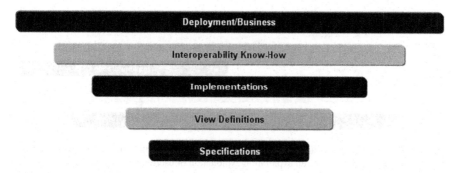

Fig. 8.2 The demand or need side of interoperability pyramid. The bottom-up approach indicating the number of potential users exploration/exploitation of ontologies

skills decreases (Fig. 8.1), when moving from the *Specifications* level towards the *Deployment* layer of everyday business activity. Remarkably, the transferring intermediate layers of *View definitions* and *Interoperability know-how* levels are underestimated in traditional vendor led implementations development.

In ontological terms one could roughly state that:

- the specification layer corresponds to a core reference ontology (say IFC for example);
- the view definition layer refers to a domain ontology (a building in construction domain) or sub domain ontology (an electrical device object in the construction domain);
- the implementations layer matches up to an application ontology;
- the *know-how* level is based on knowledge which enables several application ontology to exchange data that is to say taking benefits of the same core reference ontology. This phase tests that the data exchange is possible and proposes some correction if necessary in the implementation layer.

The *View definitions* layer is commonly seen as a subset of the specifications schema (Hietanen 2006). But thinking carefully one suddenly realizes that the scope of these views is not limited into complete overlapping with specification layer. It is true that *View definitions* actually provide multiple perspectives into the same specifications, but, and to understand the big picture of interoperability this is crucial: **it also allows a derivation of information that is not explicitly defined in layers below**. In this scheme additional processes, transitions or specific paths of behaviour for derived entity based on lower level information may be acquired. For example some of the derived spatial information may naturally be included in the specification level, like the explicit degree value to define spline geometry, a convex hull of point set or < *marquee* > tag in HTML, but equally well these can be handled in view definition level as dynamic manipulations of specifications layer. Further examples of these are, the derivation of spatial enclosures, combinatory forces, or proximity based fluid of field descriptions, which are usually formalized for a software end. Therefore the end-usage is by definition richer

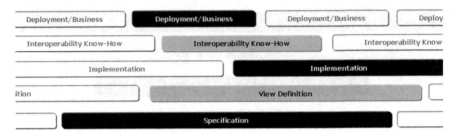

Fig. 8.3 Skewed interoperability pyramid in reality, which is the result of the top-down ontological opportunities facing the bottom-up exploration/exploitation of user-end

than its ontological base: If a picture is worth 1000 words, following our examples it seems fair to state that 3D models of spatial representation are worth more than 1,000 pictures.

This leads to layers that are theoretically neatly organized in a pyramid shape. But in reality the pyramid is highly skewed and distorted, because of overlappings that are only partial (Fig. 8.3). This is the picture even with any commonly recognized standards and proprietary data formats, so from the usage point of view any data opens up far more potential usage possibilities than a specification definitions originally ever wished for. The same is in fact true in the *Interoperability Know-how level*, which is best seen in numerous examples when a software usage or data definitions are taken in extensive use beyond their intended purpose.[4]

It may be true that there is a high concentration of skilled professionals working at the ontological definition level, but this group is also sufficiently small if compared to numerous amounts of players when moving towards the implementations and deployment layers. This "wisdom of crowds" leads into different interpretations or implementations of the concepts described in the core reference ontology. Therefore we focus on the demand side effect of interoperability describing the demand side of software development that can be seen as the pulling force that eventually challenges the flexibility and therefore the adaptive capabilities of various ontological definitions.

In the following text we challenge the traditional top-down approach of business administration and software development and provide alternative examples to outline how the *Interoperability Know-how layer* serves as an active component in steering the *Implementation layer* and adding requirements down to the ontological bases of the *Specification layer*. Most strikingly the needs of the *Deployment layer* are an open-ended pool of user-driven activity, which shifts the interest from

---

[4]Examples of these qualitative leaps are for example usage of Maya (and alike software) as a tool for architecture that has lead into completely novel idea *blob architecture* or the path from SGML to HTML, which eventually enabled the markup language popular in printing industry to transform into Internet publishing.

proper usages to creative misuse. Today the ownership of a format or even data content is simply not good enough for effective business, but setting them free might be.

8.4 BIM and Overwhelming Spatial Knowledge

In sharing information of the building and urban design activities level, two competing methods seem to be possible. In short they can be described as exhaustive (or detailed) and general (or loose), although in reality the classification is often quite indistinct and may greatly depend on the observer. Examples of these different approaches and their uses are the utilization scenarios of GML and KML. Neither can yet be called *de facto* standard for spatial data transfer while both have what it takes to become one; for profoundly different reasons however.

It is interesting to note that the richer professional level file formats mentioned earlier – GML and IFC – are indeed progressing on their way to wider use. The corresponding developing organizations however have different tactics. IAI (behind the IFC standard) works hard to achieve one universal implementation, while OGC has allowed for several co-existing application schemas (i.e. implementations) for GML. This also implies that their potential drawbacks should differ.

GML is already used all over in wildly varying application schemas. All these application schemas will not be supported indefinitely. This leads into backwards compatibility issues. As an example of backwards compatibility only think of all those text documents created before the WordPerfect (and later MS Word) breakthrough. Can you display them now as intended back then? Unfortunately you're sometimes lucky to get even the plain text out.[5] So currently, instead of just one GML, we have many still workable – application schema that are sometime fragmentary. IFC however does not even have a working implementation yet but at the end only one is expected – a complete and detailed one. The drawback of this scheme is that due to its aimed comprehensiveness and required level of knowledge, it also effectively inhibits reaching the critical mass necessary for large-scale implementations (Fig. 8.4).

Fortunately the world is not completed. The inventor of blank paper didn't rush forward to make rules to exploit the usage, but left the functional definition open. It is the same with data structures: You never know what can be baked from the same ingredients. The point to make here is that any given piece of information or data structure is defined according to an original application or software requirement. But several different applications (software) can reuse these data structures to achieve a different requirement. Naturally this is very context and user dependent.

---

[5]For example, early contributions of the father of AI research, Marvin Lee Minsky, have vanished for good, due to simple software backward compatibility issues.

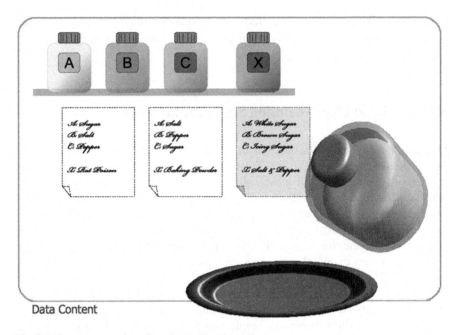

Data Content

Fig. 8.4 Smart aggregation of nearly identical ingredients

The growing computer literacy brings about more and more occasions where talented laymen may solve their intellectual need themselves if only a proper platform to build on is given.

8.5   Consumers' Pull of Product Scale

To simplify things somewhat, let us assume that there really is a clear distinction between products, buildings and cities. A product is an instance, a building is an individual entity and a city is a world populated by individual entities. A first observation may be that in reality this shift form minor products to large scale urban agglomerations is more a slider than a three-stage switch, but it becomes clear that in fact each level may be defined as an entity with its constituent parts. This chosen definition of nested partitioning in part helps explaining why, for example the term *building product model* was such short lived and why more generic discussion of ontologies in building sector become appropriate. It also helps to put contemporary thinking in perspective.

Architects and designers have long ago entered into product oriented development scheme, where the design process is more a task of combining certified (or standardized, tested, quality approved, law suit minimized, and so forth) components into house aggregate than the traditional process based on availability of raw material. So to be honest, when setting the hard-core professional role a bit aside, actually one must admit that the so-called professional activity doesn't considerably differ from ordinary laymen supermarket shopping activity. Therefore it is not surprising that companies, for example in furniture industry, have taken advantage of professional-feel computation tools to support their customers' possibilities for making plans of their own.

Naturally at the bottom line the disagreements are found on style, or lack of it. We should realize that the provider wants to push the designer (or any client) towards buying the maximum amount of their products. Thus their design software looks more like a boring order form than an intelligent software agent able to combine adequately their product. We are certain that not only designer professionals need to have a capability to combine products of different providers, but also generally people feel slightly uncomfortable with the idea of adopting only one registered trademark lifestyle. Despite this small drawback the single provider's point of view has already span-up a new kind of do-it-yourself activity, but something more is needed for enhanced creativity.[6]

To give a test for this, we thought of giving it a quick try. We will illustrate our opinion that the designer of any system cannot have a control over future usage of it. So we'll assess the unused potential of freely downloadable *Furnish* software family (*Pro & Lite* versions). *Furnish* is a spin-off development of *DesignTime* (or *RunTime*)[7] by Geac Computer Corporation Limited and both tested version of software are released as freeware. Especially the *Lite* version is distributed under several names, probably best known as *IKEA home planner* (Fig. 8.5).[8]

Despite the providers' attempt to secure intellectual property of their designs the software contains the pieces of furniture installed in a single 'library' in program's system folder. With a minor crack[9] every layman can get the same professional-feel functionality out of this freely distributed software. In the *Pro* version of *Furnish* additional features are available and the users are able, for example, to import and export CAD files in DXF-format,[10] to render[11] their homes in enhanced detail and

---

[6] [http://www.ikea.com/ms/en_US/rooms_ideas/ckl/default.html].

[7] The software originally used for design and pre-production phases in fashion and apparel industry.

[8] Commercial versions are shipped in Visual Configurator software family. Other freeware are provided by:

- Club 8; BoConcept: [http://www.boconcept.com/Default.aspx?ID=10648]
- KVIK 3D (fi): [http://www.kvik.com/fi-FI/drawing/kvik-3d.htm]
- Flexa 3D: [http://www.flexa.dk/Default.aspx?ID=372]
- Montana Furnish Lite: [http://www.montana.dk/] > List of Models > Draw Program

[9] Technically speaking this we suppose is a crack only because it is not strictly speaking allowed by the license agreement. Despite such personal usage is a clear win-win situation for customers, distributors as well as software providers.

[10] Abbreviation for Drawing eXchange Format. This, in recent development clearly outdated, format was developed by AutoDesk in 1982 for CAD interoperability and has since evolved to *de facto* open standard.

[11] Software uses UC Berkley originating Pixie rendering engine that is distributed under GNU Lesser General Public License (Free Software Foundation 2007).

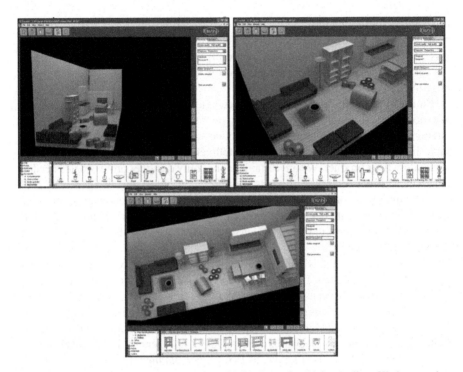

Fig. 8.5 Furnish snapshots of ordinary house with furniture of multiple suppliers: Kitchenware by KVIK & IKEA, sofa by Club 8, childrenware by Flexa and shelves by Montana. In these pictures only missing piece are the personal items

eventually to get the up to date price of their dreams. It is important to stress that all these data are already downloadable from Internet and are available to anyone with sufficient skill about Interoperability know-how. Most surprising of all, a whole new market could open up with minor conversion from currently proprietary data format. These conversions permit easy and free access to digital copies of products for any virtual environment.

So where's this all taking us in data specifications? On one hand the semantic web as described by W3C[12] has not yet kicked in and has even evoked some resistance in the Web community.[13] But, on the other hand, behind the scene Google has built a little piece of "semantic" web of its own with its georeferencing based Google Earth and its KML content.[14] Indeed many service providers are currently

---

[12] W3C Semantic Web specifications page [http://www.w3.org/2001/sw/].

[13] Sceptical reaction from web user community in Wikipedia [http://en.wikipedia.org/wiki/Semantic_Web#Skeptical_reactions].

[14] All equipped with an interface towards the rest of the net by an open API [http://code.google.com/intl/fi/apis/earth/] and the fact that KML is supported by most digital globe software a.k.a. earth browsers. For example current release description of KDE Marble [http://edu.kde.org/marble/current.php] or NASA WorldWind 1.4 release notes [http://sourceforge.net/project/shownotes.php?release_id=486507&group_id=69528].

Fig. 8.6 Snapshots of W3C Markup Validation Service results January 30th 2009: four out of six major web sites didn't pass the most basic html-validation process. From left: W3C Semantic Web page [http://www.w3.org/2001/sw/], Wikipedia Main page [http://en.wikipedia.org/wiki/Main_Page], Wikipedia Semantic Web page [http://en.wikipedia.org/wiki/Semantic_Web], Google Search page [http://www.google.com/], SourceForge front-page [http://sourceforge.net/] and Facebook Login page [http://www.facebook.com/index.php] (Results with errors presented in inverse coloring for clarity)

expanding the so-called Web 2.0, which the renowned W3C sweeps away as "a piece of jargon".[15] In any case, many content rich services do not comply with W3C standards, especially ones with user generated content, although most of them can be accessed through specific APIs. The simplistic, but extendable nature of KML complies well with something called 'the useful minimum' approach to sieve necessary and sufficient content for end use. Only once the feasibility is demonstrated is it time to gradually move towards full utilization. Since the core of KML semantics is spatial information it is inherently useful for sharing GIS based spatial content (Fig. 8.6).

The major benefit of Google's KML file format is, that it allows embedding of user defined data in a KML-model. It is certainly not the only spatial data format with this ability, but it is the lightness of the initial schema that makes it an interesting target for user modifications and one to one interoperability agreements. Its flexibility makes KML not only a beautiful companion for GML, but also a good competitor. KML developers say that it is up to the users to decide on the necessary semantics.

There are already more than just weak signals that KML may soon be another OGC standard along with GML, because its role among popular applications like Google Earth will promote its use like web browsers promote the use of the HTML language. This suggests that KML is to GML like the envelope is to a letter. GML defines which data should be stored because it is an interchange format. KML is an implementation format using the data defined in GML and making these data interpretable by Google Earth application. The importance of KML will depend on the success of those applications. It may be worth noting that the idea of the so called semantic web largely depends on the popularity of the interchange formats based on XML (GML, KML, IFC, etc.).

---

[15] Transcript of a 2006 *IBM developerWorks* interview with Tim Berners-Lee [http://www.ibm.com/developerworks/podcast/dwi/cm-int082206txt.html].

8.6   Scale Leaps Through the Universe

This trend in shift from professional tools to penetrate everyday usage is analogous to vendors who want to increase their sales by proposing their products in TV-shopping. Remarkable work towards ubiquitous computing usage is done in CASA UCL to link up various key activities of urban design and analyses to Google's SketchUp, Earth and Maps API (Hudson-Smith 2007; Hudson-Smith et al. 2007). At their best, these examples lead into free usage of urban analysis functionality (Gibin et al. 2008) or routing and geocoding (Gilmore 2008) for practically anybody; or at least without need for proprietary GIS. The current innovations are made in the level of intelligent usage and a combination of existing open geodatabases, which already at the moment are rich enough to produce a user-driven pull of interoperability.

Similarly building industry could benefit from the same approach. It often finds itself somewhere in the middle of scales and created some confusion trying to guide the unguidable. CAD-programs are the tools of choice for building industry since physically a building resembles more a chair than a city, not to mention a landscape. They evolved in mass production oriented industries, which were one of the first to utilize 3D product models intensively (to control manufacturing etc.). From that background the logical conclusion seemingly was to use product modelling tools for buildings too. However the findings were symptomatic: houses are so much more complicated than chairs that such a model is almost incomprehensible. Due to performance problems there simply wasn't any software to display it either. Also there is usually more than one person designing a house and their plans always overlap. Hence the best practice has been to use partial models. IFC is an attempt to bring these partial models together by enabling data exchange across the field. The purpose is to eliminate the need for multiple inputs.[16]

Incorporation of 3D data in KML schema suggests it could also be used to share BIM content. The recent addition of user defined extended content especially in XML format makes it applicable for building large-scale urban models with access to dedicated BIM and GIS data. These models could be created in variety of custom designed information model formats (e.g. IFC, CityGML) and even their basic KML representation automatically generated from the original data. The publicly accessible models would carry unclassified information content and serve as link to detailed information to authorized users either by query or direct download. The big idea of course is that the data creation methods (application base, work paths etc.) need not be changed at all; rather the finalized entities would be transferred to appropriate representations.

Fortunately some patterns seem to be converging here. Taking freedom to imagine the necessary associations and linking the previous analogy of LOD in data formats to the scale jumps between physics, chemistry and biology; we realize that

---

[16]This may sound minor, but duplicated data may in fact be one of the biggest problems with current BIMs. Besides rendering the model untrustworthy manner by duplicating input data, it is roughly four times more inefficient (because of the need for filtering before data exchange).

an implementation and further emergence of a large, universal file format is not too different. The actual problem caused by exponentially increasing number of entities and their innumerable arrangements can be sensed even in a modest sized stock of building blocks.

For more advanced usage of BIMs the key feature to overcome these multi-scalar view and specification difficulties is bound to a concept, which the gaming industry knows as Level of detail (LOD). At the specification level formats like KML have moved from implicit threshold definition to explicit LOD coding and IFG has taken first steps into that direction too. The need for explicit threshold definition is necessary to screen the system from a combinatory explosion and prevent it choking to incoming data. The specifications are largely missing scaling definitions that are commonly found in intelligent raster formats organized in pyramid manner (like MrSID etc.) It is more commonly handled at software end and requires heavy calculations of convex and concave hull, bounding boxes and envelopes or vertex splits and progressive meshes. (Slater et al. 2002) Taking this into the specification layer clearly leads into lighter or more efficient implementation layer as Google Earth has already proven. Additional resources would be welcome at the user-end.

8.7   Open Problems and Research Challenges

A major challenge of understanding the progressive nature of technological advancement is related to re-thinking the interoperability as addressed above. All above-mentioned interoperability issues, which by and large are led by advances in the *Interoperability know-how* layer, could make direct references to more a generic evolutionary base. The challenge for development is the commonly known Darwinian concept of **pre-adaptation**. Following the argumentation of theoretical biologist Stuart Kauffman, the idea of pre-adaptation simply means that a part of an organism might turn useful in an environment even though the development of that part was never a favoured characteristic itself. Kauffman (Brockman 2003) explains the idea of pre-adaptation with Gertrude, an incredibly ugly squirrel with flappy skins in armpits. Its evolution to flying squirrel happened only because this characteristic turned the jump into soar and enhanced its success in evolutionary selection. But importantly for us, in a strict sense **it was never designed.** The same can be found similarly from the evolution of a swim bladder or mammal ear that never was designed for the purpose we currently recognize them for. Following Kauffman's argumentation the same is by and large the case in the evolution of the technosphere as well. To take an example of computer: The early machine for ballistic calculations and code breaking was never thought of as the Internet. We simply didn't see that coming. Moreover in the Internet case, we realize exactly the same: It was never designed for Facebook or multi-player role gaming. We simply didn't see those coming either. If there is anything to learn from these general examples, it is that the strongest or even the most intelligent are not the ones who survive, but the ones that are most efficiently breeding and adapting. To support even more complex pre-adaptation in an ultimately

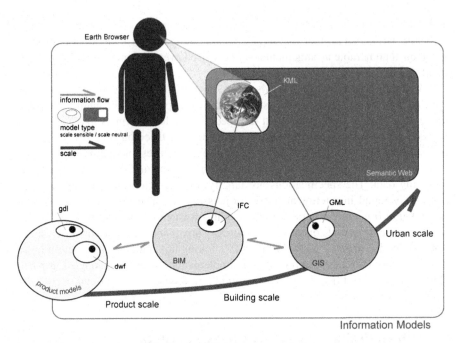

Fig. 8.7 Emergence of second reality from digital representations

open universe the characteristics that really count are bound with overwhelming information, flexibility and diverse by-products.

Similarly also GML, IFC and GDL based objects all provide in their current state a digital representation that is potentially far more valuable than the objects themselves. When considering Internet repositories and data warehouses already being filled with different digital representations of everyday objects, it is easy to see that they actually provide undergrowth of large-scale virtual environments. A simple example of a multi-scale 3D repository is the 3D warehouse of SketchUp (Google 2011), which contains spatial models at all scales, from building products[17] to hard core architecture competition entries[18] and digital cities.[19] Thinking only an additional implementation of registered EPC-type (Electronic Product Code[20]) ID to provide a unique identity to objects and the linkage between virtual and real environments is ready for (Fig. 8.7).

---

[17] http://sketchup.google.com/3dwarehouse/cldetails?mid=5ab1f8c0846734ee4f78b7b58252a6e9 &ct=hpr2.

[18] http://sketchup.google.com/3dwarehouse/details?mid=cc75568f48b9f3d76d73725a44b1c29b.

[19] http://sketchup.google.com/3dwarehouse/cldetails?mid=4c1c0aca4c6df7b6b15cd835a6effb08& ct=hpr1.

[20] EPC is the successor of UPC (Universal Product Code) and EAN (European Article Numbering) systems familiarly met in product barcodes for example in ordinary department store products.

Implementation layers with advanced LOD are currently able to provide a simulation of real time physics and other modelled interaction. If we compare, say, the development of game engines, it is clear that major leap in technology was made, not in attempts of protecting gained knowledge, but setting it free. Games like *Quake* and *Doom* some 10 years ago changed the scene. Not only was the true 3D environment groundbreaking, but also its open 'free to hack' attitude unseen. The first opened up a possibility to replay parts of a game as recorded demo sessions, but the latter was an enabler of *machinima*. Film industry had been for a while able to use 3D animation in real time, but unless you happened to own 300,000 dollar Silicon Graphics environment, you should think other business. New game engines quickly filled the gap and created a new genre of movies based on 3D engine called *machinima* (contraction of *machine and cinema*) (Carless 2005). Actually the step towards the beneficial use of representations of real environment is so short that it is nearly taken.

Looking up all digital representations scattered around Internet in form of products, buildings and cities, it is easy to see that we are literally just one step away of the potential of uploading ones everyday life in massive quantities into Second Life-type environments to augment social interactions when needed. Chosen examples in this article are meant to outline potential emergent development paths of available standards of spatial representation that are far from being controlled by any specific level of interoperability, but lead from the open-ended user creativity. More generally speaking examples are chosen to appreciate the complex wisdom of Jean Baudrillard's prophetic words outlining the true future prospective of IT development: "Information can tell us everything. It has all the answers. But they are answers to questions we have not asked, and which doubtless don't even arise" (Baudrillard 1990, 219).

References

Baudrillard, J.: Cool Memories. Verso, London (1990)
Brockman, J.: The adjacent possible – a talk with Stuart Kauffman. http://www.edge.org/3rd_culture/kauffman03/kauffman_index.html (2003). Accessed 5 Feb 2011
Carless, S.: Game Hacking. O'Reilly Media, Sebastopol, CA (2005)
Free Software Foundation: GNU lesser general public license. http://www.gnu.org/licenses/lgpl.html (2007). Accessed 5 Feb 2011
Gibin, M., Singleton, A., Milton, R., Mateos, P., Longley, P.: Collaborative mapping of London using google maps: the LondonProfiler, CASA working papers series, Paper 132. http://www.casa.ucl.ac.uk/working_papers/paper132.pdf (2008). Accessed 3 Feb 2011
Gilmore, J.: Introducing google's geocoding service. http://www.developer.com/lang/jscript/article.php/3615681 (2008). Accessed 4 Feb 2011
Google: 3D warehouse. http://sketchup.google.com/3dwarehouse (2011). Accessed 5 Feb 2011
Hietanen, J.: IFC model view definition format. International Alliance for Interoperability. http://www.secondschool.net/one/IAI_IFC_framework.pdf. (2006)
Hudson-Smith, A.: Digital urban – The visual city, CASA working papers series, paper 124. http://www.casa.ucl.ac.uk/working_papers/paper124.pdf (2007)

Hudson-Smith, A., Milton, R., Dearden, J., Batty, M.: Virtual cities: digital mirrors into a recursive world, CASA working papers series, Paper 125. http://www.casa.ucl.ac.uk/working_papers/paper125.pdf (2007)

Institute of Electrical and Electronics Engineers: IEEE Standard Computer Dictionary: A Compilation of IEEE Standard Computer Glossaries. Institute of Electrical and Electronics Engineers, New York (1990)

OGC: OGC® KML. Open geospatial consortium. http://www.opengeospatial.org/standards/kml/ (2008) Accessed 5 Feb 2011

Slater, M., Steed, A., Chrysanthou, Y.: Computer graphics and virtual environments. Addison Wesley, London (2002)

Chapter 9
Ontology-Based Interoperability
in Knowledge-Based Communication Systems

Stefan Trausan-Matu

9.1 Introduction

One of the main ideas of this chapter is that for assuring interoperability for different kinds of applications, the existence of a well designed shared structure of concepts, a so-called "ontology", has a major importance. The structure should be well designed in order to capture the relations and the properties of concepts in the considered domain, and to allow the inference of new properties. A carefully developed ontology may be easily used as the main component of different *Knowledge-Based Systems* (KBS), similarly with a human being, which uses the same knowledge in performing a large range of activities.

KBS are software applications in which there is an explicit representation of knowledge, in a so-called knowledge base. There may be declarative ("know that") or procedural ("know how") knowledge. The ontology of a given domain is an important part of the declarative knowledge, containing at least the basic concepts of the domain and the relationships among them. This fact enables the reuse of an ontology in various Knowledge-Based Systems for the given domain.

Another important idea discussed herein is that ontologies have a role not only in KBS, which are traditionally based on the individual cognition paradigm considering the knowledge which is in someone's (e.g. an expert) mind (paradigm which proved to be limited, see for example, Brown (1999)). Ontologies may have a central place also in applications based on the opposed, socio-cultural idea, which considers that knowledge is socially constructed (Vygotsky 1978), in which communication and, in particular, dialogue has a major role. In fact, *dialogism* is a basic theory in the socio-cultural approach, considering that everything is a dialogue (Bakhtin 1981).

S. Trausan-Matu (✉)
Computer Science Department of the Politehnica University of Bucharest, Romania
e-mail: trausan@gmail.com

G. Falquet et al., *Ontologies in Urban Development Projects*, Advanced Information and Knowledge Processing 1, DOI 10.1007/978-0-85729-724-2_9,
© Springer-Verlag London Limited 2011

Dialogism can be used as a theoretical substrate for developing software tools for supporting collaborative applications which use also ontologies (Trausan-Matu et al. 2007).

The socio-cultural paradigm is present not only in explicit dialogic tools as instant messenger (chat) or discussion forums. It is also the substrate of the so-called Social Web (Web2.0), which includes also *folksonomies* (Mika 2005), which are opposed to ontologies in the sense that they are constructed by a community and not mainly by an individual (in folksonomies people add tags on web resources, the side effect being that they make a classification and a social conceptualization).

In this chapter we will try to integrate the two paradigms, cognitive and socio-cultural. We will show how socio-cultural concepts may be represented in an ontology and how an ontology may be used in a socio-cultural dialogic system. We will discuss how the same domain ontology may be used in a couple of different Knowledge-Based Systems: an expert system for giving advice related to urbanism and civil-engineering regulations, and a system that uses the ontology and natural language processing techniques for assisting participants to a virtual chat conference for design or e-learning. In this second system is illustrated also the possibility of adding new concepts in the ontology. The two applications considered are typical for the two paradigms: One is starting from the idea that the ontology provides the knowledge usually possessed by a human expert. The second enables humans to construct knowledge together through dialogue.

Even if based on different paradigms, both applications may be seen as involving knowledge communities that share a domain ontology and maybe a top level socio-cultural ontology. The idea that links these kinds of applications is that they use, in fact, different ways of communication and, in particular, the way of entering into a dialog: database query, hypertext browsing, keyword-based search engine, intelligent search engine, expert system dialog, controlled natural language, question answering, and natural language dialog. All these offer access, in different degrees, to socio-cultural knowledge construction.

The chapter continues with a section introducing the basic ideas of Knowledge-Based Systems, the role of ontologies in developing KBS and the reuse opportunities that they offer. The following section will be dedicated to a socio-cultural top-level ontology. The fourth section discusses the dialogistic character of any information system. The next sections introduce the above mentioned two application examples. The chapter will end with conclusions.

9.2 Artificial Intelligence, Knowledge-Based Systems and Ontologies

Artificial Intelligence is an interdisciplinary domain in which researchers try to develop "intelligent" computer programs that behave like intelligent humans in solving complex problems and that may communicate using human-like means, e.g. natural language. One of the ideals to be reached by artificial intelligence is to develop so-called *expert systems* that could enter in dialog, answer questions and provide solutions to problems in the same way a human expert would do.

Expert systems are Knowledge-Based Systems, which intensively and explicitly process important amounts of knowledge, similarly to an intelligent human person. Moreover, KBS are computer programs in which a clear difference is kept between the knowledge they use and the procedures for processing it. This division permits the incremental development of the so-called knowledge bases, while the processing procedures remain unchanged and are usually reused for a wide range of applications. This possibility is crucial for the development of computer programs for problems which are usually solved by humans which posses a large amount of knowledge in problem's domain. The reason is, first of all, psychological: It is very hard for a human to describe the whole amount of knowledge it uses. The constructing of knowledge is much easier in an incremental process. It is easier to understand what knowledge the system lacks by examining its behavior, by entering into a dialog with it, if possible.

Another important consequence of the separation of the knowledge base and the inference engine is the reuse of the knowledge bases for several different purposes (e.g., constructing a solution, understanding a solution or generating explanations). However, for this purpose the base should be carefully developed, in order to be sufficiently general. One perspective in this idea is to construct the knowledge base starting from an ontology, which should be viewed as a "theory" of the considered domain. An ontology is a particular kind of knowledge base, containing declarative knowledge and being a skeleton for further knowledge acquisition activities. In fact, this was the context in which the term "ontology" started to be used in knowledge engineering in the beginning of the last decade of the twentieth century: For developing the knowledge base of an intelligent program, "knowledge engineers" realized that it is very useful to have a skeleton of the main concepts and relations of the considered domain, a so-called ontology.

Viewing knowledge bases as ontologies determines important advantages for developers of Knowledge-Based Systems. First of all, an ontology is developed as a coherent framework for the reality and therefore it facilitates knowledge acquisition and machine learning. It is easy to add a new concept in such a framework by finding one or some more general concepts and defining some differences between the new concept and the more general ones.

Ontologies are very important in applications that extract knowledge from texts (text mining) and, in general, to applications for the Semantic Web (Berners-Lee et al. 2001). For this kind of software they offer the substrate for semantic analysis and, very important, the possibility of defining a measure of semantic neighbourhood, based on the lattice structure (based on the hypernymic order relation) of ontologies (Hirst and St-Onge 1998). This semantic closeness is very important in text analysis for example in the retrieval of texts that do not contain a given word, but they contain a synonym or a semantically related word.

From a knowledge representation perspective, ontologies are semantic networks that state what kinds of concepts exist and what abstraction-particularization (generalization/ specialization) relations hold among them. If a concept is a

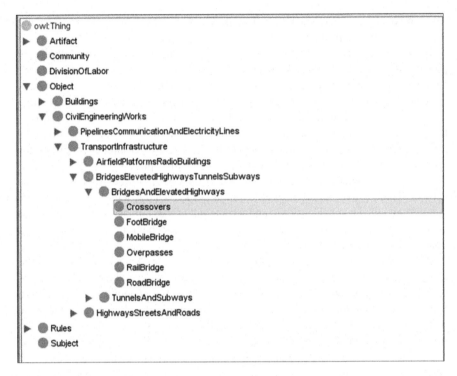

Fig. 9.1 A fragment of the urban development and civil engineering ontology

particularization (specialization?) of another concept, it has all the features of the more abstract concept and, maybe, some particular ones, For example, in Fig. 9.1, the fact that the concept "BridgesAndElevatedHighways" has "Crossovers", "FootBridge", "MobileBridge", "Overpasses", "RailBridge" and "RoadBridge", implicitly enumerates the only possible cases. Moreover, all these concepts inherit properties (e.g. regulations) that belong to "BridgesAndElevatedHighways" or its ancestors (the Protégé environment - http://protege.stanford.edu - was used for the development of the ontology and the image is a screen-shot from it).

Ontologies offer reuse, simplifying computing in a similar way with Object-Oriented Programming (whose idea has common ancestors with ontologies in frames (Minsky 1975)). For example, an ontology may be seen as a library of concepts and relations that may be used for many applications. Another important resemblance is encapsulation and centralization, which simplify changes: When some concept or relation changes, it is enough to make a modification in a single place and all the descendant applications will inherit the new version.

However, ontologies do not cover all kinds of knowledge representation. In addition to declarative knowledge representation, there is a need also for procedural knowledge, saying what to do in a given context. Such type of knowledge may be represented by production rules, which are pairs *condition – action*: IF *condition* holds, THEN PERFORM *action*. Conditions usually contain patterns and variables that may be linked to facts. A production rule system has a conflict resolution strategy that selects the rule that will be applied from the rules that may be applied.

9.3   A Top Level Socio-Cultural Ontology

In the socio-cultural paradigm, knowledge is seen as constructed and shared by communities of people acting in a more or less concerted way. In order to assure a coherent behaviour, people obey some explicit (for example, written) or implicit (for example, tacit) rules. Individuals (subjects) in a community may have different roles (for example, leader, professor, student, etc.) and their activities are associated with different types of work achieving some outcomes (or objects). As a consequence, a division of labor, that means a classification of different types of work should be considered.

A very important role in achieving the outcomes is the existence of mediators between subjects and objects, the usage of artifacts, of tools (Vygotsky 1978). A remarkable example of artifacts is the human language, which is a major tool enabling humans to collaborate (Vygotsky 1978).

All the above concepts are the ingredients of the Activity Theory of Yrjö Engeström (1987), which emphasizes categories (subjects, objects, and communities), mediators (general artifacts, social rules and division of labor) and relations between them (see also Fig. 9.2). This theory provides a theoretical framework

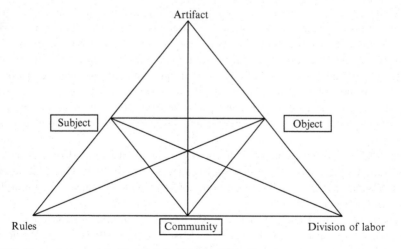

Fig. 9.2 The main concepts of the Activity Theory of Yrjö Engeström

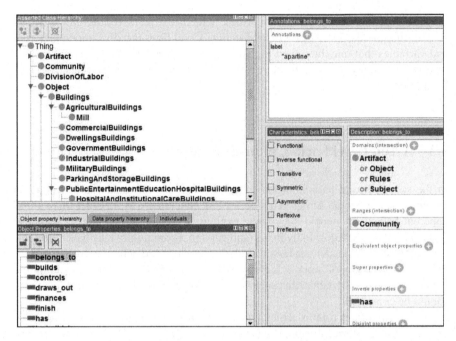

Fig. 9.3 The relations of the urban development and civil engineering ontology, emphasizing the domain and range of the relation "belongs_to"

that has been used for developing an ontology for urban development (Trausan-Matu 2007) that has as basic concepts the components of the above mentioned two group of entities.

If we want to integrate the socio-cultural paradigm with the cognitive, knowledge-based one, an ontology of the socio-cultural concepts is useful. This ontology may be used as a top-level ontology, from which should be specialized concepts for the different socio-cultural communication and information systems. Starting from the Theory of Activity, each of the six entities is a basic concept (or "class") in the socio-cultural ontology. These concepts may have attributes, sub-concepts (that may be also sub-concepts of several other concepts, i.e. multiple inheritance of properties is allowed), and relations with other concepts (see Fig. 9.3).

In addition to generic concepts, the ontology contains also individuals (instances). For example, the "Subject" class has 12 instances (see Fig. 9.4). One of these, the "LocalAuthority" instance has several relations ("provides", "releases", "controls", etc.) with other individuals.

The idea of developing an ontology for the socio-cultural top concepts (a top-level ontology) starting from Engstrom's ideas (Engström 1987) is new. We do not know about other expert systems or ontology-based systems for urbanism or any other domain using such a top-level ontology.

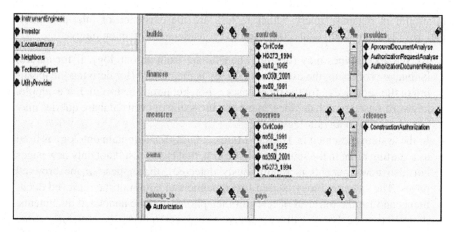

Fig. 9.4 The "LocalAuthority" individual and its relations with other individuals

9.4   Types of Dialog in Information Systems

In order to provide the needed advice to various types of users and to different kinds of questions, an intelligent information system should consider several ways of dialogical interaction. Any information act is, in fact, dialogic. Moreover, as Bakhtin emphasized, any text is a dialog (Bakhtin 1981): Even if you write something and you upload a document on the web, this is a potential dialog with the readers of the text. Bakhtin's dialogism is extending Vygotsky's ideas (Wertsch 1991), it is one of the most important representant of the socio-cultural paradigm.

Different ways of querying in information systems may be considered as different ways of entering in dialog. A classification of querying types, on an increasing scale of the degree of dialogism is:

(a) database query
(b) hypertext browsing
(c) keyword-based search engine
(d) semantic web search engine
(e) intelligent search engine
(f) expert system dialog
(g) controlled natural language
(h) question answering
(i) natural language dialogue.

From the above list, only natural language dialog and question answering are, at least for the moment, the less satisfactorily implemented. All the other ways of information querying are, more or less, possible to implement.

The degree of dialogism, in our perspective is including the importance of contextual information, which is extremely important in natural language dialogue and minimum in database query. Other factors are the existence of inter-animation patterns (Trausan-Matu et al. 2007) and the consideration of an ontology.

- All the above types may (or must) beneficiate from an ontology. If for natural language processing the use of an ontology is mandatory (for deriving the meaning of the sentences), for the other cases is not, but it may be useful. For example, keyword-based search engines, hypertext browsing or even database queries may beneficiate from an ontology.
- In the system presented in Trausan-Matu et al. (2002), a domain ontology is used as a starting point in the serendipitous search, that has as result not only new pages but also new concepts (serendipitously detected), that appear in the browsed pages. The same ontology is used for semantic annotation of the retrieved documents and for the retrieval of relevant metaphors from the annotated documents. A collection of dynamically generated web pages reflects the structure of the domain ontology. In addition, the ontology is driving the construction of the user's model and the filtering of the amount of concepts and facts presented, in order to provide personalization. This multiple usage of the same domain ontology is an exemplification of the basic idea of this chapter, that a same domain ontology may be used for several applications, for the above querying styles (e.g. expert systems or intelligent information systems), but also for others, like diagnostic expert systems, intelligent e-learning (Trausan-Matu et al. 2002) or intelligent tools for supporting collaboration (Trausan-Matu et al. 2007).

9.4.1 Expert Systems for Providing Intelligent Advice

Even intelligent search engines, which extend the power of what Google can do, lack the ability to enter into a dialog, to provide an actual advice or plan of actions. What they can do (very well, is true) is to provide relevant documents in which you may find the topics that you mentioned what you need. An alternative is the development of more dialogical intelligent information systems (Trausan-Matu and Neacsu 2008), which provide an extended range of types of query answering, which are closer to the idea of a true dialog.

An expert system was implemented that enters into a dialog with users, for providing information about topics related to getting urbanism authorizations for new buildings. The Jess production rule system (http://www.jessrules.com/jess) was used. A program in Jess is a collection of rules that can be matched to the existing data in the working memory. Each rule has a first, matching part, and a second, action one, which modifies the working memory or prints something. A rule may have variables that are linked to values in the working memory using pattern matching. For example, a rule that prints the information that local authorities may provide is below exemplified. In this rule, the variables $?p, $?r, and $?c are matched to all the available data, in the working memory, regarding what the local authority provides, releases and controls.

Do you want to learn what documents you need when building a house? (yes or no) yes
Have you reveive the authorization? (yes or no) no
Do you own the property? (yes or no) yes
Do you have the budget? (yes or no) yes
Did you asked for Urban Certificate? (yes or no) no
Solution: Go to the local authority
Do you want to know more on the subject? (yes/no)
yes
LocalAuthority provides:
    - AprouvalDocumentAnalyse
    - AuthorizationRequestAnalyse
    - AuthorizationDocumentRelease
  releases:
    - ConstructionAuthorization
  in accordance with:
    - no10_1995 (see the web-site: ~#en http://www.pptt.ro/content/legea_nr__101995_privind_calitatea)
    - no350_2001 (see the web-site: ~#en http://www.cdep.ro/pls/legis/legis_pck.htp_act?ida=30200)
    - no50_1991 (see the web-site: ~#en http://www.cdep.ro/pls/legis/legis_pck.htp_act?ida=1322)
Try again? (yes or no) yes
Do you want to learn what documents you need when building a house? (yes or no) yes
Have you reveive the authorization? (yes or no) yes
Have you paid the taxes? (yes or no) no
Solution: Pay the taxes
Do you want to know more on the subject? (yes/no)
yes
The Investor has to pay
    - AprovalDocumentReleaseTaxe
    - ConstructionTaxe
    - AuthorizationTaxe
    - DesignTaxe
Try again? (yes or no) yes

Fig. 9.5 A dialog in the expert system session

```
(defrule local_authority
  (declare (salience 1))
  (print go_to_local_authority)
  ?f <- (object (is-a Subject)
                  (:NAME "LocalAuthority")
                  (provides $?p) (releases $?r) (controls
                  $?c))
  (not (answer ?))
  =>
  (printout t (slot-get ?f :NAME) " provides: " crlf)
  (foreach ?x $?p (printout t " - "(instance-name ?x) crlf))
  (printout t " releases: " crlf)
  (foreach ?x $?r (printout t " - "(instance-name ?x) crlf))
  (printout t " in accordance with: " crlf)
  (foreach ?x $?c (printout t " - "(instance-name ?x) crlf))
```

In Fig. 9.5 is illustrated a simple dialog that, among others, presents what the "LocalAuthority" can provide, release and control. An important observation is that the data is obtained from the ontology and it may be different if the ontology changes.

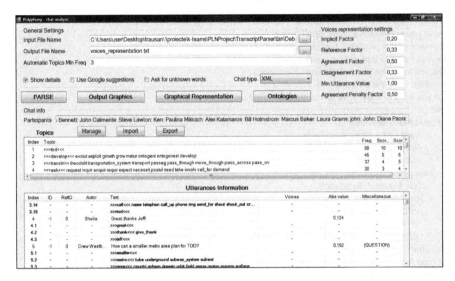

Fig. 9.6 Topics detected from a chat on urban development

9.4.2 Ontology-Based Support for Dialogue in Chats

Specialists in the urbanism domain have started to use environments, instruments and facilities specific to Web2.0, the so-called *Social Web*, which includes folksonomies, forums of discussions and on-line conversation. The same domain ontologies from the previous sections may be used by intelligent tools that provide useful abstracting facilities for analyzing the interactions in the above mentioned instruments. Such an ontology-based system was developed that detect the topics of instant messenger chat conversations, the threads of discussion and the important utterances. The system visualizes a graph of the conversation (Fig. 9.7) and allows the expanding of the domain ontology (Fig. 9.8). The application may be used for analyzing what was discussed and in what degree participants are implied in the chat conversation. For example, the automatic analysis may emphasize the main topics of discussion in a group of urbanism specialists (see Fig. 9.6).

Topics maybe detected from the frequent words discovered in the text. The application uses the WordNet (Miller 1995) lexical ontology for detecting similar concepts (concepts which are at a small semantic distance – see the section about intelligent search) and a domain ontology, which extends WordNet with domain-specific words and relations which are not present in the lexical ontology.

Natural language technology is used for the identification of discussion topics, for the segmentation of the conversation, for identifying implicit references among utterances and for graphical visualization. The generated diagrams allow identifying the participants which had an important contribution in the conversation. The domain ontology may be extended with the new topics identified by the system, as illustrated in Fig. 9.8.

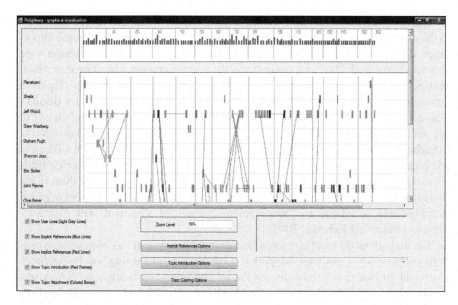

Fig. 9.7 Visualization of the conversation graph

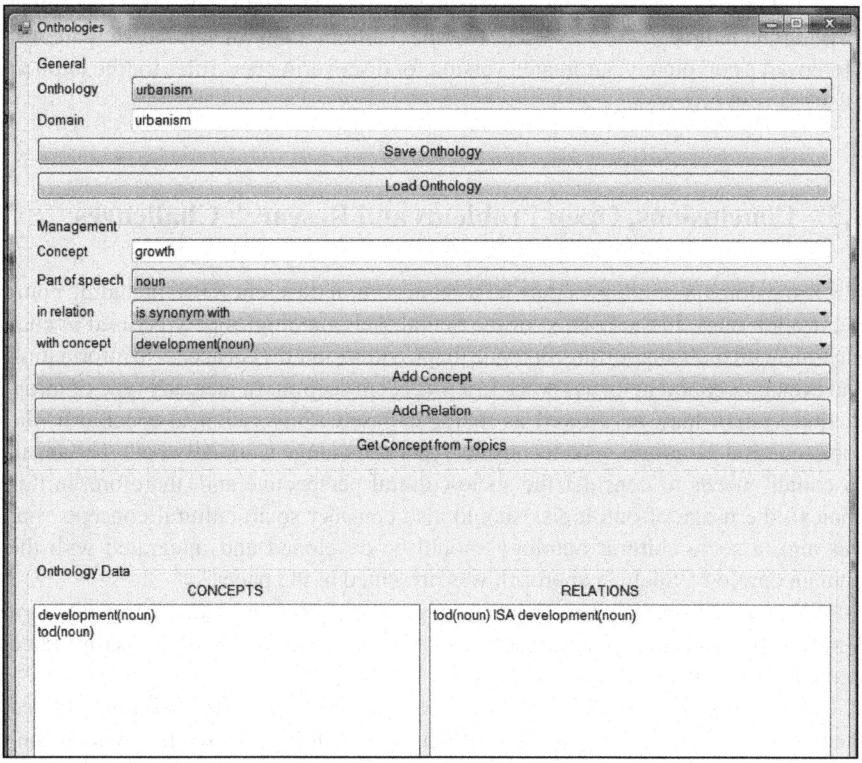

Fig. 9.8 Extending the domain ontology

The visualization of the conversations (Fig. 9.7) shows threads of related utterances in the discussion, allowing to identify important chains of argumentation, the importance of each utterance (the small vertical lines in the upper part of the image – see Trausan-Matu et al. 2007, for details) and the inter-animation (the degree in which participants collaborate effectively, in which their discussion threads display a structure similar to polyphonic music– see Trausan-Matu et al. 2007, for details). These facilities empower us to identify the important conversations and chains of argumentation from a library of online chats like, for example, those at http://www.cyburbia.org or http://www.planetizen.com, in the domain of urbanism (Trausan-Matu and Rebedea 2009). Moreover, in combination with the topic detection facility, it may be used for identifying new concepts and relations and to add them in the domain ontology. For example, in Fig. 9.8, the new concept "tod" (transit oriented development) is related to "development", which is synonym with "growth" (Trausan-Matu and Rebedea 2009).

The topic detection and conversation visualization system has been used in analyzing chats for Computer-Supported Collaborative Learning in Politechnica University of Bucharest, Romania and Drexel University, Philadelphia, USA. A new version is now under development in the EU FP7 project LTfLL (Learning Technology for Lifelong Learning, see http://www.ltfll-project.org/).

Further work will consider more complex semantic distances (than only synonymy) and more elaborated interaction patterns (Trausan-Matu et al. 2007). Machine learning techniques will be used for the identification of discourse patterns. Moreover, a completely automated version for discovering new rules for the implicit relations is in progress.

9.5 Conclusions, Open Problems and Research Challenges

The same domain ontologies may be used in several different KBS, including communication ones. In the context of the Social Web, ontologies may be used in conjunction with tools supporting dialogue for providing intelligent access to information and even procedural help, as shown in a precedent section. In fact, any type of information system may be viewed as dialogue-based. This vision is specific to the socio-cultural paradigm, which considers that knowledge is socially built. Urbanism essentially needs to consider the socio-cultural perspective and, therefore, in this context, the usage of ontologies should also consider socio-cultural concepts. For this aim, a socio-cultural ontology should be developed and integrated with the domain ontology. Such an approach was presented in the paper.

Dialogue may not only beneficiate from supporting tools provided by an ontology. It may also be a source of new concepts to be included in the ontology, as illustrated in the above section.

There are many open problems and research challenges related to ontologies and their relation to the socio-cultural perspective. An ontology should be a shared conceptualization, as the very much cited definition of Gruber (1993) states. This status is at the basis of its potential use in different applications for a large number of potential users. However, it is many times very difficult to have an agreement on the structuring the concepts among human experts in a given domain. Moreover, there are opinions that even it is sometimes impossible to obtain a categorization (Lakoff 1987). Related to this, it is not yet clear how to construct ontologies starting from data provided by socio-cultural structures like folksonomies.

It is not yet clear how to integrate ontologies and knowledge provided in social networks. They are based on different if not totally opposing paradigms: ontologies follow a cognitivist approach, which usually describe knowledge which is in the mind of an expert, while the socio-cultural view considers that everything is socially constructed.

Another fundamental problem is related to the extent to which the knowledge may described as an ontology and to which expert systems may become similar in power with humans. It seems that there are types of knowledge, for example tacit or experiential which may not be represented in ontologies. The metaphor: "stocks are very sensitive creatures" is giving us very valuable insights in the behavior and characteristics of stocks, we even could understand them by comparing to ourselves, as very sensitive creatures, having the experience of being living creatures (Trausan-Matu et al. 2002).

Starting from the problem of metaphors, we should say clearly that Natural Language Processing is far from being similar to human capabilities and many opinions (for example, Winograd and Flores 1986) say that it will never be, limiting the possibilities of extracting ontologies automatically and contradicting optimists that see ontologies and associated description logics as providing full support for powerful language technologies.

Acknowledgments This research was performed partially under the EU COST action Towntology. I want to thank to Traian Rebedea and Anca Neacsu, who implemented my ideas in operational systems.

References

Bakhtin, M.: The Dialogic Imagination: Four Essays. University of Texas Press, Austin (1981)

Berners-Lee, T., Hendler, J., Lassila, O.: The Semantic Web, Scientific American, May 2001

Brown, JS.: Learning, working & playing in the digital age. AAHE Conference on Higher Education, www.johnseelybrown.com/learning_in_digital_age-aspen.pdf (1999). Accessed 22 Dec 2010

Engeström, Y.: Learning by Expanding: An Activity Theoretical Approach to Developmental Research. Orienta-Konsultit Oy, Helsinki (1987)

Gruber, T.R.: A translation approach to portable ontologies. Knowl. Acquis. **5**(2), 199–220 (1993)

Hirst, G., St-Onge, D.: Lexical chains as représentations of context for the detection and correction of malapropisms. In: Fellbaum, C. (ed.) WordNet: An Electronic Lexical Database, vol. 13, pp. 305–332. MIT Press, Cambridge (1998)

Lakoff, G.: Women, Fire, and Dangerous Things: What Categories Reveal About the Mind. University of Chicago Press, Chicago (1987)

Mika, P. Ontologies are us: A unified model of social networks and semantics. In: International Semantic Web Conference, Lecture Notes in Computer Science, pp. 522–536. Springer, Berlin Heidelberg (2005)

Miller, G.A.: WordNet: A lexical database for english. Commun. ACM **38**(11), 39–4 (1995)

Minsky, M.: A Framework for representing knowledge. In: Winston, P. (ed.) The Psychology of Computer Vision. McGraw-Hill, New York (1975)

Trausan-Matu, S., Maraschi, D., Cerri, S., Trausan-Matu, S., Maraschi, D., Cerri, S., Trausan-Matu, S., Maraschi, D., Cerri, S.: Ontology-centered personalized presentation of knowledge extracted from the web. In: Lecture Notes in Computer Science, vol. 2363, pp. 259–269. Springer, Berlin Heidelberg (2002)

Trausan-Matu, S.: A socio-cultural ontology for urban development. In: Teller, J., Lee, J., Roussey, C. (eds.) Ontologies for Urban Development, Studies in Computational Intelligence, vol. 61, pp. 121–130. Springer, Berlin Heidelberg (2007)

Trausan-Matu, S., Stahl, G., Sarmiento, J.: Supporting polyphonic collaborative learning. E-ser. J. **6**(1), pp. 58–74. Indiana University Press (2007)

Trausan-Matu, S., Neacsu, A.: An ontology-based intelligent information system for urbanism and civil engineering data. In: Teller, J., Tweed, C., Rabino, G. (eds.) Conceptual Models for Urban Practitioners, pp. 85–92. Società Editrice Esculapio, Bologna (2008)

Trausan-Matu, S., Rebedea, T.: Ontology-based analyze of chat conversations. An urban development case. In: Teller (ed.) Proceedings of Towntology Conference, Liege (2009)

Vygotsky, L.: Mind in society. Harvard University Press, Cambridge (1978)

Wertsch, J.V.: Voices of the Mind. Harvard University Press, Cambridge (1991)

Winograd, T., Flores, F.: Understanding Computers and Cognition. Ablex, Norwood (1986)

Chapter 10
Transformation of Urban Knowledge Sources to Ontologies

Javier Nogueras-Iso, Javier Lacasta, Jacques Teller, Gilles Falquet, and Jacques Guyot

10.1 Introduction

Since the development of ontologies from scratch requires much time and many resources, the activity of knowledge acquisition constitutes one of the most important steps at the beginning of the ontology development process. This activity is essential in all the different methodologies for ontology design as a previous step to the conceptualization and formalization phases. And as its name indicates, this activity is devoted to gather all available knowledge resources describing the domain of the ontology and identify the most important terms in the domain (Gandon 2002).

This chapter is focused on the study of methods and techniques for the (semi-) automatic processing of knowledge resources that may alleviate the work of knowledge acquisition. This task is known as ontology learning in the literature of ontological engineering (Gómez-Pérez et al. 2003a; Antoniou and van Harmelen 2004). The aim of ontology learning is to apply the most appropriate methods to transform unstructured (e.g., text corpora), semi-structured (e.g., folksonomies, HT ML pages) and structured data sources (e.g., databases, thesauri) into conceptual structures. The methods of ontology learning are usually connected with the activity of ontology population, which also relies on (semi-)automatic methods to transform unstructured, semi-structured and structured data sources into instance data (i.e., instances of ontology concepts).

J. Nogueras-Iso (✉) • J. Lacasta
Computer Science and Systems Engineering Department, University of Zaragoza, Spain
e-mail: jnog@unizar.es; jlacasta@unizar.es

J. Teller
LEMA, Université de Liège, Belgium
e-mail: Jacques.Teller@ulg.ac.be

G. Falquet • J. Guyot
Centre universitaire d'informatique, Université de Genève, Switzerland
e-mail: Gilles.Falquet@cui.unige.ch; guyot@cui.unige.ch

G. Falquet et al., *Ontologies in Urban Development Projects*, Advanced Information and Knowledge Processing 1, DOI 10.1007/978-0-85729-724-2_10,
© Springer-Verlag London Limited 2011

The rest of this chapter will be devoted to review the state of the art in ontology learning and population from different types of source data, and to show how these techniques can be applied to practical examples in the urban domain. Section 10.2 analyzes existent methods for ontology learning classified according to the type of source data. Then, Sect. 10.3 describes experiences of transforming sources to ontologies in the urban domain. Finally, this chapter ends with some conclusions, open problems and research challenges.

10.2 State of the Art in Ontology Learning

10.2.1 Transformation of Corpora into Ontologies

The task of identifying, defining, and entering the concept definitions in large and complex application domains can be lengthy, costly, and controversial, since different persons may have different points of view about the same concept (Velardi et al. 2001). In order to save resources, ontologists recommend referring, in constructing or updating an ontology, to the documents available in the field. As stated in Velardi et al. (2001), although concept names do not always have a lexical correspondent in natural language, especially at the top most levels of the ontology, often a correspondence may be naturally drawn among certain domain concepts and domain-specific terms like: domain named entities (e.g., proper names), domain-specific multiword terms (e.g., travel agent, reservation list, ...), domain-specific singleton words (e.g., hotel, reservation).

Because of the accessibility and availability of corpora in different domains, there are many works in the literature of ontology engineering describing ontology learning methods using as input a corpus of texts that are representative in the domain. These methods are mostly based on the use of natural language processing, clustering techniques, machine learning and statistical analysis (Gómez-Pérez and Manzano-Macho 2003b).

Independently of the particular techniques used for specific parts of the different approaches for ontology learning based on corpora, Cimiano (2006) identifies and formalizes the following subtasks involved in this type of methods: acquisition of the relevant terminology; identification of synonym terms and linguistic variants (possibly across languages); formation of concepts; hierarchical organization of the concepts; learning relations, properties or attributes, together with the appropriate domain and range; hierarchical organization of the relations; instantiation of axiom schemata; and definition of arbitrary axioms.

10.2.2 Transformation of Dictionaries into Ontologies

Dictionaries are semi-structured resources that are infrequently updated; domain dictionaries, in particular, are suitable for extracting terms and their relationships (e.g. hyponyms, meronyms, and synonyms) as well as their definitions (Soergel et al. 2004). Dictionary definitions form a closed domain in the sense that the set of words used in definitions are defined elsewhere in the dictionary (Jannink 1999).

There are different works on ontology construction that use dictionaries as primary sources. Usually, these methods are usually based on the use of natural language processing and statistical analysis. For instance, Jannink (1999) describes a method for converting a dictionary into a directed graph, which could be considered as an initial ontology draft. For the graph extraction, each word and definition grouping is transformed to a node and each word in a definition node is transformed into an arc to the node having that head word. Kietz et al. (2000) provide a methodology for the development of domain-specific ontologies where the domain-specific concepts are acquired from a dictionary focused on the domain. These domain-specific concepts are linked to a core ontology that serves as top-level structure. Additionally, several natural language processing heuristics (e.g., analysis of noun-phrases, compound terms together and other patterns) to establish a taxonomy of dictionary concepts. Another example of this type of methods is the work of Rigau et al. (1998). It presents a method for learning lexical ontologies from monolingual machine readable dictionaries. In this method each dictionary definition is analyzed in order to find a hypernym of the word being defined. Later, a word sense disambiguation algorithm is applied on the hypernym to find the correct corresponding meaning from a range of concepts in an upper-level lexical ontology such as WordNet.

10.2.3 Transformation of Schemata into Ontologies

Schemata such as relational database models, Entity/Relationship (ER) models, object-oriented models or even unstructured schemata (e.g., XML documents) are directly considered in the literature of ontology engineering as model-driven ontologies (Borgo 2007) or information ontologies (van Heist et al. 1997).

Thus, it is very usual to find methods that based on mapping techniques enable the reverse engineering of schemata to derive ontologies. Volz et al. (2003) use the term lifting for this type of ontology learning as it mainly consists in lifting or mapping definitions from the schema to corresponding ontological definitions. Astrova and Stantic (2005) introduce a general accepted classification of ontology learning techniques based on schemata is the following approaches based on the analysis of schemas; approaches based on the analysis of instances; and approaches on the analysis of user queries.

Approaches based on the analysis of schemas establish a set of rules for mapping the constructs in a source schema (i.e., for a relational schema the constructs would be relations, attributes, tuples and constraints) into semantically equivalent constructs in the ontology (i.e., classes, attributes, instances and axioms). There are several tools implementing this transformation from databases to ontologies such as OntoStudio,[1] KaOn Reverse,[2] or ODEMapster.[3] OntoStudio is a commercial

---

[1] http://www.ontoprise.de/de/en/home/products/ontostudio.html

[2] http://kaon.semanticweb.org/alphaworld/reverse/

[3] http://www.neon-toolkit.org/wiki/ODEMapster

modeling environment for the creation and maintenance of ontologies, which allows to import structures, schemas and models. OntoStudio includes a mapping tool with which heterogeneous structures can be mapped onto each other. KAON Reverse is a prototype for mapping relational database content to ontologies enabling both storage of instance data in such databases and querying the database through the conceptualisation of the database. ODEMapster is a plugin of the NeOn toolkit (an open-source environment for ontology engineering) that allows to create, execute, or query mappings between ontologies and databases. The mappings are expressed in R2O language, which is a mapping language between ontologies and databases. Additionally, within this first category but considering XML data as primary resources, we must mention the work of Volz et al. (2003). This method transforms XML Schemas into regular tree grammars, where non-terminal and terminal symbols are matched later with concepts and roles in the output ontology.

Within the category of approaches based on the analysis of instances, we include methods that, in addition to the analysis of schemas, also analyze instance data of those schemas to discover additional hidden semantics. For instance, the method proposed by Astrova (2004) analyzes key, data and attribute correlations to identify hidden semantics in relational databases. There are also works that apply strategies of Formal Concept Analysis to derive an ontology from instance data (Nogueras-Iso et al. 2007). FCA analyzes similarities and dissimilarities among attribute values of database tuples to generate an output concept lattice.

Within the third category, approaches based on the analysis of user queries, user queries enable the refinement of ontologies. This is the case of the work described by Kashyap (1999). User queries may suggest different refinements: create new entities and attributes; drop entities and attributes not referenced in the queries; or suggest subclass relationships. Another approach related to this category is the work of Astrova and Stantic (2005), which extracts the semantics by analyzing HTML forms. HTML forms are the most popular interface to communicate with relational databases for data entry and display on the Web.

10.2.4   Transformation of Thesauri into Ontologies

A thesaurus is a lexical ontology that defines a set of terms describing the vocabulary of a controlled indexing language, formally organized so that the a priori relationships between concepts (e.g., synonymous terms, broader terms, or narrower terms) are made explicit. The applicability of thesauri for search and retrieval in digital libraries has promoted the creation and diffusion of well-established thesauri in many different domains. As stated in Hepp and de Bruijn (2007), hierarchical classification standards, thesauri, and such taxonomies are likely the most promising sources for the creation of domain ontologies at reasonable costs, because they reflect some degree of community consensus and contain, readily available, a wealth of category definitions plus a hierarchy.

Among the works related to the transformation of thesauri into ontologies, we must cite first a set of works that transform thesauri from its native format into Semantic Web languages such as RDF, OWL or SKOS (a W3C initiative for the representation of knowledge organization systems such as thesauri, classification schemes, subject heading lists, taxonomies, and other types of controlled vocabulary). The output of these methods (van Assem et al. 2004, 2006; Golbeck et al. 2003; Wielinga et al. 2001) cannot be categorized as a formal ontology because the relationships between concepts are still ambiguous.

Other works are more ambitious and try to transform the ambiguous BT/NT relationships of thesauri into more formal relationships such as *is-a* or *part-of* hierarchies. The ISO 2788 guidelines for monolingual thesauri contain a differentiation of the hierarchical relationship into generic, partitive and instance relationships. However, because the main purpose of thesauri was to facilitate document retrieval, the standards allow this differentiation to be neglected or blurred. But in contrast to thesauri, ontologies are designed for a wider scope of knowledge representation and need all these logical differentiations in relationships (Fisher 1998).

For instance, Clark et al. (2000) describes the experience of transforming a technical thesaurus (Boeing's technical thesaurus) into an initial ontology. In particular, this work introduces algorithms for enhancing the thesaurus connectivity by computing extra subsumption and association relationships. An important characteristic of technical thesauri is that many concept names are compound (multi-word) terms. They implemented a graph enhancement algorithm for this task, which automatically inferred these missing links using word-spotting/natural language processing technology. Additionally, they also used natural language processing to refine the RT relationship into finer semantic categories.

Another remarkable work with the aim of automating the refinement of relationships is the one done with the AGROVOC thesaurus (Soergel et al. 2004; Kawtrakul et al. 2005). It introduces a semi-automatic approach for detecting problematic relationships, especially BT/NT and USE/UF relationships, and suggesting more appropriate ones. Upon the experience obtained with the transformation of AGROVOC into an ontology, their approach is mainly based on the identification of patterns and the establishment of rules that can automatically applied. The method is based on three main ideas. Firstly, they try to find expert-defined rules. Assuming that concepts are associated with categories (e.g., geographic term, taxonomic term for animals, …), experts may define rules that can be generally applied to transform BT/NT relationships of concepts under the same category into *is-a* or *part-of* hierarchies. Secondly, they propose noun phrase analysis to detect *is-a* hierarchies. If two terms in a BT/NT relationship share the same headword, this relationship can be transformed into *is-a*. Alternatively, if two terms are in the same hierarchy of hypernyms in Wordnet, their relationship is also transformed into *is-a*. Thirdly, in the case of RT relationships, which usually are under-specified relationships, refinement rules, acquired from experts and machine learning, are applied. If we identify a particular case of conversion of an RT relationship between two terms, we may derive a general rule for the hypernyms of these two particular terms and apply it again to all their hyponyms related through RT.

10.3 Practical Use Cases

The practical use cases described in this section use the URBAMET thesaurus as an input source to improve and build an ontology. URBAMET was produced by the French Centre for Urban Documentation for indexing bibliographic notes in the URBAMET bibliographic database. The first version of this thesaurus was released in 1969 and it contained 2,300 terms. Nowadays, it contains around 4,200 terms (labelled in French, English and Spanish) and has been used for indexing 230,000 documents.

10.3.1 Use of Text Mining Techniques

This subsection presents a methodology for the incremental development of a shared urban ontology that uses a urban thesaurus as a primary source. Figure 10.1 shows the main themes of the thesaurus and the hierarchical relation of terms under the transportation theme. As it can be observed in the figure, the terms of this thesaurus denote (sub-)domains and/or concepts. For instance, while *road and traffic* represents a subdomain, *utility vehicle* represents a concept. The thesaurus hierarchy of BT/NT relationships cannot be considered as a hierarchy of concepts, but as a hierarchy of sub-domains.

The methodology proposed here for the development of an ontology consists in the use of text mining techniques on indexed documents to: analyze the thesaurus; update it restructuring the domains; and find (new) domain terms to build ontologies.

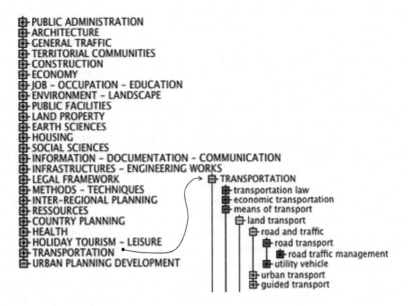

Fig. 10.1 Main themes (domains) of the Urbamet thesaurus

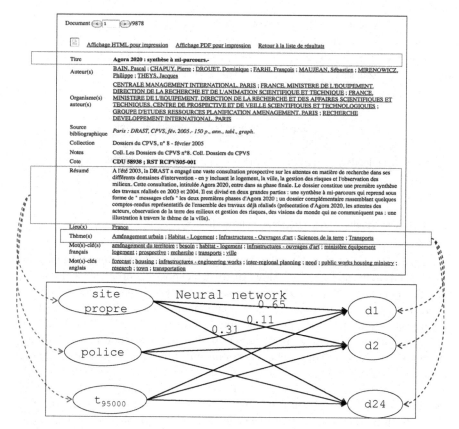

Fig. 10.2 Neural network classifier for the Urbamet thesaurus

To analyze the urban thesaurus, this methodology proposes the applicability of a neural network classifier that uses the Urbamet bibliographic database as training corpus. For the creation of the training corpus, around 10,000 abstracts, together with their manual assigned themes, have been extracted from Urbamet. This means about 70 indexed words per document and a final vocabulary of about 18,000 words (stems). Then, the classifier builds a neural network by reading the training files and applying the Winnow learning technique. Figure 10.2 depicts an example of the neural network classifier employed to analyze the correspondence between the set of terms in the abstracts of the Urbamet database and the main themes (domains) assigned to the documents. The neural network contains weighted arcs from a word or pair of words to a domain. A weight of term i for domain j represents how strongly i draws to j.

The neural network was trained with 80% of the corpus, using the remaining 20% for testing purposes. As a result of the performance of the generated classifier, the classifier discovers the main domain of each tested document with probability: 59% for the first proposed domain; 16% for second choice; 7% for third choice. That is to say, the classifier has a probability of 82% in first three proposals (random choices=23%).

In \out	Transportation	Traffic	Tourism	...
Transport	45%	24%	3%	
Circulation	10%	40%	1%	
Tourism	1%	1%	49%	

In \out	Legal	Methods	Urbanism	Infra...
Legal	8%	3%	5%	3%
Methods	2%	4%	4%	13%
Urbanism	17%	14%	24%	4%
Infrastructure	2%	11%	1%	22%

Fig. 10.3 Some results obtained from the confusion matrix

In general, it can be stated that the classifier is effective: the Urbamet classification corresponds to the text contents. However, to detect possible problems and restructure the domains, the methodology proposes an analysis based on the creation of confusion matrices. The objective is to find domains which are poorly classified. Figure 10.3 shows two excerpts of the complete in-out 24×24 matrix. Each cell M_{ij} represents the percentage of document in domain i classified in j. Ideally M_{ii} should be 100%. On the one hand, this confusion matrix allows to find not clearly separated domains. For instance, see the confusion between *Traffic* and *Transportation* in Fig. 10.3 (*top part*). Probably, it would be a good idea to merge the domains and create new subdomains. On the other hand, this matrix also allows to find orthogonal domains. For instance, *Legal framework* and *Methods* are orthogonal to the other domains (see *bottom part* of Fig. 10.3). Documents are rarely only about *Law* or *Methods*, they usually present legal aspects of *Urbanism*, *Transportation*, etc.

Finally, the analysis of the "most classifying" (highly weighted) terms in the neural network may help to find new domain terms. The methodology proposes the comparison of the top 50 terms of a domain with the thesaurus terms for this domain. This may help to discover the emergence of new subdomains, or new domains which span other domains. For instance, *Computer Science* emerged from *Mathematics*, *Automation, Electronics*.

10.3.2 Merging of Thesauri

This subsection presents the work done to transform the urbanism thesaurus of URBAMET into a more formalized ontology. The main goal for the transformation of this thesaurus has been to enrich it with more concepts. It must be taken into account that urbanism can be considered as an intersection of different domain areas such as economics, politics culture or civil engineering. In this context, the process

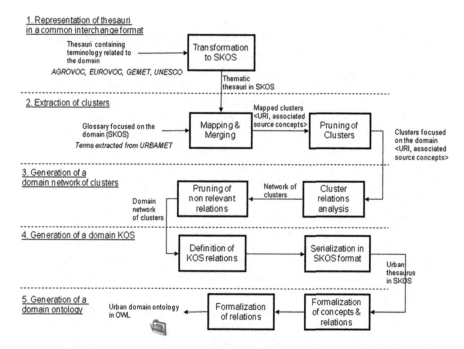

Fig. 10.4 Workflow for the generation of an urban domain ontology

to develop an urban domain ontology, providing explicit and formal specification of the knowledge behind the urbanism discipline, makes necessary to revise all these cross-domain areas and capture all the relevant concepts.

Therefore, the transformation methodology proposed is based on the merging of source thesauri containing concepts from cross-domain areas. Figure 10.4 remarks the different tasks involved in the process, showing the inputs and the produced results. Five different phases can be highlighted within the process:

1. Representation of input thesauri in a common format. This task is devoted to the transformation of the input thesauri into SKOS (Miles et al. 2005), a W3C initiative for the representation of Knowledge Organization Systems. Apart from URBAMET, the thesauri used as input for the method are: GEMET (the GEneral Multilingual Environmental Thesaurus of the European Environment Agency),[4] AGROVOC (the FAO Agricultural Vocabulary),[5] EUROVOC (the European Vocabulary of the European Communities)[6] and the UNESCO thesaurus.[7] They provide a shared conceptualization in the areas of economics, politics, culture and environment.

---

[4] http://www.eionet.europa.eu/gemet

[5] http://www.fao.org/aims/ag_intro.htm

[6] http://europa.eu/eurovoc/

[7] http://www.ulcc.ac.uk/unesco/

2. Extraction of clusters. This is the main step and consists in the detection of intersections between concepts in the different input thesauri, through the analysis of their lexical similarities. Additionally, this analysis takes advantage of the multilingual support given by the input thesauri. Each set of mapped concepts is grouped into a cluster, which is the name given to a concept in the output ontology. A cluster represents a group of equivalent concepts and is identified with one of the URIs of the original concepts. But previous to this and because top terms of input thesauri are usually very generic, we must identify core concepts specific to the knowledge area in the cross-domain thesauri. Thus, a reduced set of terms in the knowledge area is added as another input in the merging process to focus on the domain. In this case we have considered the *urban planning* concept of URBAMET and the recursive chain of *related* and *narrower* concepts.

   Additionally, not all the clusters obtained in the mapping process are useful; many clusters contain terms not related to the desired domain. Therefore, only the clusters that contain a concept from the selected list of terms and those with at least one concept directly related (through *broader*, *narrower* and *related* relations) to another one in a cluster of the first case are kept. The rest are considered as not relevant and they are pruned from the system.

3. Generation of a domain network of clusters. This step consists in connecting the clusters previously extracted. The relations between the concepts assigned to the different clusters are converted into relations between the clusters that contain them. The relations between clusters are labelled with: the types of relations, which are derived from the original types of relations between concepts; and a weight that represents the number of occurrences for each original relation type between the concepts of the inter-related clusters.

   Besides, it must be noted that the output network may be still too complex and/or contain spurious clusters. Therefore, a process to prune the less relevant relations has been created. This process receives as input the complete network of concepts and a weight threshold to determine if a relation is maintained. All the relations with a weight below the threshold are pruned. After the pruning, all the clusters that do not have at least one relation with another one are also eliminated.

4. Generation of a new thematic thesaurus. The next step is to transform the network of clusters into a thesaurus. The generation of the thesaurus consists in taking the clusters of the network and organizing them into a hierarchical model. The clusters are transformed into concepts of the new thesaurus; one of the labels of the original concepts within the cluster is selected as preferred label. With respect to the thesaurus structure, each relation is marked with the type that has more occurrences. Additionally, those concepts that do not have broader relationship are marked as top terms. Finally, the generated structure is reviewed to verify that the BT/NT relationships structure does not contains cycles. If any cycle is found, it is removed by replacing the BT/NT relationship that generates the cycle by a *related* relationship.

5. Formalization of the thematic thesaurus. The last step of the defined process is to transform the obtained thesaurus into a formal model that allows more complex

Table 10.1 Formalization of *is-a* relations

Weight threshold	Nr Concepts	Nr RT	Nr BT/NT	Nr *is-a*	% *is-a* relations
1	276	346	224	51	22
2	105	98	52	30	57
3	66	56	37	18	48
4	48	22	30	12	40
5	19	14	6	5	83

forms of information inference. In the developed formalization system prototype, the following tasks have been performed: transformation of each thesaurus concept into a class, identification of relationships with higher semantics (*is-a*), and serialization into OWL format. The transformation of the thesaurus concepts into OWL classes requires the transformation of their identifiers, and the registration of their preferred and alternative labels as *rdfs:label* properties. With respect to the relations, to determine which narrower relations can be transformed into *is-a* relationships, the following heuristic has been used: "a narrower relationship is transformed into an *is-a* relationship if the related concepts contain the same headword (substantive) in at least one of their labels (preferred or alternatives) in any of the available languages". The relationships that are not transformed are left as they were and have to be manually converted.

Table 10.1 shows the results obtained from the formalization process. For each thesaurus generated upon a different network of clusters, we measure the percentage of *is-a* relations detected from the total number of relations according to the heuristic previously described. Additionally, the table contains the number of original concepts in each generated thesaurus, the number of RT and *BT/NT* relationships, the number of *BT/NT* relations that have been detected as hidden *is-a* relationships.

Table 10.1 shows that the highest percentage of identified *is-a* relationships happens with weight 5 (relations found in all of the five input thesauri). However, this does not automatically means that this is the best of the generated models. Since it does not contain many concepts and relations, it cannot be considered as representative. From the other four, the model with weight 2 also provides a relevant percentage of identified *is-a* relationships. Its main problem comes from the set of concepts identified as thematically relevant for which it has not be found any relationship contained in two of the original models (53 concepts). This shows that the concepts are relevant but that there is no common criteria about how these concepts are related. Here, more work must be done to identify other types of relationships apart from *is-a* relationships, and to establish additional relationships between unrelated concepts.

For further details about the algorithms applied in the different tasks of the proposed method, we refer to Chap. 3 of Lacasta et al. (2010). This work describes additional experiments of this method to test the viability for another urban thesaurus (URBISOC), and in the hydrological domain.

10.4   Conclusions

Although to build high-quality ontologies some kind of manual processing is indispensable, there are ontology learning methods that can alleviate the task of ontology construction. This chapter has been devoted to present different ontology learning methods that make profit of existent sources for building ontologies. In general, we must say that there are not industrial applications for ontology construction. Quite the opposite, depending on the application domain and the availability of sources, ontologists must choose the best ontology learning method in each case.

Additionally, this chapter has shown two different use cases in the context of the urban domain where heterogeneous sources have been transformed into urban domain ontologies. On the one hand, the first use case has demonstrated the use of automated classification, with a neural network, for evaluating the quality of the URBAMET thesaurus hierarchy, finding parts that must be re-structured, and identifying new emerging terms that correspond to new concepts already present in the documents but not yet introduced in the thesaurus. On the other hand, the second use case has presented a method that takes as input URBAMET and a set of different thesauri and obtains, as a result of a merging and pruning process, a more consistent and formalized ontology with multilingual support.

10.5   Open Problems and Research Challenges

The process of generation of a formal model in the urban area presents a set of open research challenges whose solution can improve the quality and liability of the obtained results. Some of these main challenges are the appropriate selection of sources focused in the domain, the ability to make profit of those sources providing multilingual support, and the improvement of techniques to formalize relationships among concepts.

With respect to the appropriate selection of sources focused on the domain, we have experienced that this is a crucial issue. The more focused the inputs (text corpora, dictionaries, or thesauri) are, the better results you will obtain. For instance, this is particularly relevant when using thesauri as inputs. Usually, the top level terms in the hierarchical structure of these resources make a general classification of the universe. If you do not focus on the relevant branches and terms of the real domain of the thesaurus, the concepts obtained as output will not be really focused on the domain of your interest.

A second challenge is the ability to make profit of resources providing multilingual support. Several techniques reviewed in this chapter combine the use of multilingual input sources such as multilingual dictionaries, thesauri with concepts labelled in different languages (e.g., GEMET or AGROVOC) or corpora (e.g. news repositories with articles in different languages). This multilingual richness is very useful because it allows capturing concepts that are particular to a specific language (cultural) scope and would disappear otherwise. However, it must be also noted that this multilingual diversity also requires efforts to establish the machines among the lexical representations of concepts in different languages. In order to face this problem, it is essential to count on publicly accessible automatic translators (e.g., Google translation service API[8]).

Finally, it is worth stressing the importance of finding techniques and heuristics for the identification of formal relationships among concepts once the ontology learning methods have proposed a draft set of concepts. In general, most works have focused on the identification of *is-a* relationships. However, more efforts should be devoted to identify other types of relationships such as *is-part-of* or *instance-of*. Here, the use of general purpose ontologies such as Wordnet,[9] OpenCyc[10] or Yago[11] can help to identify relationships among concepts. Thanks to their structure, Wordnet is especially useful for the identification of *is-a* and *is-part-of* relationships, and OpenCyc and Yago are appropriate for the refinement of RT relationships.

References

Antoniou, G., van Harmelen, F.: Ontology engineering. In: A Semantic Web Primer, pp. 205–222. Massachusetts Institute of Technology (2004)

Astrova, I.: Reverse engineering of relational databases to ontologies. In: Proceedings of the 1st European Semantic Web Symposium (ESWS), LNCS, vol. 3053, pp. 327–341 (2004)

Astrova, I., Stantic, B.: An html-form-driven approach to reverse engineering of relational databases to ontologies. In: Databases and Applications, pp. 246–251 (2005)

Borgo, S.: How formal ontology can help civil engineers. In: Ontologies for Urban Development. Studies in Computational Intelligence, vol. 61, pp. 37–45. Springer, Berlin / Heidelberg (2007)

Cimiano, P.: Ontology learning and population from text. Algorithms, Evaluation and Applications. Springer Science + Business Media, LLC, New York (2006)

Clark, P., Thompson, J., Holmback, H., Duncan, L.: Exploiting a thesaurus-based semantic net for knowledge-based search. In Proceeding 12th Conference on Innovative Application of AI (AAAI/IAAI'00), pp. 988–995 (2000)

Fisher, D.H.: From thesauri towards ontologies? In: el Hadi, W.M., Maniez, J., Pollitt, S.A. (eds.) Structures and Relations in Knowledge Organization: Proceeding 5th International ISKO Conference, pp. 18–30, Lille, France (1998)

Gandon, F.: Distributed Artificial Intelligence and Knowledge Management: Ontologies and multi-agent systems for a corporate semantic web. Scientific Philosopher Doctorate Thesis In Informatics, INRIA and University of Nice – Sophia Antipolis, Doctoral School of Sciences and Technologies of Information and Communication (S.T.I.C.) (2002)

Gómez-Pérez, A., Fernández-López, M., Corcho, O., Gómez-Pérez, A., Fernández-López, M., Corcho, O., Gómez-Pérez, A., Fernández-López, M., Corcho, O.: Ontological Engineering, chapter Methodologies and Methods for Building Ontologies. Springer, London (2003a)

---

[8]http://code.google.com/intl/es-ES/apis/ajaxlanguage/

[9]http://wordnet.princeton.edu/

[10]http://www.cyc.com/opencyc

[11]http://www.mpi-inf.mpg.de/yago-naga/yago/

Gómez-Pérez, A., Manzano-Macho, D.: A survey of ontology learning methods and techniques. Deliberable 1.5, OntoWeb Consortium (2003b).

Golbeck, J., Fragoso, G., Hartel, F., Hendler, J., Parsia, B., Oberthaler, J.: The National Cancer Institute's thesaurus and ontology. J. Web. Sem. 1(1), 1–5 (2003)

Hepp, M., de Bruijn, J.: GenTax: A generic methodology for deriving OWL and RDF-S ontologies from hierarchical classifications, thesauri, and inconsistent taxonomies. In: LNCS, Proceedings of the 4th European Semantic Web Conference (ESWC 2007), vol. 4519, pp. 129–144, Innsbruck, Austria. Springer, Berlin/Heidelberg/New York (2007)

Jannink, J.: Thesaurus entry extraction from an on-line dictionary. In: Proceedings of Fusion '99 (1999)

Kashyap, V.: Design and creation of ontologies for environmental information retrieval. In: 12th Workshop on Knowledge Acquisition Modeling and Management (KAW'99), Banff, Canada (1999)

Kawtrakul, A., Imsombut, A., Thunkijjanukit, A., Soergel, D., Liang, A., Sini, M., Johannsen, G., Keizer, J.: Automatic term relationship cleaning and refinement for AGROVOC. In: Workshop on The Sixth Agricultural Ontology Service, Vila Real, Portugal (2005)

Kietz, J.U., Maedche, A., Volz, R.: A method for semi-automatic ontology acquisition from a corporate intranet. In: Proceedings of Workshop Ontologies and Text, EKAW'2000, (2000)

Lacasta, J., Nogueras-Iso, J., Zarazaga-Soria, F.J.: Terminological Ontologies: Design, Management and Practical Applications, 197 p. Springer, New York/Dordrecht/Heidelberg/London (2010). ISBN: 978-1-4419-6980-4

Miles, A., Matthews, B., Wilson, M.: SKOS core: simple knowledge organization for the WEB. In: Proceedings of the International Conference on Dublin Core and Metadata Applications, pp. 5–13, Madrid, Spain (2005)

Nogueras-Iso, J., López-Pellicer, F.J., Lacasta, J., Zarazaga-Soria, F.J., Muro-Medrano, P.R.: Building an address gazetteer on top of an urban network ontology. In: Teller, J., Roussey, C., Lee, J. (eds.) Ontologies for Urban Development: Interfacing Urban Information Systems. Studies in Computational Intelligence, vol. 61, pp. 157–167. Springer, Berlin/Heidelberg (2007)

Rigau, G., Rodríguez, H., Agirre, E. Building accurate semantic taxonomies from monolingual mrds. In: Proceeding 17th International Conference on Computational Linguistics and 36th Annual Meeting of the Association for Computational Linguistics COLING-ACL'98, Montreal, Canada (1998)

Soergel, D., Lauser, B., Liang, A., Fisseha, F., Keizer, J., Katz, S.: Reengineering thesauri for new applications: The AGROVOC example. J. Dig. Inf. 4(4), 1–19 (2004)

van Assem, M., Malaisé, V., Miles, A., Schreiber, G.: A method to convert thesauri to SKOS. In: Proceedings of the 3rd European Semantic Web Conference (ESWC-06), Budva, Montenegro, LNCS, vol. 4011, pp. 95–109. Springer, Berlin/Heidelberg/New York (2006)

van Assem, M., Menken, M.R., Schreiber, G., Wielemaker, J., Wielinga, B.: A method for converting thesauri to RDF/OWL. In: McIlraith S.A., Plexousakis D., van Harmelen F. (eds.) Proceedings of the Third International Semantic Web Conference (ISWC 2004), Hiroshima, Japan, LNCS, vol. 3298, pp. 17–31. Springer, Berlin/Heidelberg/New York (2004)

van Heist, G., Schreiber, A.T., Wielinga, B.J.: Using explicit ontologies in KBS development. Int. J. Hum. Comput. Stud. 46(2/3), 183–292 (1997)

Velardi, P., Fabriani, P., Missikoff, M.: Using text processing techniques to automatically enrich a domain ontology. In: Proceedings of the International Conference on Formal Ontology in Information Systems, FOIS 2001, pp. 270–284 (2001)

Volz, R., Oberle, D., Staab, S., Studer, R.: OntoLiFT prototype. Wonder Web Delivarable Dll, Institute AIFB, University of Karlsruhe (2003)

Wielinga, B.J., Schreiber, A.T., Wielemaker, J., Sandberg, J.A.C.: From thesaurus to ontology. In: Proceedings of the 1st International Conference on Knowledge Capture, pp. 194–201, Victoria, British Columbia, Canada (2001)

Part III
Case Studies

Chapter 11
Developing and Using Ontologies in Practice

Christopher Tweed

11.1 Introduction

The previous sections have presented and described ontologies developed for use in a wide range of applications linked to the urban built environment domain. In many cases these ontologies have been developed through university-based research projects to achieve interoperability between different software systems. The interface, therefore, is between systems. In contrast, this section of the book seeks to explore some of the issues that arise when ontologies are introduced into working organisations. What happens at the user-ontology interface? And how does an ontology impinge on the working practices of an organisation? Although it is beyond the scope of the COST Action C21 to answer such questions, we can begin to consider what shape the answers may take.

The section is structured around a set of case studies that either describe the use of ontologies in real organisations—for example, the English Heritage thesauri—or more speculative pieces on the problems of developing ontologies for specific domains—such as for road building—or for time-limited purposes—such as the use of an ontology to integrate different actors involved in urban regeneration in Bari. The ontologies also vary according to the size of the community they address. The development of IFC classes for the construction industry is intended to address a global community; the English thesauri, to provide the basis for a national database; and the regeneration ontology in Bari, a local group of stakeholders.

C. Tweed (✉)
BRE Centre for Sustainable Design of the Built Environment, Welsh School
of Architecture, Cardiff University, UK.
e-mail: TweedAC@cardiff.ac.uk

G. Falquet et al., *Ontologies in Urban Development Projects*, Advanced Information
and Knowledge Processing 1, DOI 10.1007/978-0-85729-724-2_11,
© Springer-Verlag London Limited 2011

It is conceivable that the type of ontology might differ depending on the purpose and breadth of the community it seeks to support. The final chapter in this section of the book tries to summarise some of the generic features of ontologies in use and to use this as a guide for future development of ontologies.

11.2 The Case Studies

The main goal in selecting and developing these case studies was to study the impact of ontologies (implied or otherwise) on organisations working on urban development. The rationale was that a better understanding of the impact of ontologies in practice will inform the development of future ontologies. The case studies are intended to provide the 'raw material' for analysis and discussion of issues surrounding the use of ontologies in practice.

The scope of the case studies depended heavily on the availability of and access to information and actors within studied organisations. Since this type of work tends to be labour-intensive, it is difficult to conduct detailed studies without significant funding or other resources.

The general aim of this task is to investigate the use of ontologies in real organisations. The specific objectives were:

- to identify methods of studying ontologies in action,
- to identify and describe specific problems resulting from the use (or absence) of ontologies in this field; and
- to develop a deeper understanding of how ontologies impact on the practices of organisations working in the urban environment.

11.2.1 Methodology and Analysis of Case Studies

The case studies used a variety of methodologies depending on the application and the domain under investigation. The methods used included literature reviews and textual analysis, interviews with key stakeholders in organisations, and participant observation during use of ontologies.

The studies were structured according to the headings down the left hand side of the diagram shown in Fig. 11.1.

This structure guided the collection of information for each of the cases and so makes it easier to compare cases. Whilst the evaluation may fall short of a complete set of guidelines, the final chapter in this section seeks to identify some generic issues that developers may wish to consider when designing future ontologies. It also identified some research challenges that need to be addressed to develop the application of ontologies in the future.

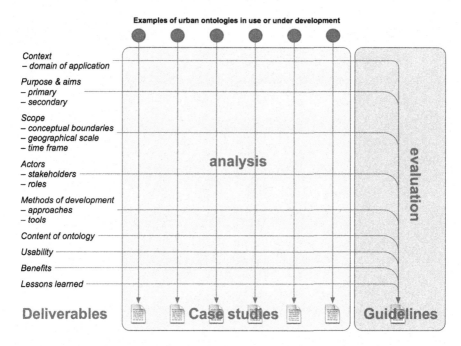

Fig. 11.1 Diagram showing the headings for studying cases and the relations between cases and deliverables

11.2.2   Selection of Case Studies

The cases were selected mainly on the basis of availability. Given the constraints on time and resources, the members of the Action were encouraged to investigate cases they were familiar with either through involvement in their development or through working with ontologies and organizations in a given domain. The aim to study ontologies in use, therefore, was relaxed to allow investigation of the development of ontologies prior to their deployment in organizations. Ideally, it would have been good to observe the life cycle of an ontology in a longitudinal study, but this was not possible, except for the notable case examining the role of ontologies in urban regeneration. Even this, however, was restricted to a relatively narrow window of observation.

The case studies that follow, therefore, cover a range of applications that are relevant to urban development. In addition, some are global in scope, some are time bounded, and some are directed towards specialised audiences.

Chapter 12
URMOPRO: An Example of an Urban Ontology for the Formalization of Morphological Processes

Eduardo Camacho-Hübner

12.1 Context

The urban morphological processes ontology (URMOPRO) has been developed to find an intermediate level of abstraction between the quantitative measures and the conceptual frameworks needed to understand the observable changes in the city-scape (i.e. morphological processes). The domain of application of this ontology is urban morphology research.

12.2 Purpose and Aims

The primary purpose of this ontology is to structure the morphological knowledge to explore urban historical databases characterizing morphological processes. Two main aims can be addressed here: first, to define the hierarchy of concepts available from morphological literature to build a primary corpus; and, second, to explore systematically the relationships between these concepts in three main directions—temporal structure, geographical scale and levels of aggregation of morphological processes.

The secondary purpose is to use the ontology to develop an exploratory approach helping end-users to understand the relationships between the different levels of abstraction involved in the description of the city form and to explore new relationships using their own capabilities and experience in the field.

E. Camacho-Hübner (✉)
Région de Genève, Suisse
e-mail: eduardo.camacho-huebner@transitec.net

G. Falquet et al., *Ontologies in Urban Development Projects*, Advanced Information and Knowledge Processing 1, DOI 10.1007/978-0-85729-724-2_12,
© Springer-Verlag London Limited 2011

12.3 Scope

12.3.1 Conceptual Boundaries

Here, the boundaries of the conceptualization are understood not only as a technical matter, but as an epistemological issue of how our knowledge can evolve. The main question is to know how can we deal with the changes of users (point of view) and the changes of paradigm (conceptual changes).

The specific concepts describing the evolution of urban forms come from many different sources and are neither totally shared nor fully characterized by the researchers in this discipline. The way our comprehension of the complexity has evolved during the process of production influences the way we define the stakes of this comprehension. The main boundaries are therefore those of the evolution of the conceptualization of the city through history. Is it necessary to freeze the conceptual framework to test hypothesis or is it during the process of conceptualization that the relevant questions emerge to the observer of these phenomena?

12.3.2 Geographical Scale

The geographical scale of the ontology is an intrinsic problem of the definition of the processes we are interested in. All the usual scales of urban phenomena should be taken into account (from typological distribution of inner spaces to landscape), but we have to deal with the lack of knowledge of the relationships between these different scales. We are interested in the problem of geographical scale as a "conceptual shift" between the usual scales of analysis and the relevant points of view (emergent scale) necessary to grasp the phenomena related to the urban conceptualization. To study this, we have started by giving a maximum relevance to the cadastral scale in which the main relationships can be reduced to three main classes of objects as it is often described in the morphological literature (plots, buildings and street systems). Then we have elaborated a set of extensions from this cadastral scale to take into account the links between the processes observed and the evolution of forms at larger (i.e. typological scale) and smaller scales (i.e. urban fabric and landscape).

This approach has been a good starting point to keep the idea of changes of scale as a change of point of view and has therefore been useful to epitomize the question of what kind of process does the scale shift illustrates into the field of morphological analysis of the city.

12.3.3 Time Frame

The temporal question has also been a central point in the construction of historical process based ontology. The main idea is to explore the evolution and enrichment of the conceptualization of the cityscape. Instead of defining a single period of validity or unalterable conceptualizations through time, we have introduced the idea of an epoch-oriented construction to seize the complexity of the relationships between the comprehension of an urban phenomenon at a given period of time and the universe of discourse produced at this same period of time to describe and typify this phenomenon. Thus, by leaving the scope open to complementary knowledge contributions or new rearrangements of concepts, we try to respect the ideas on the evolution of ontologies and concepts defined as the main hypothesis of this work. The formal modelling of these evolutions is still an open problem needing further developments.

12.4   Actors

12.4.1   Stakeholders

This ontology has been developed mainly for research purposes. But, even if at this stage it is still difficult to define other end-users than researchers, the main partner of this work is the heritage conservation department of Geneva in Switzerland – Direction du patrimoine et des sites.[1] This ontology might therefore be useful for conservation issues.

12.5   Methods of Development

12.5.1   Approaches

Two complementary approaches were considered during the process of construction of the ontology: the top-down approach aiming to characterize the morphological processes defined in the literature (Fig. 12.1), and, the bottom-up approach, using the systematic exploration of the historical database to find out if new concepts and relationships were needed to grasp the complexity of the evolutionary processes of the city (Fig. 12.2).

12.5.1.1   Sources

The sources used for the top-down approach are glossaries and dictionaries of urban morphology and historical geography. These sources are (de Dainville 1964; Larkham and Jones 1991; Caniggia and Maffei 2001; Gauthiez 2003; Conzen 2004).

---

[1] http://etat.geneve.ch/geopatrimoine/viewer.htm

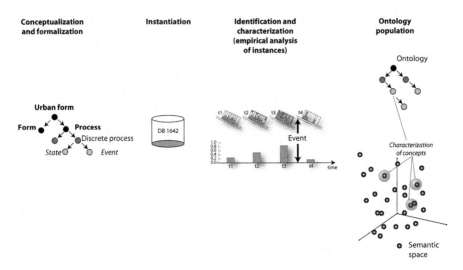

Fig. 12.1 Top down approach

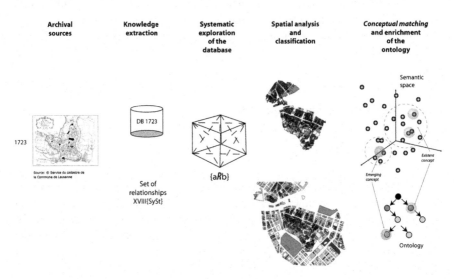

Fig. 12.2 Bottom-up approach

12.5.1.2 Tools

The URMOPRO ontology has been developed under Protégé version 3.1.1.[2]

---

[2](http://protege.stanford.edu/).

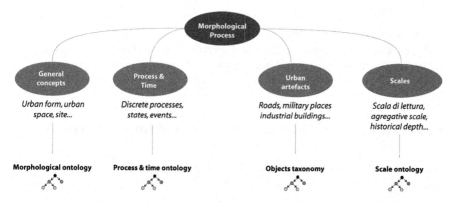

Fig. 12.3 Conceptual structure

12.6 Contents of the Ontology

The urban morphological processes ontology is structured as follow: general concepts of the morphological field, process and temporal structure of urban evolution and transformations, scale(s), secondary classification of urban artefacts (buildings, roads…) and relationships between concepts (mereological, temporal, topological and semantic relationships).

Figure 12.3 illustrates the structure of the first level of the conceptual mind map used to structure the ontology of morphological processes. Each branch resumes the main concepts related to the general description of the ontology, the formalization of the concept and the characterization of different cases observed in the database.

12.7 Usability

No usability tests have been developed yet. The ontology should be implemented in a next stage into an exploratory interface to help management and visualization of the morphological knowledge. Usability tests should be integrated to these future developments.

12.8 Benefits

The main benefits of this conceptualization are:

– Empowerment of the researchers in the field of the urban morphology by determining different levels of complexity of the urban phenomena.

– Definition of a common ground that helps dealing with the linguistic and semantic differences of the same discipline.
– Links between the highly cognitive and speculative tradition in the study of the city and empirical methods of analysis helping to characterize complex processes.

12.9   Lessons Learned and Perspectives of Improvement

As our work is the first step in the development of an ontology for the formalization of morphological processes, it is mainly determined by a qualitative heuristic approach. It is still too early to give a useful critique of the adopted method, but we can nevertheless highlight some of the difficulties encountered. Each one of these difficulties offers very interesting hypotheses for future developments and improvements:

1. Managing the right level of conceptual complexity between both contradictory points of view of the morphological approach: reductionism and relativism. These include temporal, scalar and cognitive issues determined by the contextual emergence of the knowledge.
2. Sources come from three main schools of morphology, mainly French, Italian and British sources. They are therefore charged with an important cultural load due to the fact that these schools depend on the territorial traditions of each country in which they have been developed. The resulting conceptualizations provide excellent examples of translation problems, not only from one language to another, but also from one conceptual framework to another.
3. Conceptual stability issues. As urban morphology has very strong historical roots, there is a high probability of redefinition of the conceptual framework, as far as new sources are studied or new points of view developed.
4. Finally, the capacity of innovation and/or redefinition of the urban form by addressing original or pioneering responses define the main limit to the completeness of the system of knowledge structured in an ontology.

References

Caniggia, G., Maffei, G.L.: Architectural Composition and Building Typology: Interpreting Basic Building. Alinea Editrice, Firenze (2001)
Conzen, M.P. (ed.): Thinking about Urban Form: Papers on Urban Morphology by M.R.G. Conzen. Peter Lang, Bern (2004)
de Dainville, F.: Le Langage des Géographes. Picard, Paris (1964)
Gauthiez, B.: Espace Urbain, Vocabulaire et Morphologie. Monum, Editions du patrimoine, Paris (2003)
Jones, A.N., Larkham, P.J.: Glossary of Urban Form. Historical Geography Monograph no. 26, Geo Books for the Institute of British Geographers' Historical Geography Research Group, Norwich (1991)

Chapter 13
OUR City Cohesion Policies: Practices of Ontologies for Urban Regeneration (OUR): The Case of the Puglia Region

Francesco Rotondo

13.1 Context

The European Union (EU) Community Strategic Guidelines 2007–2013 place particular emphasis on the specific needs of certain zones, such as urban and rural areas. The guidelines encourage an "integrated approach" towards cohesion policy, not only stimulating growth and creating jobs, but also pursuing certain social and environmental objectives.

Furthermore, the European Parliament, in its report on the urban dimension within the context of enlargement,[1] welcomed the incorporation of sustainable urban development in cohesion policy.

Forthcoming EU urban regeneration policies attempt to consolidate these successes with new policy initiatives directed towards the regeneration of deprived urban areas, with the JESSICA[2] policy a case in point. In this context, ontologies could play a significant role in developing and managing these new policies thereby strengthening integration, sharing ideas and increasing knowledge of problems specific to urban regeneration. Furthermore they could, in the context of the European Union, present a multilingual tool capable of demonstrating concepts, shared definitions and the relationships between them.

At present, institutions dedicated to the management of regeneration policies at all levels, whether EU, regional or municipal, often demonstrate real difficulty in terms of interpreting the language used by an architect, a planner, an ecologist or an economist due to discipline-specific terminology. Urban regeneration may

---

[1]Report on the urban dimension in the context of enlargement, rapporteur: Jean Marie Beaupuy, A6(2005) 0272 on 21.9.2005.

[2]Joint European Support for Sustainable Investment in City Areas.

F. Rotondo (✉)
Dipartimento di Architettura e Urbanistica, University of Basilicata, Bari, Italy
e-mail: f.rotondo@poliba.it

G. Falquet et al., *Ontologies in Urban Development Projects*, Advanced Information and Knowledge Processing 1, DOI 10.1007/978-0-85729-724-2_13, © Springer-Verlag London Limited 2011

therefore mean different things in different disciplines. Ontologies could be a useful tool in ordering, integrating and making transparent a range of possible meanings associated with a policy.

13.2   OUR Domain of Application: Significant Elements of Urban Regeneration and Its Multiple Dimension

Urban regeneration is an integrated urban policy approach mixing multiple dimensions: economic, social, cultural, spatial and environmental. New urban planning and design methods replaced rationalist architectural codes and conventions by locating some key points which, when seen alongside the Leipzig Charter on sustainable European cities,[3] echo the aspirations of urban regeneration policies and strategies. This may be expressed, for example, in the upgrading of the physical environment and encouraging sustainable urban transport, the strengthening of the local economy and labour markets, or in the promotion of proactive education and training policies for children and young people in deprived urban areas. The recommendations of the Charter summarize strategies put forward by the New Urbanism movement (Dutton 2000) or those already declared in the *New Charter of Athens* (2003) by the European Council of Town Planners (2003) and embrace:

- The creation of high quality public spaces and their reinforcement within city structure;
- The improvement of energy efficiency in buildings and the modernization of infrastructure networks favouring a compact city form;
- The use of greenery as a bio-infrastructure to enhance the sustainability of cities;
- The encouragement of mixed-use neighbourhoods, buildings and blocks (shops, offices, apartments, and homes on the same site), with a wide diversity in demographic make-up in terms of age, income level, culture, and race;
- The promotion of well-conceived social housing policies, with suitable and affordable housing;
- The participation in urban policies which lead to a better level of education and training contributing to achieve their ambitions and to ensure equal opportunities on a long-term basis.

All of these elements are of crucial importance to deprived urban neighbourhoods not only in reducing inequalities but also in preventing social exclusion and improving the physical environment. Indeed, new EU initiatives, JASPERS[4] and

---

[3] The *Leipzig Charter* is a document by the Ministers responsible for urban development policy of the EU member states, edited in its final draft version on 2 May 2007, available on line at: http://europa.eu.int/comm/regional_policy/index_en.htm.

[4] Joint European Resources for Micro to Medium Enterprises.

JESSICA, and several particular measures of the European Regional Development Funds (ERDF) will support, from 2007 to 2013, exactly such policies within urban regeneration.

13.3   Conceptual Boundaries

The multi-dimensional nature of urban regeneration processes encouraged by the European Union is therefore evident when seen in the context of the concrete objectives of urban regeneration itself and the support of specific European policies which target those objectives. To a region implicated in such European policy making it is therefore of primary importance to manage the multi-dimensional nature of the problem, by drawing upon different skills and competencies and sharing the same words and objects whether physical, economic or social (European Commision 2006). Ontologies could be a potential way of organizing this complex and multi-faceted task, as we attempt to outline in the following paragraphs.

13.4   Purpose and Aims of a Possible Ontology for Urban Regeneration (OUR)

According to Gruber (1993), an ontology is an explicit, formal and shared conceptualization of a particular domain. The conceptualization process represents the attribution of unambiguous meanings to terms defining knowledge in that precise domain (domain ontology). Guarino (1998) defines an ontology as a set of logical axioms designed to account for the intended meaning of a vocabulary.

A domain ontology for urban regeneration is therefore expected to express the viewpoints and satisfy the informational needs of multiple stakeholders and interest groups, including, yet by no means limited to, town planners, environmental agencies, municipalities, police departments, owners and sellers of real estate, third sector associations. These actors use different jargons and pursue different, occasionally conflicting tasks, even if they manage similar or related domains. Reports of the experience of ontology development in many fields of application,[5] underline that different jargons and informational needs are hard to accommodate in a consensual ontology. In the case of OUR, it is not strictly necessary to arrive at a unique definition of a term, if, as may be the case, the obtaining of a common definition proves impossible. Rather, it is sufficient that all agents involved in the same or similar activities are at least informed and have the possibility of knowing others definitions. For example, in an "Objective 1" region such as Apulia in Italy, it is necessary that the Environmental Management Department, the Regional Planning Office, the

---

[5]Examples of ontologies are available at http://protege.stanford.edu/download/ontologies.html.

Transport Bureau and the Economic Planning Bureau are aware of other definitions thus avoiding a scenario in which each of them promotes different and possibly incoherent funding policies on the same urban regeneration objective. Such a situation is not simply theoretical. Consider, for example, the different funding for the construction of cycle paths within the previous phase of cohesion policies (2000–2006), which may be considered one of the objectives of urban regeneration. Promoted by the Transport Bureau, this particular objective may take on a more functional image, useful in increasing the possibilities for movement in an urban context. This clearly does not correspond with an altogether different definition of a cycle path associated with leisure and nature, which could be built with natural materials such as compact sand and bordered by green hedges, perhaps intended as tourist routes through the countryside. Indeed, such a vision including all of the above elements was conceived during the same policy phase by the Environmental Management Office. In the same period the Regional Planning Office promoted urban regeneration processes in which it funded the same objective, in this case encouraging an alternative method for commuters to reach the work place, schools etc.

13.5   OUR (in) Practice: Geographical Scale, Context Bonds and Content of the Ontology

With reference to the case of the Apulia Region, as well as representing a large number of situations especially within the "Objective 1" regions of the EU, in the case of OUR, we have started to create the ontology from the point of view of a town planner. The 110 terms identified in describing the domain were then submitted to other agents, identifying alternative definitions of concepts and related objects, illustrating them with images and showing their relationships in a dynamic chart which changed its representation according to the interests of the agent managing the ontology.

The chosen agents are all interested in developing urban regeneration policies at a regional level and they are directly involved in the elaboration of the specific regional measures to apply the European programmes such as the next JESSICA, or what is referred to as the Operative Program in the ERDF.

A working group of five professionals was established including a civil engineer working within the field of public service utilities, a biologist specialised in ecology, an architect specialised in urban planning, an agronomist and an economist within the field of structural fund management. They were guided through the process by the author and one of his students (Fig. 13.1).

The survey was conducted using the well known SWOT (Strengths, Weaknesses, Opportunities, Threats) analysis method, in an attempt to establish whether the ontology could be a useful tool in their public administration offices, whether the prototype used basic words and definitions and whether there was any conflict or disagreement regarding such definitions and relationships.

Following an outline of the meeting the participants were engaged in the analysis of the ontology.

Fig. 13.1 The meeting of the working group involved in study in the Apulia Region

The "Editor" page within the software provides the space in which definitions and relations between terms may be entered, as shown in Fig. 13.2.

A total of 110 definitions within the urban regeneration domain have so far been entered into the OUR, ranging from somewhat abstract or complex terms such as "urban decline" or "social and economic cohesion" to a definition of concrete objects such as "cycle path", "chicane" or "green corridor". For each definition there is the possibility of indicating a reference and a URL with a link to a corresponding image (as shown in Fig. 13.3), therefore attempting to pinpoint the disciplinary knowledge at the base of the term, meaning that the knowledge base may be enlarged by users from different fields.

Having edited the ontology, the Townto-Browser offers the possibility of surfing the ontology to reveal relationships, the level of integration of particular terms and their general value, as is shown in Fig. 13.4.

Since its conception and creation, OUR has been tested with the groups described above who work within different departments of the Apulia Region. This has resulted in 25 definitions of the original 110 being modified and the addition of a further 9 definitions of existing terms, demonstrating no agreement on those terms. The most striking difference observed has been between the definitions inserted by the Transport Department and those made by the Environmental Management Department.

Leading on from this, the next step could be the integration of the ontology into a Geographic Information System (GIS) for the Apulia Region (currently under

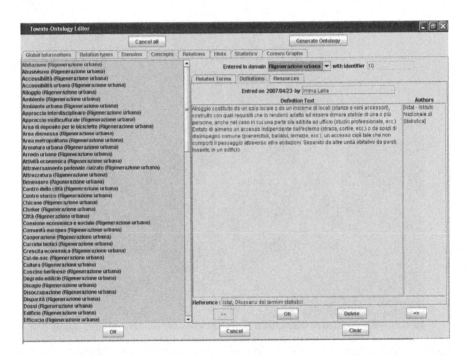

Fig. 13.2 The Towntology editor offers the possibility of adding as many definitions as necessary simply using the arrow keys. In this example, the definitions of terms, for example, "abitazione" (house), are in Italian

construction) linking terms to actual examples from around the region focusing on each city where regional departments are involved in planning urban regeneration policy.

Having a unique domain ontology could reduce the possibility of overlapping decision making and could offer the possibility of integrated policy making by sharing the same knowledge base. Indeed, with regards to the ontology running on a GIS, it may be possible to highlight locations where urban regeneration policies either have been, or are in the process of being applied, with all the resulting terms and relationships.

13.6   Lessons Learned: User Needs and Requirements

After this first, yet significant, experience in collecting impressions from participants it is possible to outline some user requirements:

– OUR could perhaps be of most use if used as an integrated tool within usual policies and policy making, rather than as an exceptional instrument;
– In order for OUR to be effective it has to be available on the web or at least on the intranet of the public office or institution involved;

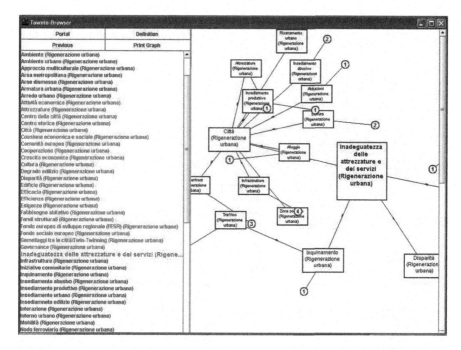

Fig. 13.3 A typical display of the townto-browser showing the term? traffico? (traffic) and other related terms

– A unique multitask interface could be developed within the "Towntology" software with which the user would simultaneously be able to locate the list of terms (possibly with a multilingual description), their definitions, their relationships and any associated imagery where applicable.

The availability of multiple on-line ontologies takes on a particular importance, especially when considering EU policies given that:

(a) Public organizations are predominantly divided into a range of departments with a high level of specialization yet a low level of integration. If ontologies were to become an integrated tool which could be applied to even standard policy, or better still if applied on a GIS, public organizations could potentially arrive at a greater integration of policy content.

(b) Ideally, OUR would be available on-line or at least on the intranet of the organization in question, as its value is determined by the possibility of being utilized by anyone involved in urban regeneration regardless of their physical working location. In this way the glossary will grow and every definition could be discussed and eventually shared in a unified way.

(c) EU cohesion policies are frequently multifaceted and complex, often with various possible implementation choices, deriving in part from the particular characteristics of the nation in which it is applied.

Taken from Rigenerazione urbana\Urban Regeneration

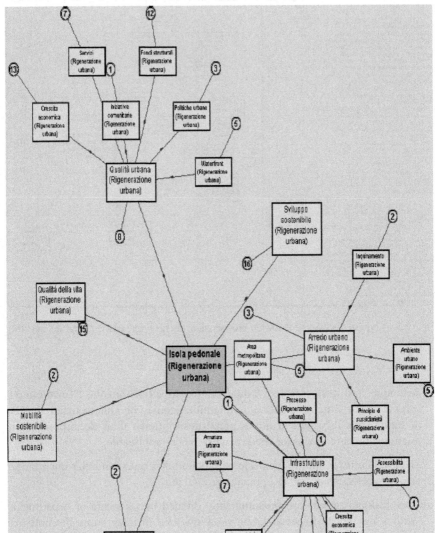

Fig. 13.4 A typical display of the townto-browser showing the term "isola pedonale" (pedestrian precinct) and other related terms

In the case therefore of single large-scale organizations, ontologies could lead towards a better cohesion in the way that different member states may apply the same EU policy.

13.7   Conclusions

Although yet to be completed it may be, considering the initial results of the experience, possible to assume that OUR is potentially a tool which could foster improved communication between stakeholders. Possible future directions for research in the field of ontologies for urban regeneration with reference to EU policies could be a compared evaluation between ontologies as seen within different languages and cultures as, for example, with a French urban renewal ontology, as has been developed by the EDU Laboratory in Lyon (Berdier and Roussey 2007), alongside another in English thereby making an ontology available in the official language of EU. A step beyond this would perhaps be the conception of a more extensive experiment involving EU offices, in which regeneration policies are developed and managed. As the user requirements highlighted by the case of the Apulia Region demonstrate, the possibility of using OUR in practice is strictly related to the wider diffusion of ontologies within public administration routine. From the first definition by Gruber (1993) of an ontology in the sphere of Artificial Intelligence, only within the last few years have we seen some experiences. The greater the increase in the availability of data sets, the more an ontology lends itself to being a useful instrument in providing clear definitions and corresponding relationships within a specific domain.

Acknowledgements I gratefully acknowledge the cooperation of officials from departments of the Apulia Region Departments for having participated in the OUR experiment and for having offered their invaluable suggestions, especially with regards to user needs. It should be added that the views expressed in this paper do not necessarily reflect those of the scientific group working with the EU COST Action C21 which sustained the project.

References

Berdier, C, Roussey, C: Urban ontologies: The towntology prototype towards case studies. In: Teller, J, Lee, J, Roussey, C (eds.) Ontologies for Urban Development, pp. 143–155. Springer, Berlin (2007)
European Council of Town Planners: The New Charter of Athens 2003. Firenze, Alinea (2003)
Dutton, J A: New American Urbanism: Re-forming the Suburban Metropolis. Skira, Milano (2000)
European Commision, Commission Staff Working Document. State Aid Control and Regeneration of Deprived Urban Areas. Vademecum. http://ec.europa.eu/competition/state_aid/studies_reports/vademecum.pdf (2006). Accessed 11 Feb 2011
Gruber, T R: A translation approach to portable ontologies. Knowl. Acquis. 5(2), 199–220 (1993)
Guarino, N.: Formal ontology in information systems. In Guarino, N. (ed.) Proceedings of FOIS'98, Trento, Italy, 6–8 June 1998, pp. 3–15. IOS Press, Amsterdam (1998)

Chapter 14
An Ontology for Urban Mobility

Chantal Berdier

14.1 Context

The development of the urban mobility ontology was first intended as a test of the Towntology prototype (Berdier and Roussey 2007). This test permitted us to integrate fuzzy concepts and to connect two ontologies (a road system ontology and an urban mobility ontology) through a concept bridge. This prototype has shown the interest of the professionals in this tool. At the same time, the "Cité des Sciences" in Paris expressed its interest in this tool, and would like to use it in an exhibition about the city.

14.2 Purpose and Aims of Ontology

This type of tool should facilitate the coordination and cooperation between various actors in the urban field. It should also prevent semantic drift between these actors and their databases. In addition, it could also provide a link between the various specialized vocabularies in this domain (road system ontology, urban mobility ontology).

C. Berdier (✉)
Institut National des Sciences Appliquees (INSA) de Lyon, France
e-mail: chantal.berdier@insa-lyon.fr

G. Falquet et al., *Ontologies in Urban Development Projects*, Advanced Information
and Knowledge Processing 1, DOI 10.1007/978-0-85729-724-2_14,
© Springer-Verlag London Limited 2011

14.3   Scope

The development of a road system ontology (Towntology) allowed us to validate the interest and the feasibility of an ontology of technical objects in which the concept definitions are easy to apprehend. The questions we addressed in this test were:

- Can we obtain the same result in other urban domains that are fuzzier, and do not represent the same structuring elements?
- Can we integrate the mobility and transport concepts, in Towntology?

14.4   Methods of Development

To obtain a sample of concepts from the domain of mobility and transport, various alternatives were possible. So, we first chose to harvest concepts using a questionnaire, and not from a bibliography. This method provides a representative sample of public expectations towards an ontolgy of this domain. The sample is not exhaustive. It was necessary to list the concepts of interest to users, to help facilitate later future tests of the ontology, but also to increase the interest in this tool.

A questionnaire was developed to identify concepts associated with the domain of mobility and transport. To ensure representativeness, the sampled public was diverse: students, junior researchers, confirmed researchers, teacher-researcher, professionals, laymen, etc. About 50 questionnaires were distributed, and from the responses we have been able to build a collection of 100 concepts, for example: Accessibility, Pollution, User, etc.

The second step of the ontology construction was to collect a set of definitions for these concepts. This was achieved in two ways: first by bibliographical searches of literature on mobility and transport, to define concepts such as accessibility, as mobility, but also of specialized dictionaries. At the same time, online searches of glossaries or lexicons were conducted on the Internet. Thus a set of definitions about urban mobility was collected. Since some concepts had several definitions and some definitions lacked precision, it was necessary to disambiguate these. This took place in association with a workgroup composed of junior researchers, experienced researchers in research departments specializing in mobility issues, and practitioners.

Subsequently each of these definitions has been inserted into the existing structure of the Towntology ontology, which is organized according to specialization relations and disciplinary domains. For example, the term "road system" recovered from the group (Generality) indicates all the traffic lanes of the public domain. On the legal plan (legal), it denotes all the urbanism regulations and the local regulations which concern the ways of the public domain (source dictionary source of the road system).

The term "accessibility" in the group (Generality) defines the degree of ease with which users can reach a place or a network and use it depending on their needs. (PORTAL Consortium (2007))

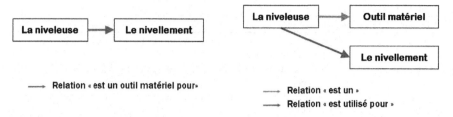

Fig. 14.1 Example of generic relations

From the sample of concepts and definitions, the development of semantic networks began by relying on the relations defined in the existing ontology. After several attempts, it turned out to be very difficult to organize these new concepts using the existing relations. Indeed, some relations were too precise, too specific, and impossible to reuse. This was particularly so for the relation: "is a material tool for". Other relations were redundant and ambiguous, entailing usage difficulties for example "is a" and "is a subset".

An important task in the definition of the relations was to simplify the usage: both by classifying the relations to eliminate ambiguities, but also to generalize them, to facilitate their re-use and avoid their duplication, and the semantic networks.

The study of the definitions of existing relations allowed us at first to identify a group of relations that can be decomposed into generic relations (Fig. 14.1).

This group consisted of the following relations:

is a material tool for
is a tool of study for
is a computing tool for
is a procedure concerning
is an operation for
is a document for
has an activity concerning
is a problem affecting

Then, with the help of the workgroup, it was possible to identify and to suppress useless, ambiguous and redundant relations like such as:

has material
is a subset of
is opposed to

The simplification and the generalization of the relations, entailed a reduction of their numbers from 21 to 12 and also involved the removal of some ambiguities, and created opportunities for re-use (Table 14.1).

From all the concepts, their definitions, and the new list of relations, the concepts were organized in semantic networks. To reach it, several successive methods were used.

Table 14.1 Meanings of relations

Relations	Signification
is a	Relation used to make the link between specific terms and their more generalized concept
is composed of	Relation used to describe the horizontal, vertical and structural composition
is use for	Relation indicating that an object is used for an operation or a particular function
is used by	Relation indicating that an object is used by a person or an organization.
is located … on, in	Relation of localization positioning an object with regard to the other one
work for	Relation indicating what sort of job works for other one.
is characterised by	Relation defining parameters or specificities characterizing an object, a material or a concept.
depends on	Synonymic relation of « is conditioned by » or " is the consequence of ". It can also be a relation between a procedure and it decision-makers or another procedure, which could be characterized by the relation "decided by".
can take the role of	Relation indicating that an object, a concept or a procedure can take a role, according to a particular situation
is coming from	Relation indicating the origin of an object, a concept or a procedure.
« tell for »	Relation used to connect terms or expressions specific in an object or a concept.

The concepts were grouped together in small groups presenting *a priori* interrelations. The double entry table below allows one to cross-compare, by relation, all the concepts, and to identify their interrelations (Fig. 14.2).

To complete this first approach, the definitions of the concepts were used, by verifying they did not contain new interrelations, to avoid possible oversights.

Finally, a set of graphs was built: (one for each relation) representing the semantic networks. This visual method allowed us to verify and to refine the networks easily (Fig. 14.3).

The final stage was to validate the networks by the previously constituted workgroup.

14.4.1   The Relation of Urban Mobility with Road System Ontology

The connection between urban mobility and road system ontology took place thanks to the concept "bridge" allowing connections between the new semantic networks built for the mobility to those existing around the urban road system (Fig. 14.4).

Roughly ten concepts were selected to connect the two ontologies. They are those concepts that qualified as a "bridge," such as: road system, car parking.

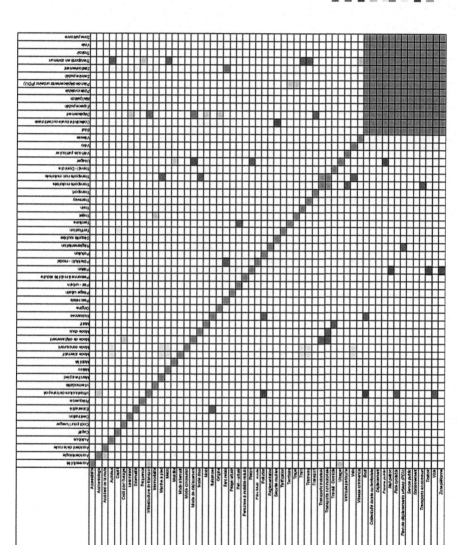

Fig. 14.2 The double entry table with interrelations

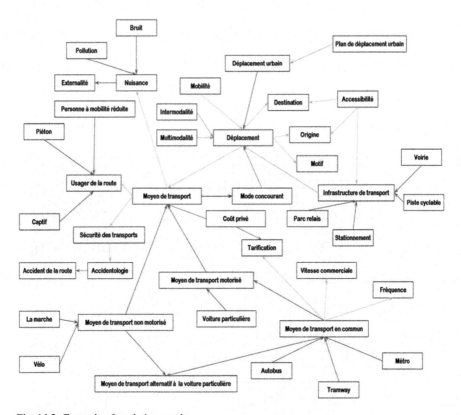

Fig. 14.3 Example of a relation graph

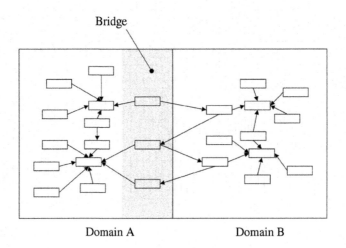

Fig. 14.4 The connection of both ontologies by "bridge concepts"

14.4.2 The Test Phase of the Prototype

The model was tested to gauge the general feeling on this type of tool and identify future improvements. It was a question of testing a prototype, containing all the definitions and network of associated relations.

To make this test, the ontology, stored in a database containing the definitions and relations, was distributed to the testers, accompanied by a questionnaire. The questionnaire concerned the function, the impressions felt during the use of the database, the errors it could contain, the identified dysfunctions, and suggested improvements.

Thirty questionnaires were issued and returned. The comments which went out again are rather homogeneous. All the testers were interested in this database, essentially because of its educational dimension, which confirms the advantages such a tool can present.

Several criticisms were formulated. They concerned:

– navigation and the layout (dysfunctions on certain pointers, typing errors, difficult navigation…);
– definitions: omissions and incoherence were noted, notably at the level of the illustrations. This indicates that it will be necessary to pay careful attention to the different browser rendering capabilities and to the association of illustration with concepts during the creation of the base;
– sources of definition which were considered vague. Some testers wanted to see more precise definitions, particularly references to the current standards and tests.

The adaptation of the precision levels of the definitions to the target audience for the ontology will be indispensable.

14.5 Lessons Learned

The experience gained during the construction of the first ontology was very useful. Indeed, it greatly aided the choice of the concepts and their relations. The construction of an ontology in the field of the urban mobility is possible. The experience with this workgroup demonstrates the educational potential of this tool. Besides, the evolutions envisaged for the current year as well as the new tests will address other types of usage, in particular for professional and individual applications.

However one aspect remains to be developed in the years to come: it is the question of the interoperability of the various databases used by different actors engaged in designing and planning cities.

The signs are promising for the development of this kind of tool:

– the museum, Cité des Sciences, Paris expressed its interest in this tool, and would like to use it within the framework of an exhibition on the city;

– the bibliographical searches made within the framework of this project, also showed that international organizations like the United Nations Organisation (UNO) or the European Union (EU) are trying to organize their vocabularies;
– finally, the test of the prototype also showed the interest of professionals towards this type of tool.

Reference

Berdier, C., Roussey, C.: Urban ontologies: The Towntology prototype towards case studies. In: Ontolgies for Urban Development Studies in Computational Intelligence vol. 16, pp. 143–155. Springer, Basel (2007)

Dictionaries and Glossaries

PORTAL Consortium: Promotion of Results in Transport Research and Learning. http://www. eu-portal.net/start.phtml?sprache=en (2007). Accessed 16 Feb 2011

Chapter 15
The Development of Thesauri by English Heritage

Christopher Tweed

15.1 Context

The computer-resident National Monuments Records (NMR) thesauri developed by English Heritage evolved from a paper-based list developed by the Royal Commission on Historical Monuments of England and have since been expanded by various means, such as one-off projects as well as continuous adjustment following their use. English Heritage (EH) has been involved in the development of several important thesauri that serve various purposes. The remainder of this case study will focus on the largest of the English Heritage thesauri, the National Monument Records Monument Type thesaurus.

15.2 Purpose and Aims of the Ontology

The main aim in developing the thesaurus is to standardise the terms archaeologists use to refer to monuments. This is intended to guarantee consistent use of terms within a number of archaeologically related disciplines. A secondary aim is to use the thesaurus to classify buildings and other structures that are listed under the English conservation legislation. This process operates in two directions: the existing monument types are applied to instances that have been erroneously classified or if the type is missing, but the thesaurus is also updated to accommodate building types that are missing.

C. Tweed (✉)
BRE Centre for Sustainable Design of the Built Environment, Welsh School of Architecture,
Cardiff University, UK.
e-mail: TweedAC@cardiff.ac.uk

G. Falquet et al., *Ontologies in Urban Development Projects*, Advanced Information
and Knowledge Processing 1, DOI 10.1007/978-0-85729-724-2_15,
© Springer-Verlag London Limited 2011

15.3   Scope

The thesaurus contains definitions of monument types including infrastructure (bridges, etc.), sites, and buildings. The thesaurus contains types that are found in England and restricts the terms to those used in England. The word 'rath' (used in Ireland to identify an ancient fort) is not found in the thesaurus. The thesaurus can contain a term for any period of history, though much of its contents could be described as archaic and historical.

15.4   Actors

Development of these thesauri involves many stakeholder organisations and individuals. English Heritage led the development but others participated in suggesting and approving candidate terms as well as revisions.

EH does not develop the software in which the thesauri are embedded. This is carried out by a company called *exeGesIS* that sells a HBSMR (Historic Buildings, Sites and Monuments Record) database which encapsulates the English Heritage definitions. The database is tied into a GIS and is marketed as a tool for the management of Historic Environment Records (HERs).

Other stakeholders are those who make use of the thesauri in English Heritage and in other organisations that have an interesting built heritage, including the National Trust, conservation bodies and local authorities.

15.5   Methods of Development

The thesauri in their present form were developed following the conversion of the Royal Commission on Historical Monuments of England from paper to computer. One part of that project involved examining lists of listed buildings and checking individual entries against types available in the thesaurus. This first project produced 200–300 new candidate terms for the thesaurus, often for buildings that had not been classified previously. New candidate terms emerge as scholars discover new types in the course of their research. The rate is roughly two or three per month, but can be more frequent than that.

Occasionally, specific projects will be carried out that can alter the overall shape of the main thesaurus, such as a study of the defence of Britain, which generated many new terms. These were considered to be too specialised and so were not added to the main thesaurus. Instead, a separate micro-thesaurus was created in which the top level terms, more or less map on to the bottom level terms in the main thesaurus. This means that if it was considered necessary the two thesauri could be merged fairly easily in the future.

English Heritage developed its own tools for creating the initial thesaurus. In the current development of a multilingual thesaurus, English Heritage is using Microsoft Excel with XML and XSLT, having tried a range of bespoke thesaurus building software packages.

The thesaurus supports three different relationships that are applied in the following order:

- equivalence—two or more terms are linked because they are considered as equivalent, one of which will be designated 'preferred,' the others classed as 'non-preferred';
- hierarchical—preferred terms are arranged in hierarchies following a 'type-of' relationship, such that, for example, farmhouse and shepherd's hut appear at the same level in the hierarchy and are both immediately below agricultural dwelling;
- associative—related terms can be associated even though they are not otherwise linked, thus making it easier for someone to find similar (but not equivalent) terms.

It is worth noting that the thesaurus has no top terms as items are grouped under classes that are not part of the thesaurus. For example, under the class name 'domestic' it is possible to find the terms: backyard, cooking pit, kennels, etc. Clearly, the term 'domestic' is not part of the thesaurus. The thesaurus is poly-hierarchic in that it will allow terms to appear under more than one class. So, for example, 'castle' appears under the class name 'domestic' as well as under the class name 'defence.' Future development is moving towards an ontological basis in which terms can appear in several places, but concepts can only appear once. In the previous example, 'castle' could continue to appear in several places in the thesaurus but the concept of 'a fortified building with towers' could only appear in one place.

15.6   Content of the Ontology

The complete thesaurus contains more than 6,500 terms and can be viewed on the English Heritage website at:

http://thesaurus.englishheritage.org.uk/thesaurus.asp?thes_no=1

A snippet is shown in Fig. 15.1 below.

15.7   Usability

English Heritage publishes its thesaurus on the Web as a freely available resource. The thesaurus also forms a central component of a larger database system developed by *exeGesIS*, as shown in Fig. 15.2. The thesaurus is now informing the

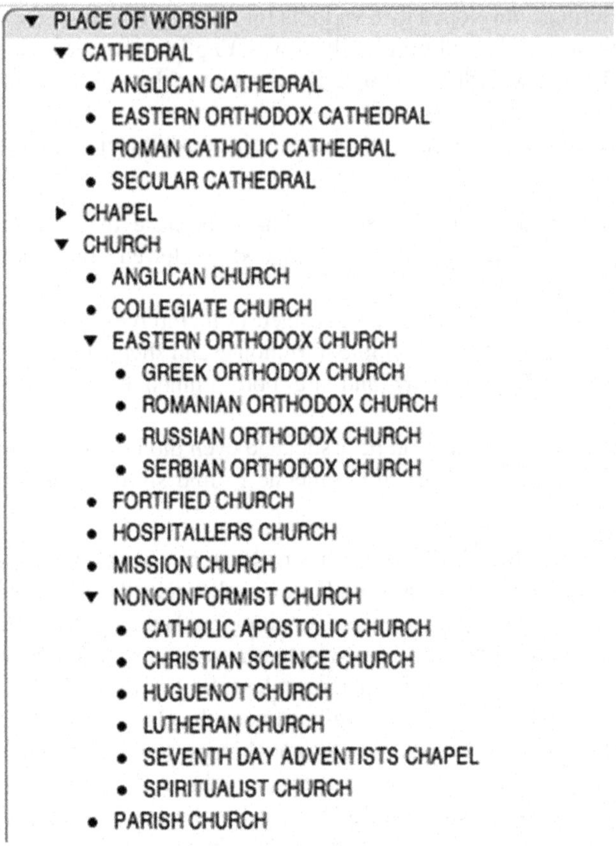

```
▼ PLACE OF WORSHIP
   ▼ CATHEDRAL
        • ANGLICAN CATHEDRAL
        • EASTERN ORTHODOX CATHEDRAL
        • ROMAN CATHOLIC CATHEDRAL
        • SECULAR CATHEDRAL
   ▶ CHAPEL
   ▼ CHURCH
        • ANGLICAN CHURCH
        • COLLEGIATE CHURCH
        ▼ EASTERN ORTHODOX CHURCH
             • GREEK ORTHODOX CHURCH
             • ROMANIAN ORTHODOX CHURCH
             • RUSSIAN ORTHODOX CHURCH
             • SERBIAN ORTHODOX CHURCH
        • FORTIFIED CHURCH
        • HOSPITALLERS CHURCH
        • MISSION CHURCH
        ▼ NONCONFORMIST CHURCH
             • CATHOLIC APOSTOLIC CHURCH
             • CHRISTIAN SCIENCE CHURCH
             • HUGUENOT CHURCH
             • LUTHERAN CHURCH
             • SEVENTH DAY ADVENTISTS CHAPEL
             • SPIRITUALIST CHURCH
        • PARISH CHURCH
```

Fig. 15.1 A small part of the English Heritage NMR thesaurus

development of a multi-lingual thesaurus through the HEREIN project, and it is intended this will be made available via the web when it is finished.

End-users can modify the thesaurus once they have signed the licence agreement, though they are not allowed sell it on as a new product.

15.8 Benefits

The thesaurus offers benefits to those working in the area of conservation and archaeology as it provides a common reference point that allows a wide range and large number of organisations to remain consistent in the terms they use.

The mechanisms controlling the addition of new terms also seems to be sufficiently flexible and fluid to allow the thesaurus to evolve as new information comes to light.

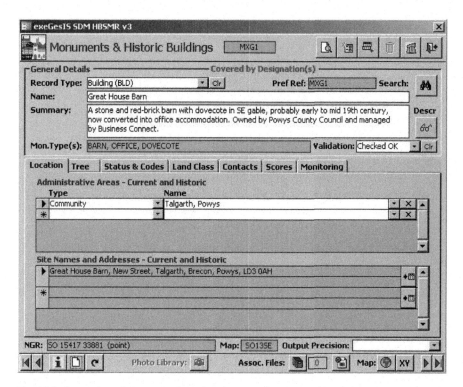

Fig. 15.2   Screenshot of the *exeGesIS* software, which uses the English Heritage thesaurus

15.9   Lessons Learned

The long period of development and refinement has allowed English Heritage to accumulate significant experience in dealing with the problems of surrounding the use of thesauri both in-house and by others. The main points are summarised here.

Ontology development always starts from some previous position, which can rarely be ignored, and must accommodate the legacy of pre-existing conceptual structures. It is rarely possible to start afresh.

Even when an ontology starts from a 'clean slate' it will invariably get "messy" over time as it gets extended and revised by its users.

Ontologies seem to work best when the user has a choice of how much she wishes to incorporate the terms. The English Heritage thesaurus works well because its users can choose how much of it they want to include.

There are always implementation issues following a change to the thesaurus. The software will need to allow for disambiguation changes, such as when the term 'axe' is divided into 'axe-tool' and 'axe-weapon.'

Chapter 16
Ontology and the Scottish Building Regulations

John Lee

16.1   Context

In this section, we discuss the notion of ontology in relation to the Scottish Building Regulations. There is no formal ontology associated with these regulations, and the interest here is partly in investigating why. This is therefore less a case-study than the study of a non-case, but we hope that it will point to some useful issues about the potential role of ontologies in cases like this, and in related contexts. The fact that the regulations are part of a legal framework seems to be important, and highlights issues about when and why it is considered important for definitions to exist and be clear, and the importance of attention to the needs and practices of the communities using the terminology. Questions that arise include which terms are defined, how terms are used that are not defined, and how in practice concepts are used and worked with.

16.2   Purpose and Aims of the Ontology

The Scottish Building Regulations provide a legislative framework within which standards can be applied to the industry involved in the design and construction of buildings. Many aspects of buildings are addressed within this framework. It is natural to suppose that the conceptual structure involved would benefit from being made as explicit as possible, so that the application of standards in individual cases can be clearly determined. In the ideal case, perhaps, it would be possible to develop intelligent systems that would automatically determine, for a given design, whether

J. Lee (✉)
Graduate School of Arts, Culture and Environment, University of Edinburgh, Alison House,
12 Nicolson Square, Edinburgh EH8 9DF, Scotland, UK
e-mail: J.Lee@ed.ac.uk

G. Falquet et al., *Ontologies in Urban Development Projects*, Advanced Information
and Knowledge Processing 1, DOI 10.1007/978-0-85729-724-2_16,
© Springer-Verlag London Limited 2011

it complies with the standards (as is done in Singapore with the CORENET system[1]). The primary purpose of an ontology in this area would thus be to exhibit and formalise this conceptual structure. Secondary purposes might include roles in education, further development of standards, etc.

16.3 Scope

An ontology as envisaged here would have scope over the complete range of building types covered by the regulations, both domestic and non-domestic. It would apply within Scotland, specifically; but one supposes that a very similar system could be used in many other countries within Europe and perhaps more widely. The time frame could be fairly long, but there would have to be sufficient flexibility to encompass innovations in building design and construction, materials, methods, purposes, etc.

16.4 Stakeholders

Legislators, design and construction professionals, and local authority verifiers (see discussion below) would be the principal stakeholders, and the principal effective roles in this context. Others, including property owners and ultimately the general public, would have important interests.

16.5 Methods of Development and Content of the Ontology

We discuss these issues together. Since there is no ontology in this area, the challenge is to investigate why this is and whether there would be a role for one. The content and methods would therefore be interdetermining. We are also not really able to address ontology construction approaches, and especially tools, in any useful way. We therefore lay out the context of the problem, with some focus on those aspects that can be thought of as conceptual structuring, and the nature of the practices involved in the use of the regulations.

The Building (Scotland) Act (2003), a piece of legislation enacted in the Scottish Parliament, completely overhauled the system of building regulation in Scotland. It removed a system that had been in place for several decades and introduced "functional" standards that prescribe how buildings should perform, or what general

---

[1] http://www.corenet.gov.sg/ Accessed on 19 October 2010.

features they should have, rather than in detail about how these should be achieved as "prescriptive" standards. This change was introduced partly to provide greater freedom for the industry, but partly in response to a need for European harmonisation of standards. The regulations imply a responsibility, placed on all concerned, to establish that particular construction practices achieve the specified objectives. The Act creates the Scottish Building Regulations, or, more accurately, the *Building (Scotland) Regulations 2004*, as a statutory means of controlling the safety and habitability of buildings in Scotland. These are in themselves quite a brief document, being a little less than 10,000 words.[2] However, they are supported by Technical Handbooks, one covering Domestic and the other non-Domestic buildings, each extending to over 700 pages.[3] The purpose of these handbooks is to interpret the regulations and provide guidance on how to comply with them. The handbooks themselves have no legal status, and alternative means of compliance can be used if found to be reliable, but in practice the handbooks are treated as an extension of the regulations themselves. There is also a Procedural Handbook describing many procedures relating to implementing the regulations.[4]

As noted, the new regulations are expressed in terms of functional standards. These standards are statements of functions the completed building must fulfill or allow. For example, Section 3.9, Private wastewater treatment systems - infiltration systems:

> Every private wastewater treatment system serving a building must be designed and constructed in such a way that the disposal of the wastewater to ground is safe and is not a threat to the health of the people in and around the building.

Any means of achieving this objective is in principle acceptable, as long as it also respects the other regulations. A consequence of this approach is that the regulations have relatively little to say in detail about the parts or other aspects of buildings themselves, and hence do not contain a rich terminology for these purposes. However, there is a curiously arbitrary quality to the terminology that is used.

At the start of the regulations document, a section headed "Interpretation" provides definitions of the following 16 key terms:

"agriculture"
"boundary"
"building site"
"different occupation"
"domestic building"
"dwelling"
"flat"
"high rise domestic building"
"house"

---

[2]http://www.opsi.gov.uk/legislation/scotland/ssi2004/20040406.htm Accessed on 19 October 2010.

[3]http://www.sbsa.gov.uk/tech_handbooks/tbooks2009.htm Accessed on 19 October 2010.

[4]http://www.scotland.gov.uk/Resource/Doc/217736/0105327.pdf Accessed on 19 October 2010.

"maisonette"
"residential building"
"residential care building"
"sanitary facility"
"sheltered housing complex"
"site"
"storey"

No other terms are explicitly defined, although a few passages might be said to have the effect of a definition, e.g. regulation 6 on "Limited life buildings", which says:

> For the purposes of paragraph 3 of Schedule 1 of the Act (which enables special provision to be made for buildings intended to have a limited life) a period of five years is hereby specified.

It is not at all clear why or how just these 16 terms are selected. Other terms are of course used, for instance in the section relating to communication in the event of an outbreak of fire (Schedule 5, section 2.11), where we find the following limitation:

This standard applies only to a building which (a) is a dwelling; (b) is a residential building; or (c) is an enclosed shopping centre.

In this case, the term "shopping centre" (enclosed or not) is nowhere defined, and nor is the term "enclosed". One might think that the terms in (c) call for definition as much as those in (a) or (b), but it seems the legislators felt otherwise.

In the Technical Handbooks, an appendix (identical in both) provides a relatively much more extensive set of definitions, numbering 118 including those already found in the regulations and also defining many terms that are used, but not defined, in the regulations. However, many terms are of course still not contained in this list. Enclosed shopping centres are discussed almost exclusively in connection with fire risk. There is a specific annex (2.C) that deals with them, noting that "The recommendations contained in this annex ... are unique to enclosed shopping centres with malls on 1 or 2 *storeys*": the italics indicate that "storey" is defined in the appendix (and, in this case, the regulations themselves), but no further definition of the other terms is offered. Nor is there a definition of the term "mall", which is widely used in the document in relation to these kinds of buildings.

A lawyer, informally queried on how one can determine whether a given building is an enclosed shopping centre, suggested that it would simply be up to the courts to decide. In practice, no doubt, this means that people will "play safe" – not necessarily a bad thing, but not helpful in terms of discovering the details of the conceptual system or ontology underlying the regulations.

These observations indicate that the ontology is in fact very implicit, and remains embedded in practices and understandings among the relevant professional and other communities involved in construction. The regulations create a framework for managing certain aspects of the activity of these communities, but do not seek to determine details of how this will apply in particular cases. Such determination requires practitioners, and if necessary the courts, to interrogate the specifics of a case and interpret the regulations to fit it. This will quite possibly entail the further definition of some of the concepts involved. However, this will happen on a case-by-case basis, and be constrained to the question whether a specific building meets a functional requirement by whatever means it may seek to do so. To understand this properly, we need to note the system whereby the regulations operate. Normally, a building requires a "warrant", showing that it is compliant with the regulations, which is issued by a "verifier", usually part of the local authority. A long process of negotiation may surround the issuing of the warrant, during which the designers/constructors and the verifier discuss whether and how the regulations are met by various aspects of the building. Eventually a warrant is issued or withheld. In the latter case, there can be appeal to the courts; however, there has been no such appeal in relation to these regulations, which suggests that the negotiation process is rather effective.

There is no attempt to generalise the outcomes of these processes. One might suppose that a very similar process may have to be carried out many times for quite similar cases. The system seems to be designed to embrace this consequence and resist further development of contentious cases.

These cases are in any event not common. There are no court cases involving the Building (Scotland) Act 2003 and/or associated legislation, other than a fatal accident inquiry in February 2008 relating to the death of a construction worker working on a farm building. The system allows in principle applications to be made for relaxation of the regulations, as noted by the Procedural Handbook, in "cases where a requirement is clearly, in whole or in part, unreasonable for a particular building" (p.34). However, as of 2008 no applications for relaxations had been received by the Scottish Government. We conjecture that this is because the generality of the regulations is such as to make relaxation all but impossible: who could suggest e.g. that wastewater should in some case be allowed to be a threat to health? The Scottish Government's Building Standards Division also offers a service to provide a "view", on behalf of Scottish Ministers, "[w]here the owner or the verifier considers there is doubt about the extent to which a building or design meets the building standards."[5] Such views are not frequently sought – only 32 have been recorded from 2005 (when the regulations were implemented) up to September 1, 2010, and these are normally expressed in somewhat specific terms. For instance, it is agreed in one view that "safe, unassisted and convenient means of access" is acceptably provided by stairs in a given working environment,[6] and it is asserted in another that similar sanitary provision is expected in a conversion as in newbuild.[7] Although the latter in particular seems generalisable, these views remain strictly "project specific".

It appears, then, that in the context of functional regulations we can have an approach that avoids any level of explicitness such as would be necessary to articulate

---

[5] http://www.scotland.gov.uk/Topics/Built-Environment/Building/Building-standards/about/minview Accessed on 19 October 2010.

[6] http://www.scotland.gov.uk/Resource/Doc/217736/0090253.pdf Accessed on 19 October 2010.

[7] http://www.scotland.gov.uk/Resource/Doc/217736/0090246.pdf Accessed on 19 October 2010.

an ontology, or would benefit from the development of one. If a useful role of ontologies might be to help structure argumentation about points and issues where there is disagreement and contention (cf. Lee and McMeel 2007), even this is sidestepped here by using language so generally that most of the conceptual structure in the discussion has to be contributed case by case. Legal argumentation often seeks to avoid too specific definitions. It is recognised that cases are very different, and the legal system seeks to provide a legislative framework that can cover them all, while exploiting a very flexible system for tailoring its application to the individual specifics. To provide in advance a system of concepts with sufficiently detailed structure to capture variations in understandings of specific issues would be to prejudice the discussions themselves by effectively limiting the range of possible variations.

Especially critical would seem to be the process whereby the verifier issues the warrant on the basis of negotiation. It is during these negotiations that concepts are tried and tested. There is a vagueness or fuzziness about many of the concepts: does this one apply in a given case, or does that one, or is there an overlap? Such questions will be settled in ways that depend on understandings that are, or come to be, shared by the participants, may be different in different cases or contexts, may change over time, etc., and are not themselves anticipated anywhere in the framework. The 16 key terms that we saw defined are simply those that the legislators, more or less arbitrarily, see a need to have clearly agreed at the start, to keep possible disagreement within reasonable bounds, but it is actually not too critical which terms these are, since the process is robust enough to develop the basis for agreement on any other terms that might arise as an issue.

This kind of flexibility is evidently welcomed by the system, because it is what helps to meet the original desideratum that designers and constructors are given more freedom than is allowed by prescriptive regulations. Hence we see that the move towards functional regulations is actually a move away from a position where, in the extreme, one might seek to determine compliance with regulations by reference to some kind of automated system. Prescriptive regulations lend themselves much more obviously to the development of a clear ontology and a system of rules whereby a design can be tested; the functional approach relies, it seems crucially, on a process that would gain little from the codification of precedent and resists automation in almost the same way as does the process of design itself.

16.6 Benefits

If there were to be benefits from introducing an explicit ontology into this framework, they would most likely have to do with the application of information technology. It is therefore interesting to speculate about the potential role of information systems here. Application could be wide, given that European standards are harmonising around the approach. One prospect is perhaps that there could be a kind of "case base" in which histories would be maintained of particular building types and discussions. Verifiers could consult this to accelerate the process of assessing a new design for compliance. Even this idea, however, is only likely to work for buildings of recognisable types with similar features. Matching a design that is significantly innovative is likely to be impracticable. An aspect, however, of this approach is perhaps evidenced by the Scottish Government in its "Fire and Rescue Framework for Scotland 2005,"[8] which suggests that in fact information technology might help in deriving the benefits of greater flexibility:

> Because of the introduction of [Integrated Risk Management Plans] and the removal of the nationally recommended standards of fire cover and associated guidance, Authorities will in future have more flexibility. Modern, intelligent information systems mean that risks can be assessed more effectively allowing a more appropriate and better-targeted response. (p.16)

Following this line of thought, verifiers, and others, would use intelligent systems, where available and in whatever way happens to be supported, to assess various qualities of a particular design, and then conduct the usual negotiations about whether these meet the standards. The use of a broad range of building performance evaluation tools can thus be actively encouraged, and would take place within a context where the outcomes of using these tools would be subjected to critical appraisal and discussion in the process of negotiation, offering a natural response to the charge that these systems cannot be assumed to be correct or reliable in application to a given design.

In such a scenario, should it become widespread, the role for an ontology will perhaps re-emerge. Standardisation among the tools will mean that lessons from application to one design can usefully be re-used in relation to another. Discussions around these are likely to be similarly enough structured that capturing their rationale becomes a worthwhile exercise. An ontology, as a basis for elaborating this structure, can once again be seen to have a value in supporting the resolution of disagreement, contention and misunderstanding.

16.7   Lessons Learned

The principal lesson learned from this discussion is perhaps the importance of seeing the complexity of practices in a given domain. Where it seems at first sight almost obvious that an ontology would be a valuable development for the application of building standards, we find that in fact there are many deep problems associated with this idea. Ontology development is often undertaken in haste on the assumption that standardisation and automation will be a good thing. Sometimes this may turn out to be literally a waste of time, but in other cases at least it will pay to probe more deeply into why a certain informality is a persistent feature of a domain.

---

[8]http://www.scotland.gov.uk/Resource/Doc/1100/0017601.pdf (All URLs accessed 19 October 2010).

Reference

Lee, J., McMeel, D.: 'Pre-ontology' considerations for communication in construction. In: Teller, J., Lee, J., Roussey, C. (eds.) Ontologies for Urban Development. Studies in Computational Intelligence, vol. 61, pp. 169–179. Springer, Basel (2007)

Chapter 17
Road System Ontology: Organisation and Feedback

Chantal Berdier

17.1 Context

The project of developing an urban ontology for road systems is to be viewed in the context of a lack of coordination tools between urban engineering actors. The aim is to fill this gap. By reducing semantic disagreement and increasing data interchange, this tool should improve urban maintenance services (road system maintenance, public spaces, etc.). It will also improve synchronising the coordination of the interventions on networks as well as the consistent elaboration of the various related urbanism documents. A first stage emerged from the creation of a road system ontology. This first link is currently under development as part of a collaborative research project with Lyon's Urban Community Services.

17.2 Purpose and Aims of the Ontology

The first goal in developing this ontology was to validate its feasibility in the town planning field. It was a question of proposing a consensual tool to allow designers of the road system plans to be trained for their profession in the roadway system school. The primary goal is educational. The second objective was to facilitate communication between local authorities and the users of urban space.

The field of the roadway system involves various actors with very different visions of this field.. For instance, a tree-planting service considers a roadway system object only taking into consideration its potential for growing trees. In addition, the originators of the roadway systems conceive this object in terms of profile, slope,

C. Berdier (✉)
Institut National des Sciences Appliquees (INSA) de Lyon, France.
e-mail: chantal.berdier@insa-lyon.fr

G. Falquet et al., *Ontologies in Urban Development Projects*, Advanced Information and Knowledge Processing 1, DOI 10.1007/978-0-85729-724-2_17,
© Springer-Verlag London Limited 2011

and choice of materials. Given the complexity of the roadway system field and the multiplicity of actors, data sources and approaches, an ontology could constitute a tool for sharing important information to optimize the report/ratio investment profitability. It is to fill the gaps that the first roadway system ontology prototype was elaborated using the *Towntology* software.

Moreover, recent developments—in particular in the use of geographical information systems—in the road system plan for Grand Lyon, make it possible to plan in the years to come integration of the road system ontology with "roadway system heritage" in the current geographical information system of Grand Lyon.

17.3 Scope

The roadway system ontology covers the full scope of vocabulary for urban roads (the different layers concerned and the materials used in each layer). It also provides definitions relating to objects and the trades involved. Additionally there is a list of road-related materials, already in use, and unrelated materials which might be thought suitable for the construction or rehabilitation of roads. This ontology is potentially interesting to laymen, and also technicians, students and specialists in the roadway field. It offers terms, images as well as different levels of detail.

17.4 Actors

The development of this ontology mobilized the participation of the engineers and the technicians of the planning of the road system for Grand Lyon. Indeed, the construction of the ontology coincided with the installation within a territorial collectivity, "Grand Lyon", of a school to deliver training and education for the various trades involved in planning and constructing road systems. The ontology is conceived as a tool of diffusion for sharing data.

17.5 Methods of Development

The first stage consisted in transcribing the contents of road systems into the dictionary in the software, *Towntology*. This first project consisted of the following tasks:

- Build the bases of an urban ontology, by structuring the terms used in the field of the urban road system within a semantic network. The following stage is the generalization of these principles in the domain of the development and urbanism.
- Analyze the contents of the most important urban databases.

- Make a first inventory of the terms and define them.
- Organize the terms between them by establishing links.
- Choose the structuring concepts and build a standard vocabulary.
- Validate this first level of structuring with end-users and enrich it.
- Develop a model to test the feasibility and the level of interest.
- Analyze the systems of construction of ontologies and choose a tool.
- Present an ontology in graphical form.
- Navigate and interrogate an ontology.
- Store an ontology in one of the ontological representation languages.
- Build a formal ontology.
- Validate the final ontology with the participation of end-users.

This first research work ended in September, 2003 and resulted in a first operational version of the urban road system ontology. It was more like a dictionary than an ontology because it does not allow users to cross-reference data.

The starting point of the road system ontology construction was the dictionary of the road system containing all the terms relative to the urban road system and to the professions connected with it. So, to allow a greater flexibility of use, the common vocabulary was differentiated to the specialized vocabulary, as well as the definition domains of the terms. The user can choose in this way if he or she wants the whole vocabulary or only the vocabulary for a given domain.

At the first level of this repository we find the terms emerging from a known and common vocabulary have no particular precision. At the second level the specialized vocabulary is known mainly by specialists. At the third level, the vocabulary yields regional terms.

The support of development of this ontology is the software *Towntology*. In addition, the terminological network was developed in XML and can be used like a thesaurus.

17.6   Content of the Ontology

The thesaurus includes more than 900 terms organized around a semantic network. The diagram below shows the different lexical tokens used in the road system ontology (Fig. 17.1).

The domain of definition requires particular attention, especially in the presence of terms having several definitions according to their usage. For example, here are eight domains retained for the structuring of the ontology. The terms in bracket indicate the abbreviation of the domain (example-ad) or the name of the (administrative) domain:

- The administrative domain (ad): it applies to all documents, decisions and administrative organisations. For example the term "road system" classified under the column (Generality) indicates all the spaces reserved and fitted out to allow the circulation of the persons, the animals and the vehicles or any means of terrestrial

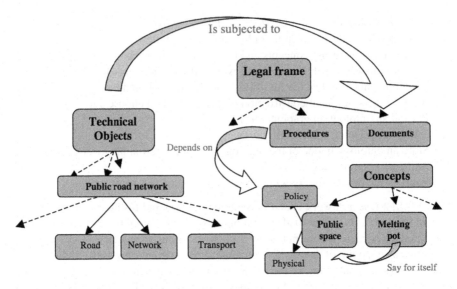

Fig. 17.1 The investigated lexical fields

transportation as well as their park. On the administrative plan (Administrative), the road system is the public service, which has for object the establishment, the conservation, the maintenance and the alignments, all the communications allocated to the traffic.

- The development domain (a): it qualifies the vocabulary of the developer. For example, the "hierarchy of ways" (development) according to developers decomposes into: the primary road system—connections between conglomerations or between districts, which is chargeable to the community in urban development zones; the secondary road system—internal traffic in a district, which is chargeable to the developer; and the tertiary road system—adjacent to the buildings and groups of buildings, which is chargeable to the builder.
- The arboriculture domain (ab): it is about the vocabulary concerning planting. For example, the "hairy" term: (arboriculture) indicates all the finest roots of a plant and its mass evokes a hair. These roots absorb the water and the mineral elements. In a road system it also denotes the graphical representation of a network of routes from a common departure point to multiple destinations.
- The construction domain (c): this domain collects everything concerning the construction in general, including the road system. For example the Coordination (Construction) is a logical organization in time and in the workspace of a building site. In the road system, the coordination consists in synchronizing the interventions on the public domain to avoid construction sites following one another in a disorganised way (intervention of the company of electricity follow-up of a repair road system; Intervention of the general Company of waters followed by a repair of road system)
- The generality domain (g): in the case of a definition having no particular domain of application, it is clarified that it is about a general definition. For example

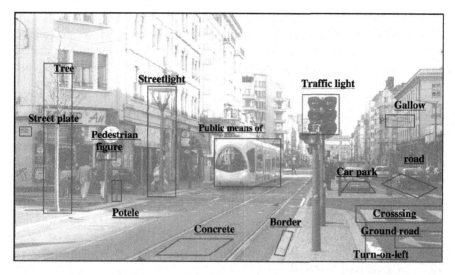

Fig. 17.2 Example of illustration appearing in the roadway system ontology (Source: Bernard Chatreau photo, www.nycsubway.org)

subsidence (Generality) is a very general concept that is relevant in the construction domain as well as in the geotechnical and road system domains.

- The geotechnical domain (gt): it is about specific definitions in the geotechnical domain. For example a core sample (Geotechnical) is a sample of ground of cylindrical shape or quite other material such as concrete; coated... its analysis allows knowing the nature and the thickness of the pooled layers and the materials.
- The Legal domain (j): this domain groups the definitions explaining the legal or statutory frame of a term. For example in road system: (Generality) All traffic lanes of the public domain. On the legal plan, it is a set of the urbanism regulations the local regulations which concern the ways of the public domain.
- The road system domain (v): the vocabulary having this indication is mainly the whole road system *engineers* and *technicians*. It applies exclusively to the road system and to the diverse networks. For example, a "boat" in a road system is the name given to the connection between a property access and the public highway. It corresponds to a slight withdrawal of the pavement and its border. Such a work implies an arrangement of the pavement and the verge which requires from written agreement from the designers of the road system.

Most of the terms are illustrated either by photography, or by a plan or by a diagram. The illustrations are very useful when they propose a graphical visualization of the terms in contact with the others (Fig. 17.2).

The user interface allows a user to interrogate and view the ontology, without having to resort to complex manipulations. This mode of global visualization introduces the concept of dynamic request, thanks to the result of a request, specified in an interactive manner, is immediately visible. The user begins with the selection of a first concept in the ontology of the urban database; she can see all links for this concept in a window, thus allowing the visualization of nodes. She can also go through the ontology vertically and horizontally using the scrolling bars.

The definition of the concept is accessible in the top part of the interface, after having chosen the domain of definition in the left part. The definitions and the other associated meta-data associated to the concept will appear according to the user, in new windows or directly in interface. In the connections graph, the user can choose the concept of her choice with an appropriate "click." This will take place in the centre of the window and will show the concept's new relations. At any time, the user can choose to print only the concepts with a certain level of specialization or in a precise domain.

17.7   Lessons Learned

The evolutions of the prototype draw largely on test results made with the potential users of the future road system ontology. This evaluation was made with local authorities, private research departments, research organizations, educational establishments. It suggests that a tool of this nature could be useful to professionals and for the beginners. The road system school which is being established in Grand Lyon would like to use road system ontology for the training of its students.

In addition to this experience, in January 2007 the research laboratory Environments and Urban Devices began collaboration with the planning of the Grand Lyon road system to organize exchanges of data that will enrich the road system ontology. This current research work, includes two main strands: building bridges between road system ontology and the integration of a "road system heritage"; and automatic data extraction (if possible) for applications emanating from another service (tree and plantations, road signs) to enrich the database.

The application "road system heritage" is a tool which allows the road system to perform its main missions, such as:

– The maintenance and preservation of the road system heritage.
– The evolution, improvement and extension of the road network.
– The road signs and traffic management.

The *Towntology* project was the first stage of the construction of a road system ontology, it continues to evolve and grow, notably through the works of the workgroup in the road system laboratory of Grand Lyon. It has ambitions to integrate the various existing applications within the planning of the road system. Research is in progress with the aim of automating data extraction from the multiple available bases within Grand Lyon: *Chorus*, for the coordination of the interventions on the public domain of road system; and *Bill*, for the lists of applicable prices in works of road system.

Chapter 18
Impact of BIMs on Business Models in Construction Industry

Jarmo Laitinen, Anssi Joutsiniemi, Juho Malmi, and Jussi Vakkilainen

18.1 Introduction

This article aims to cast some light on the dilemma of data transfer and storage by offering examples and experiences of the ontological approach at a building scale. The world of Geographic Information Systems is not alone facing the fact. In many a field it is nowadays impossible to conduct 'business as usual' without the aid of sophisticated computer based tools. Our view is that in recent decades these tools have become so effective they produce more information than can be easily stored or even handled by contemporary methods. Building industry thinks in terms of building projects that have some distinct phases. Generally speaking the three main ones are:

- design;
- maintenance;
- demolition.

J. Laitinen
ICT in Construction, Department of Civil Engineering, Faculty of Built Environment, Tampere University of Technology, Finland
e-mail: jarmo.laitinen@tut.fi

A. Joutsiniemi
Institute of Urban Planning and Design, School of Architecture, Faculty of Built Environment, Tampere University of Technology, Finland
e-mail: anssi.joutsiniemi@tut.fi

J. Malmi • J. Vakkilainen
Virtual Building Laboratory, Department of Civil Engineering, Faculty of Built Environment, Tampere University of Technology, Finland
e-mail: juho.malmi@tut.fi; jussi.vakkilainen@tut.fi

G. Falquet et al., *Ontologies in Urban Development Projects*, Advanced Information and Knowledge Processing 1, DOI 10.1007/978-0-85729-724-2_18,
© Springer-Verlag London Limited 2011

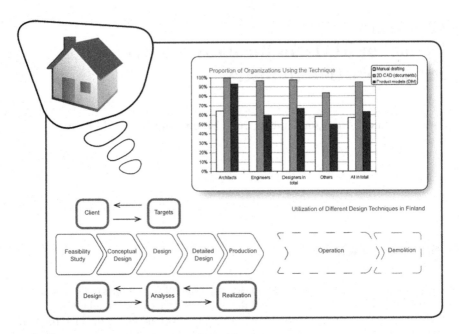

Fig. 18.1 Phases of design and construction

In the light of the above, information loss is unavoidable after completion of each phase. Further more, the conventional phasing is becoming increasingly inconvenient when identifying problem points in BIM data transfer. One expression of BIM ideology is that the information content of the models concerning a particular building should always mirror its current state. From BIM data analysis' point of view, it doesn't really matter whether the building actually exists, but if it does an outdated model may not represent it sufficiently. This also implies that unless BIM's are utilized during maintenance phase (i.e. operation) it's hard to imagine them being available for demolition stage planning. State-of-the-art BIM approaches usually focus on the design phase, since it is conceived as being most hectic period of activity and because many solutions out there are best suited for handling design phase data (Fig. 18.1).

Something that strikes anyone dabbling with BIM as mysterious is, how did buildings ever get erected before. This becomes evident when modelling existing buildings from original plans. One is easily inclined to bet high on there being not a structure in the world with coherent building instructions or documentation. The situation arises mostly from the fact that a set of drawings allows for a design that is not exactly possible in three dimensions. Experiences in modelling show that one should not be fooled to think even trained professional designers to be unerring. A building is a complex entity, ever more so in fact. But what exactly is the importance of such fact to the information modelling scene. Surely the problem will go away once BIM is properly implemented in design? Don't bet on it. In addition to being complicated to start with, buildings are also alive. So even if coherent 2D documents were originally produced from design stage BIMs they are bound to get obscured over time. Maybe it's the decisions made on building site, as sound 3D form doesn't after all guarantee practical assembly. Or, perhaps it's simply that 2D- documentation gets obfuscated when alterations are superimposed on them. Either way it all boils down to the question of BIM documentation. Even if it must be assumed that building plans always have an inherent margin of error there is no point in widening the gap between plans and reality by not applying as sophisticated methods in documentation as was used in design. This is particularly true because of yet another factor, the fact that more powerful design tools drive a vicious circle. As the everyday tools of the trade get more complicated ever more complicated building solutions become standard. It is already quite impossible to design modern machine of a house by ways of planar drawing. The situation calls for data transfer capabilities inside the design team at the very least. Should it also call for new approach to storing the information produced in the process? From our viewpoint the answer is yes of course. As to why so, is the most important question this text needs to answer.

18.2   Purpose and Aims of BIM Approach

18.2.1   Primary Aims

When asking the purpose of a new industry based technique the answer is always more or less the same: "It'll save you/us money and effort". Underlying this of course is the elementary logic that a technology that fails to achieve either or both is worthless for a business. The most simplistic business model in building industry is the one where the construction team is completely separated from the end user. In this model it is sometimes possible to evaluate projects simply by looking at the ratio of market value to building cost. Such strategy is also the toughest nut to crack for BIM approach for reasons discussed later in this chapter. For now it is sufficient to acknowledge that greatest savings theoretically achievable by BIMs lay elsewhere in building life cycle. Thus if benefits can be merited to usage of BIM technologies in planning stage, shift towards their implementation should be inevitable (Fig. 18.2). Which happens to be the case in the industry. What then, are the benefits?

- model based quantity takeoff;
- model based scheduling;
- model based energy analysis.

BIM based quantity takeoff and scheduling have had good reception in the industry mostly because they can immediately cut the price tag for the developer. Such result is achieved by means of combining automated cost analysis to comparison of multiple design solution from the very early stages of project. Something, though, about buildings that often amazes laymen is their real cost. The common misconception is that the building costs equal the price tag while in truth it's quite the opposite. As a matter of fact most money in general is spent on the maintenance during the buildings' life cycle. Most of the life cycle bill comes directly from heating up or cooling down the place during operation. Also this

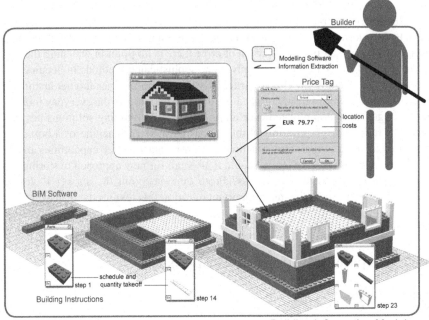

Fig. 18.2 Building information models (BIMs)

cost could easily be reduced but the responsibility lies in the hands of the consumer. Energy efficient buildings will remain poorly available until there is real market demand for them.

Predominant problem arising from present-day use of BIM's is industry's lean toward developing and embracing planning stage solutions. As said it is obvious that data exchange within design teams is already working. What happens to all that information after construction starts? It's turned into 2D construction documents and this is often all that gets stored. One of the main issues behind this problem is that since there is no de facto standard for overall data exchange, every project develops its own transfer schemes. While this kind of solution works fine for short-term purposes of design stage there is no guarantee what information can easily be extracted from each designer's model in future. To grasp the meaning of the statements above following points have to be considered:

- To exchange data in design team is in essence similar to data storage. Information must be extracted from an original model and input to other systems. Only, in case of storage one cannot tell what those systems will be. Thus the data structure of the storage model must also be known.
- The tools of trade are proprietary, which means that documentation of their inner data model need not exist in public domain. Hence they cannot be trusted to carry the information to future.

- Buildings' normal lifespan is vast compared to anything in modern information technology.

Clearly, what the industry needs is a data transfer/storage enabling file format whose structure is in the public domain. In other words, that it is open source code. It is understandable that such talk may disappoint proprietary software selling companies. What must be understood though is that open source file format does not entail free open source software (FOSS) that would compete with existing solutions. It is doubtful whether a transfer/storage format would be of any use in developing new programs. This is of course because its data structure was not designed for in program efficiency.

18.2.2   Secondary Aims

While the basic academic interest lay in research and propagation the use of technologies securing future usefulness of modern BIMs, there certainly are a number of interesting short-term benefits that could arise to mainstream as side products of standardised data transfer solutions. Most of these techniques already have small-scale implementations in closed software families. First one to mention is the building industry's long-lived dream of total automation from designers table to building site. Basically the main aspects of the idea are accomplished in Lego® Digital Designer software, in playroom scale. This CAD type program allows for design of Lego models while producing building instruction and price data automatically. The desired design can be ordered for delivery via the postal service. For those not willing to design there is a vast and ever-growing collection of designs by other users. Another one worth mentioning is the growing use of simple augmented reality solutions. Some mobile devices boasting GPS chips and motion sensors already use the available information to align content from e.g. Google Earth to real world. Maybe quite soon information model content can be viewed on site to help building. After the completion it could be used to spot faulty elements or dysfunctional devices that are hidden, etc.

18.3   Scope

What is the scope for building information models? In the previous chapter we came to listing some emerging technologies already unconventional enough to blow the hat of some commonsensical practitioners. While not going as far as to announce the break through of any particular technology any number of such now bizarre things are bound to become common-day in near future. The sensible answer lies somewhere in the vicinities of anything that has to do with building and can be profitable. How about endless real-life playgrounds for future gaming? Or real-life gaming in enhanced environments?

Since this text is purposed to appear together with a collection of studies into what we conceive to be the information model equivalent in spatial information world, it's probably best to stick to methods enabling BIM-GIS interaction. An apparent relationship between built entities and spatial information exists. All real, and most planned buildings have specific locations. This seemingly banal fact has some fascinating implications when looked at from the perspective of some recent representation techniques. An especially interesting tool is something called earth browser, a term referring to software like Google Earth. These programs offer an intuitive new platform to decipher relationships between urban and building scale data, and perhaps enhance information flow across that interface. How this goal could be achieved is chiefly to do with search techniques, such as:

- GIS based systems as search, navigation and organization tools for BIM data
- GIS based systems as communication tools between planning and public, investors etc.
- GIS based systems as regulatory tools for building

Things like Google Earth have been hanging in the air for quite a while already. Our guess is that the concept of digital globe is good enough to stay afloat even though just a fraction of its potential has yet been implemented. For the first time in history there is a coherent, scale free and interactive representation of earth. This allows for using the (virtual) planet as query machine. What better organization method could there be for building data? The uses of this technique are obviously not limited to queries to building and spatial data but also have to them a communicational side. Public authorities could easily use digital globes to visualize new development plans and communicate building regulations even in 3d.

18.4   Time Frame

In the time scale of information technology the idea of building information models as the means of sharing data is not exactly a newcomer. The development of what was to become the IFC file format was started already in 1994 and the controlling body for the development, IAI (Industry Alliance for Interoperability or International Alliance for Interoperability since '96), was formed the following year. Currently there are a few BIM exchange and storage formats, most of which are based on IFC schema. In present situation BIMs are satisfactory for information exchange purposes. There are practically no experiences yet of using BIMs for long-term storage. A widely approved view though is that the techniques available are still ill suited for building life cycle management. A rough estimate of BIMs' development stages and time implementation of is as follows:

- as planned: in use;
- as built: implementation possible today;
- as used: implementation in near future.

The information content of contemporary BIMs is often limited to as-planned stage, meaning that the use of BIM technology is discontinued during the construction. Present means should be sufficient for as-built stage models as well; the update is seldom done however, since as-built models are often perceived as pointless unless also life cycle management is to be BIM based. Recent adoption of IFC on national government level in several European countries for gathering more of the information created in planning process will probably push through attempts to implement as-used BIMs.

18.5 Actors

Each building project is a virtual enterprise, as the saying goes in the industry. To produce a building, an ad hoc "corporation" is formed with the usual goal of designing and manufacturing a product to fill a market demand. This is ideally speaking, of course. In the real world the affair is seldom conceived as such. Rather, it is everyone for themselves. Different actors in the design and construction teams take competitive positions towards the limited amount of capital available in the project. In the eyes of an individual actor, BIM is mostly reckoned a as means to produce the regular output with less effort, i.e. engine of surplus profit. Problems related to this issue are chiefly responsible for hindering the information model revolution in building industry. In this sense the actors in building process have dual roles as stakeholders in single enterprise and as individual stakeholders (Fig. 18.3). The different stakeholders in planning and construction stages are:

- client;
- developer;
- designers;
- contractor;
- public authority.

18.6 Roles

The relationships between different stakeholders are described in the figure above. The important notice is that each one listed may consist of multiple sub-actors. It depends greatly on the point of view how accurately any such categorization can describe the building process. Even belonging to the same subcategory doesn't always mean exactly identical interests.

18.7 Approaches

There are two model approaches to solve data exchange at work in building industry. On the one hand there are big software conglomerates offering overall solutions in form of internally interoperable software families and on the other is the ideal of

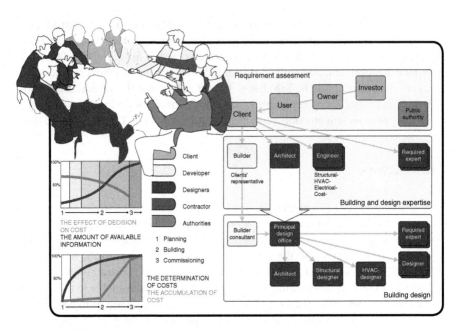

Fig. 18.3 Stakeholders involved in planning and construction

open standards for data exchange that would allow the user to choose from a variety
of software for each task. In many senses the situation resembles what is happening
in countless other domains leaning heavily on IT. Because of such setup the prime
software developing companies have quite limited interest towards pushing open
standards. From their point of view supporting openness is more as insurance in case
they should fall from grace. The most enthusiastic advocate for universal standards
is public sector; governments etc. have hard time justifying the use of proprietary
systems since it decreases their level of control. Currently IFC is the only available
BIM file format on the open source side of the fence. Actually, it is the only one
offering exchange across software families. The situation has both positive and negative effects. The major good thing is that one can be pretty sure whenever a software
company decides to begin supporting openness they'll choose IFC. Nevertheless
even open standards need competition to excel and at the moment there is none.

18.8 Tools

Each discipline inside the building industry has its own specific set of tools.
Traditionally information has been exchanged via 2d documents. One can think
such documents as an archaic data exchange format, whose use is strenuous since
all output and input stages have got to be done manually. Non-automatic data transfer

gives rise to myriad of software categories defined by similarities in input data type and insertion methods. Below is a brief list defining some of the conventional software types:

- drawing;
- design;
- calculation;
- scheduling;
- analysis.

BIM software can read in data from existing model and/or produce original information models i.e. only two kinds of tools are needed:

- modelling;
- analysis.

18.8.1   IFC Data Model

The Industry Foundation Classes (IFC) is an open data model designed for representation of building industry information contents with aim to facilitate interoperability in the building industry. The original file format for IFC is STEP Physical File (SPF) or STEP-file for short. The Standard for the Exchange of Product model data (STEP) is an ISO standard (ISO 10303) for computer-interpretable representation and exchange of industrial product data. The customary language used for coding STEP-files is called EXPRESS (plus variants). Wide adoption of XML in variety of fields has influenced also IFCs, and actually there already is an implementation of IFCs in XML. This probably due to the fact that also STEP-XML exists to define XML representation of the EXPRESS schema.

Confusion sometimes arises from the use of the IFC in two separate meanings:

- industry Foundation Classes data model;
- IFCs in STEP-file format (.ifc).

The official recommendation by IAI is that the abbreviation IFC is reserved for the STEP-file and the data model itself should be referred to as IFCs.

18.9   Usability

The bottom line is that IFC stands and falls at the mercy of usability. While there are positive indicators of the IFC usability, also concerns exist. The biggest problem is supposedly common to all schemas as huge as IFCs. Defining the implementations at program level seems on quick look nearly impossible. It took some 10 years to finalize the IFCs. How long will it take to define all the ways IFCs should be used, one can only guess.

As said in various ways above, IAI is trying to achieve overall data exchange capabilities in building industry through IFC. This means in action that it doesn't matter whether one is an analyst or a designer dabbling with software from CAD to scheduling, the background information one needs could nevertheless be pulled from the same file and the results put back into it. This is at the moment only a dream. Even so, the use of IFC is increasingly steadily, largely since it is the only solution offering even fractional BIM functionality across software families. Another contributing factor is the adoption of IFC by large property holders, especially governments, with hopes that in future useful information could be pulled out of the files. Be that as it may the present standard of storing building information in 2d-drawings and separate written descriptions shouldn't be very hard to beat.

18.10   Benefits

Trying to list the benefits of large-scale shift from 2D and dummy 3D to BIM usage is futile. The effect will be more or less similar to that of the printing press on publishing. Throw the emerging automation of design techniques into the bargain and maybe the effect on building will become comparable to the net effects of printing. For the sake of argument, a brief overview of what's behind these claims is in place. The benefits from information modelling are due huge improvement in following two areas:

- information exchange;
- data manipulation.

The relationship between the two is bidirectional in such way that while either in itself is beneficial, the combined effect is more than the sum of its parts. The role of BIM is to offer the interface between information generating and manipulating software. Ideally this would mean total elimination of duplicate datum input. This by it self should yield substantial decrease in need of effort in design process, since most of the work involved traditionally consists of copying from one system to another. A positive side effect is the reduction of human error. Together the use of smart software and data exchange leads to increase in two key factors:

- predictability;
- comparability.

These developments owe largely to time and resources saved by reduced manual labour. The time it takes to actually design a building isn't changed by modern methods, what is though, is the ability to test the effect of each design solution beforehand. In early design there is often a multitude of variants for the overall design. Now also these can be assessed better, since astonishing amounts of information can be produced even from very crude BIMs. Another saying often heard in the industry is that building is all about risk management. From that point of view building information modelling offers advances in:

- costs assessment;
- construction scheduling;
- crisis simulations (e.g. fire, earthquake);
- environmental analysis;
- etc.

18.11   Lessons Learned

Perhaps the most important lesson learned during the past development of information modelling technology in building industry is one of top down design and information technology. In many cases it is truly challenging to create large coherent systems to replace some already accepted fragmentary ones, provided that they already yield substantial benefits compared to more traditional methods. This is exactly true about virtual building environments (VBEs).

Many existing ICT tools and skills in the real estate and construction companies (RECC) form fragments of VBEs. However, to join these fragments into efficient and effective working frameworks is a formidable challenge. The transition from the earlier document based processes into seamless Virtual Building Environments includes substantial technological and organizational challenges. The technical challenges are mainly related to the different internal data structures of the software products, which cause difficulties in the file based data exchange between the different tools used in the RECC processes. Moreover, the obstacles in the human behaviour and business processes are at least as challenging. The VBE technologies have already had impacts on the RECC business network, and these changes are rapidly increasing.

One of the most interesting ways to tackle the problems in implementing large file formats such as IFC, is something commonly described as the Useful Minimum approach. The solution suggested by the useful minimum is to focus; to reduce the scope of implementations. If resources are not adequate for reaching good enough quality on a large scope, then reducing scope while maintaining the same level of resources should result in better quality. If the selected smaller scope satisfies the criteria of a useful minimum it will be taken into real use and will drive demand for the larger scope. This will eventually result in a quality implementation of the larger scope. From what it seems at present, whether such approach is taken intentionally or unintentionally, will determine if IFC will prevail. BIM solutions will at any case take over the industry one way or another.

Chapter 19
Some Observations on the Case Studies: Lessons Learned and Current Challenges

Christopher Tweed

Given the broad range of applications for ontologies, how can we analyse the relations between ontologies and their social and cultural contexts? The source of many of the issues we stumble upon in dealing with ontologies in the real world, can be found in philosophy. Perhaps not surprisingly, philosophy delivers some plausible tools for analyzing the role of ontologies in the applications we have discussed above.

A central concern of phenomenology is how things are revealed and presented to us in everyday life. Without delving into the detail of phenomenological analysis it is still possible to enlist some of its main concepts to extract interesting observations about ontologies in use. Reflecting on the case studies above we note that people are often not aware of using ontologies. Ontologies are implicit but not revealed during many everyday activities connected to urban planning and design. But without knowing it, people are using ontologies that are embedded in the systems (software and otherwise). It is often only when the software comes to the fore that its ontological underpinnings are exposed. In a second type of usage, an ontology can be developed specifically to reveal characteristics of a problem in the urban modelling domain. By focusing on an ontological description, it forces its developers to clarify the entities and relations inherent in the problem and from which a possible solution may emerge.

Anthony Steinbock has developed a trenchant reworking of Edmund Husserl's later phenomenological thinking and presented it as consisting of three main dimensions: static, genetic and generative (Steinbock 1995). These provide convenient concepts to aid a broad analysis of ontologies.

Static analysis of an ontology might consist of an investigation of the contents and structure of an ontology and how its elements are related (or not) to each other. This type of analysis should also describe an ontology's relation to a domain. It should consider the entities represented in an ontology and how these represent the

C. Tweed (✉)
BRE Centre for Sustainable Design of the Built Environment, Welsh School of Architecture, Cardiff University, UK.
e-mail: TweedAC@cardiff.ac.uk

G. Falquet et al., *Ontologies in Urban Development Projects*, Advanced Information and Knowledge Processing 1, DOI 10.1007/978-0-85729-724-2_19,
© Springer-Verlag London Limited 2011

domain, as well as examining the domain to see what has been omitted in an ontology and the consequences of doing so. We are familiar with these general kinds of questions about ontologies, but it is helpful to be reminded that they need to be asked every time we propose an ontology to serve a given purpose or to provide the basis for an application that will represent a domain within an organization. The familiar error is in mistaking the map (or model) for the territory.

A static analysis should examine the fit between an ontology and the purposes it is intended to serve within an organisation. Most of the examples provided in this volume are intended to support interoperability between systems. For this type of purpose, it is possible to design ontologies that mimic mechanical functions in the way they exchange information. Such ontologies are almost identical to engineering components, but as soon as they are required to be used directly by people they acquire a human-technology interface, which ushers in a larger set of concerns and demands new approaches. It is beyond the scope of this volume to describe these methods, but examples of the type of issues to consider are mentioned in some of the case studies above—for example, see the study on building regulations and technical standards.

These kinds of problems are not new. The difficulties of creating and maintaining conceptual models for interoperability have been explored in depth before, for example in the research on prescriptiveness of Computer Aided Architectural Design (CAAD) at edCAAD in the 1980s (Bijl 1989), and in consecutive European COMBINE projects (Augenbroe 1994, 1995). One conclusion to be drawn from these studies is that the social and organisational framework in which such developments take place are almost as important as the content of the ontology. Even the most perfect fit between ontology and purpose will eventually diverge as the needs and expectations of users drift away from the current ontological provision. There needs to be a strategy for accommodating these changes and coherent plan for revising and maintaining an ontology. Otherwise, an embedded ontology risks inhibiting the ability of an organisation to respond to the changing landscape of a given domain. This highlights the need to consider the life-cycle of ontologies.

A genetic analysis of an ontology, as the name suggests, takes account of its *genesis*—how it changes over time. Whereas static analysis focuses on the product (the ontology), a genetic analysis focuses on the process by which the product is developed, maintained and eventually retired. Several of the case studies above refer to the evolution and maintenance ontologies, so it is worth considering genetic aspects in more detail.

From a cursory glance, it is possible to identify different lifecycle models applied to ontology. Two different models are shown schematically in Fig. 19.1.

A historical ontology, as suggested in Fig. 19.1 (a), grows indefinitely. Some ontologies are required to preserve their histories and as such become cumulative. Dictionaries, for example, are rarely allowed to forget. They must serve as the record of a language and as such are required to accommodate old as well as new words and meanings. New words are often introduced and archaic terms remain accessible. The English Heritage thesauri described above provide a good example of this type of development since they must retain all previous entities and can still

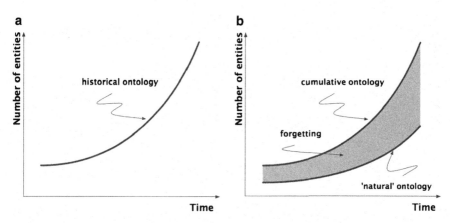

Fig. 19.1 'Natural' and cumulative ontology development

be expected to admit new terms as archaeological research discovers new objects and building types.

The difference between a cumulative ontology and a 'natural' ontology, as shown in (b), is the 'forgetting' that takes place among people. Forgetting is usually cast in a negative light, as something to be prevented as far as possible, but it is also what keeps an everyday ontology manageable. Meanings of familiar words change. For example, it is easy to accept today the widespread use of a term such as 'the economy,' but this has really only been common parlance within the past 40 years (Hacking 1999). It is important, therefore, to revise meanings as well as forget entities. Unlike informal systems that are subject to the vagaries of social construction, formal ontologies do not forget without deliberate actions by their authors. It seems, therefore, for formal ontologies to remain manageable they must be routinely purged of redundant entities. In contrast to the thesauri, IFC classes may benefit from 'forgetting' so that the total set remains minimal.

The process of critiquing and renewing ontologies creates a disjunction between successive ontologies. Figure 19.2 shows two different versions of this process. In Fig. 19.2a, the successive ontologies are linked because of a lack of separation in time. The second ontology is a revision of the first. In Fig. 19.2b, however, the ontologies are separated and it is more like starting over. This separation between ontologies throws light on the context in which this process takes place. In the urban regeneration example, an ontology served as a tool for bringing together disparate actors to complete a time-bounded task. The lifespan of the ontology was deliberately limited from the outset. It was always intended that the ontology would be thrown away after the task it supported had been completed.

The process is no longer about editing or revising a continuous ontology. This opens the generative dimension.

Generative analysis reminds us that ontologies are created by people within a specific setting. As such, they are cultural artifacts. They are products of the conditions that exist at a given time within a specific community or group. The extent to

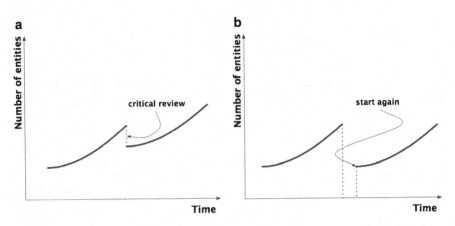

Fig. 19.2 Disjunction between successive ontologies

which an ontology receives widespread approval will be a measure of the general coherence of a cultural group. Such communities may be defined by any number of shared characteristics. They are what Steinbock refers to as normatively constituted. For any ontology to work, requires some degree of intersubjective agreement within its community of application about its terms, relations and their meanings. Agreement beyond a community may be less easily secured. A generative analysis should remind us that an ontology we develop for a particular purpose may only be valid for a bounded community of practitioners. Ontologies developed for road engineers, for example, may not be comprehensible to others. The COMBINE projects mentioned previously are good examples of the incommensurability of different models. Despite an ambitious plan to serve multiple evaluation tools and models from a single, centralised description of a building design, neither of the projects succeeded in producing a convincing prototype. As the paper on IFC classes suggests, it is almost impossible to integrate pre-existing models by overlaying another layer. IFC classes may be thriving but it is probably because they are being embedded in the next generation of Building Information Models (BIMs) rather than applied to existing software systems. They are also being modified to accommodate much wider variation in building descriptions than they were originally intended to.

19.1   Some Questions for Future Developers of Ontologies

Static, genetic and generative analyses do not provide a design method for ontologies. They merely serve as guides to some important characteristics of ontologies in relation to the domains they seek to serve. These three headings suggest further directions to explore the relationship between ontologies, the purposes they are intended to serve, the applications they support and the audience they address. They could provide the broad framework for developing ontologies by suggesting the kinds of questions that need to be asked. The sequence of asking, however, is probably in the reverse order: from generative through genitive to static. So, for example, an ontology developer might begin with the generative aspects by asking:

1. Who belongs to the community that will be served by this ontology?
2. How will the ontology help the community grow (purpose)?
3. How much agreement is there about definitions of entities in this community?
4. What is the cultural context (linguistic, disciplinary) for the ontology's development?
5. What assumptions are embedded in the starting points for development (legacy)?
6. Who will feel excluded by these definitions?
7. How can end-users be involved in the development and maintenance of the ontology?
8. What are the mechanisms for critique and renewal of the ontology?
9. Who will have the authority to make changes?

Similarly, a genitive analysis would suggest the following:

1. What is the intended lifespan of the ontology?
2. Will it provide a cumulative record of the domain?
3. How often will the ontology need to be revised?
4. What is the rate of change in the target domain?
5. Will the ontology be allowed to 'forget' entities?
6. What will the status of historical terms be?
7. How large can it grow and still be manageable?

Finally, a static analysis could entail a further set of queries:

1. What aspects of the domain does the ontology reveal?
2. What aspects does it obscure and exclude?
3. What is the appropriate level of complexity?
4. Does the ontology support current working practices?
5. How is the ontology likely to impinge on the domain?

Those these fall short of a method they should prompt debate prior to and during the construction of an ontology and hopefully will throw light on critical aspects.

19.2   Open Research Questions and Challenges

The authors of the above papers were asked to identify open questions and challenges in future research on urban ontologies. Their responses are summarized here.

Broadly, the research challenges fall into two main categories: those involving technical difficulties in exchanging data between different software tools, including migrating existing datasets into new tools; and secondly, challenges that are mainly conceptual, such how to accommodate multiple ontologies for a given domain and translate between them. The technical challenges should not be underestimated, but they are often less interesting than conceptual difficulties. Closer examination, as the previous discussion might suggest, reveals strong connections between technical and conceptual challenges, to the extent that almost all of them could be recast as socio-technical in nature. Technical developments suggest new concepts and methods and new conceptions drive technical developments.

The key questions and challenges to emerge are:

1. *Translation between ontologies in: (a) different domains; (b) different conceptualizations; (c) different languages.*

   The problem of sharing ontologies derived from different disciplinary, intellectual and cultural origins is a recurring theme in the work described above. It is likely to remain a major focus for research in the design and deployment of ontologies in urban planning and design for the foreseeable future. There are no quick fixes to these issues and the solutions are likely to result from careful and painstaking research into developing systems that will allow multiple ontologies to coexist. The key research challenges will then become how to map between them easily and quickly.

2. *Development and evolution of ontologies over time.*

   This challenge is closely related to (1). In one sense, the transition from one version of an ontology to a later one is a translation between two different ontologies. The difference, however, is the speed at which this takes place and the degree of common ground in both. Since they are versions, one might assume they share many concepts.

3. *Integration of ontologies into (a) decision making tools; and (b) spatial systems, such as Building Information Models (BIM) and Geographical Information Systems (GIS), to permit formal specification of spatial objects and relations.*

   This challenge is linked to (1) above and (4) below, but it is subtly different. Integration of ontologies into planning and design tools suggests that existing frameworks for such tools are often arbitrary and conceived with only a single tool in mind. The challenge of integration is to persuade developers, practitioners and policy makers of the need for formal ontologies as a foundation for their work. Successful persuasion requires demonstration of the efficacy of ontologies.

4. *Interoperability.*

   The continuing development of software systems dealing with spatial entities suggests new ways that they might interact to offer new features. Laitinen and Joutsiniemi suggest that their work on BIM could be extended in scope to embrace GIS. In their response, they highlight the emergence of "earth tools", such as Google Earth, as an example of a coherent, scale-free and interactive representation of earth that could open the doors to systems that would, for example, support search, navigation and organization tools for BIM data.

5. *User participation in the development of ontologies.*

   Franceso Rotondo and Chantal Berdier both see great potential for using urban ontologies as the basis for developing participative tools that will help practitioners work with the people who will be directly affected by planning decisions and designs. Despite the difficulties of developing, taming and maintaining folksonomies—user-generated taxonomies—there may be opportunities to create new types of ontologies with significant end-user input. The problems in doing so are entwined with the problems of translating between different conceptualizations of a domain, in this case between "experts" and the general public.

Within these questions there are many hidden challenges. If ontologies are to make their mark on real urban planning and design activities, research needs to make significant advances. While there is clear potential for research in this area to underpin the future development of tools, both as software and in other forms, we should be mindful of the conclusion reached by John Lee at the end of his paper:

Ontology development is often undertaken in haste on the assumption that standardisation and automation will be a good thing. Sometimes this may turn out to be literally a waste of time, but in other cases at least it will pay to probe more deeply into why a certain informality is a persistent feature of a domain.

Or, to put it another way, if you have a hammer in your hand, you will tend to see the world as consisting of things to hit.

References

Augenbroe, G.: The COMBINE project, An overview. Proceedings of the First ECPPM Conference, Dresden (1994)

Augenbroe, G.: COMBINE 2 Final Report. CEC Publication, Brussels (1995)

Bijl, A.: Computer Discipline and Design Practice — Shaping Our Future. Edinburgh University Press, Edinburgh (1989)

Hacking, I.: The Social Construction of What? Harvard University Press, Cambridge (1999)

Steinbock, A.J.: Home and Beyond: Generative Phenomenology after Husserl. Northwestern University Press, Evanston (1995)

Index

G. Falquet et al., *Ontologies in Urban Development Projects*, Advanced Information and Knowledge Processing 1, DOI 10.1007/978-0-85729-724-2,
© Springer-Verlag London Limited 2011